The
Essential
Guide to
Knowledge Management

ISBN 0-13-032000-5

9 780130 320001

Essential Guide Series

The Essential Guide to Knowledge Management

E-Business and CRM Applications

AMRIT TIWANA

Prentice Hall PTR, Upper Saddle River, NJ 07458
www.phptr.com

Library of Congress Cataloging-in-Publication Date

Tiwana, Amrit.
 The essential guide to knowledge management : e-business and CRM applications / Amrit Tiwana.
  p. ·cm.
 Includes bibliographical references and index.
 ISBN: 0-13-032000-5
 1. Knowledge management. 2. Electronic commerce. 3. Customer relations. I. Title.
 HD30.2.T498   2001
 658.4/038 21   12188469

Editorial/Production Supervisor: *Kerry Reardon*
Project Coordinator: *Anne Trowbridge*
Acquisitions Editor: *Miles Williams*
Editorial Assistant: *Richard Winkler*
Manufacturing Manager: *Alexis Heydt*
Marketing Manager: *Kate Hargett*
Art Director: *Gail Cocker-Bogusz*
Interior Series Designer: *Meg Van Arsdale*
Cover Designer: *Bruce Kenselaar*
Cover Design Director: *Jerry Votta*

© 2001 Prentice Hall PTR
Prentice-Hall, Inc.
Upper Saddle River, NJ 07458

Prentice Hall books are widely used by corporation and government agencies for training, marketing, and resale.
The publisher offers discounts on this book when ordered in bulk quantities.
For more information, contact

 Corporate Sales Department
 Prentice Hall PTR
 One Lake Street
 Upper Saddle River, NJ 07458
 Phone: 800-382-3419; FAX: 201-236-7141
 E-mail (Internet): corpsales@prenhall.com

Printed in the United States of America

10 9 8 7 6 5 4 3 2 1

ISBN 0-13-032000-5

Prentice-Hall International (UK) Limited, *London*
Prentice-Hall of Australia Pty. Limited, *Sydney*
Prentice-Hall Canada Inc., *Toronto*
Prentice-Hall Hispanoamericana, S.A., *Mexico*
Prentice-Hall of India Private Limited, *New Delhi*
Prentice-Hall of Japan, Inc., *Tokyo*
Pearson Education Asia, Pte. Ltd.
Editora Prentice-Hall do Brasil, Ltda., *Rio de Janeiro*

In memory of my father

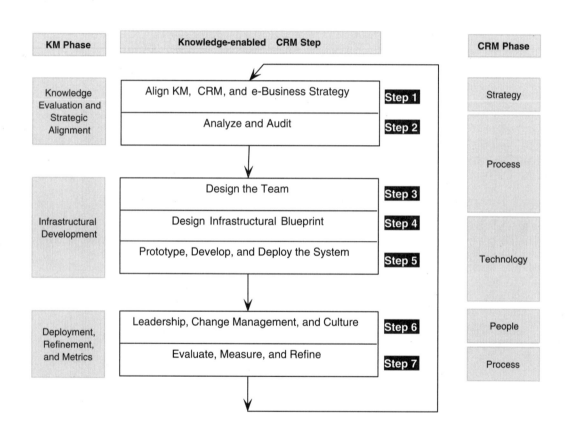

KM Phase	Knowledge-enabled CRM Step		CRM Phase
Knowledge Evaluation and Strategic Alignment	Align KM, CRM, and e-Business Strategy	Step 1	Strategy
	Analyze and Audit	Step 2	Process
Infrastructural Development	Design the Team	Step 3	
	Design Infrastructural Blueprint	Step 4	Technology
	Prototype, Develop, and Deploy the System	Step 5	
Deployment, Refinement, and Metrics	Leadership, Change Management, and Culture	Step 6	People
	Evaluate, Measure, and Refine	Step 7	Process

Contents

Preface

In the digital economy, traditional thinking is proving its futility. Assumptions from the old economy that most of us are comfortable with do not carry over to the now-mainstream digital economy. The proof is in the mirror. MrWakeup.com calls my phone at 7 A.M. to wake me to a fresh cup of Starbucks.com coffee brewed in a coffee maker bought at Gevalia.com. As I munch on a bagel that WebGrocer.com delivered last night, I read the *New York Times*.com delivered every 10 minutes to my wireless hand-held purchased from OfficeDepot.com. I am still waiting for a new suit that I ordered from LandsEnd.com, but I know that FedEx.com will send me an e-mail as soon as the package is delivered at my door. After a shower and quick shave with a DrugStore.com-delivered razor, I pick the navy blazer that I got from Overstock.com, get dressed, and drive to the subway station. I can't help but notice the blooming flowers that my neighbor bought at Garden.com, and so religiously waters with his Web-based X10 pump controller. A short drive filled with PhoneFree.com commercials brings me to the subway station.

I swipe the MARTA smartcard that WebVan.com delivers on the last day of every month as I notice the gloomy look on the newspaper vendor's face. A train finally arrives as I step away from the LastMinuteTravel.com banner only to end up sitting right under a big AtlantaYardSale.com sign. Do I care? Not when I listed my old notebook PC on eBay just the night before. The only "e-free" part of my day—my train ride—was ruined last year when Palm Computing took the Web wireless.

As I begin to pull out the latest issue of *Business Week* that I ordered at Magazineoutlet.com from my briefcase, I remember that I left my presentation Zip disk on my desk at home. I need not panic, because in just a few minutes I'll get into my iMac at home from my work PC through the Web. I continue browsing through my copy of

Business Week and highlight a couple of interesting tidbits with my C•pen digital highlighter. As I step out of the train, I toss my magazine into the trash; I'll soon have all the highlighted material on my desktop PC as soon as I *dock* my highlighter. Thank God, I still write with a *real* Waterman fountain pen that I got from Ashford.com that uses real ink that I can always find at Onvia.com. The calendar in the hallway reminds me that Mother's Day is close. The card from Sparks.com must be in the mail.

As I step out of the station in downtown Atlanta, I remember that life was not this way a few years back. More daunting is the realization that all this is just the tip of the iceberg. Electronic commerce is hardly a whiff of the impending change of which e-business is a harbinger.

Whether by choice or lack thereof, we are all bearers of the Chinese curse-blessing, "May you live in interesting times." While the newspaper boy is among the many left far, far behind, the dot-com era is unstoppably altering the structure of our economy. This book is written for those who do not want to be left behind, and for those who are keen to understand how e-business success is defined by knowledge and relationship capital—the only meaningful assets in the digital economy. Because it is meant to *explain* the underlying ideas behind relationship management and e-business applications of knowledge management to nontechnologists, I assume no significant prior knowledge of e-business or knowledge management. For readers who might want to dig deeper into the technicalities of knowledge management, I'd suggest taking a look at excerpts and chapters from my previous knowledge management book (freely available at www.kmtoolkit.com). Think of this book as a continuing dialogue between us, and feel free to carry on the conversation with me at *atiwana@acm.org*.

Amrit Tiwana
Atlanta, Georgia

ACKNOWLEDGMENTS . . . .

No book is a solo effort. Much credit for this one goes to my editor Miles Williams (the source of the idea), and to my friend Ashley Bush, whose unfailing encouragement and heated intellectual debates have found their way into what you hold in your hands.

I am intellectually indebted to Eph McLean, Arun Rai, Bala Ramesh, Herbert Simon, and Peter Keen, who have taken the time to express their ideas, opinions, and differences with gracious humility. To repeat Isaac Newton, I can see far because I stand on the shoulders of giants. I also want to thank my mentors, colleagues, students, and collaborators from whom I have only learned. Most above all, this was an impossible task without the support of my virtually and globally distributed family who are finally going dot-com!

Prologue

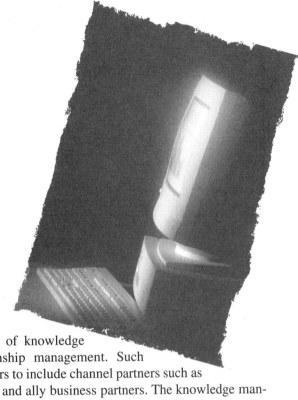

This book explains the application of knowledge management in e-business relationship management. Such relationships extend beyond customers to include channel partners such as distributors, suppliers, collaborators, and ally business partners. The knowledge management focus here is not enterprisewide, but customer-centric. I use the term knowledge-enabled customer (and channel) relationship management (KCRM) to describe this concept throughout the book. KCRM extends beyond traditional customer relationship management (CRM) and eCRM (CRM on the Web) in its strong knowledge management (KM) focus.

WHAT THIS BOOK IS ABOUT . . . .

This book is not about knowledge management in general, but customer-centric knowledge management in e-businesses. The purpose of this book is to explain the fundamental concepts and applications of knowledge management in e-business and customer relationship management. It is *not* supposed to be a toolkit for actual implementation. Detailed technology design for knowledge management is not described here; a higher-level *explanation* of the strategy-driven technology blueprint is instead the focus. Readers interested in that level of detail are pointed to two other books of mine, *The Knowledge Management Toolkit* (Prentice Hall, 2000) and *Web Security* (Butterworth Heinemann, 1999).

Intended Audience

This book is primarily intended for a nontechnical audience. This includes three types of readers: (1) managerial readers—CEOs, CIOs, corporate management, business development managers, and strategists—who are interested in e-business and relationship management applications of KM, (2) nontechnology managers such as sales, marketing, field support, and help desk staff interested in understanding knowledge management applications, and (3) information systems (IS) staff—e-business developers, Internet specialists, Web-enabled CRM developers, senior IS executives—who want to understand various business facets of knowledge management applications in an e-business context. Although basic familiarity with the Internet and computers is expected, no assumptions of prior technical knowledge are made. If you come across a term that you have never encountered before, or one that is technical, look for an explanation in a nearby sidebar or in the glossary at the end.

How This Book Is Organized

Specifically, you will understand seven broad areas of KCRM that are described along a conceptually simplified seven-step roadmap (see the table on page xxiii). The roadmap consists of three phases: (1) evaluation and strategic alignment, (2) infrastructure development and technology deployment, and (3) leadership, change management, measurement, and refinement.

Specifically this book will explain how the following issues are addressed in the context of knowledge management applications in an e-business relationship management context:

Align Strategy and Technology

The first step of the roadmap explains the key issue of aligning e-business strategy and technology investments. We identify opportunities for knowledge management in various categories of e-business to examine opportunities for strengthening relationships with customers and across the channel. We see how gap analysis methods are used for strategy analysis, how various critical success factors (CSFs) influence technology choices, and how an e-business vision is translated into digital capabilities.

Chapter	What is Covered	Roadmap Step
Part 1	Fundamentals	
1	Introduction, structure of this book.	
2	Understanding e-business, customer relationship management, and knowledge management; understanding how the three intersect to deliver KCRM.	
3	A seven-step roadmap metaphor-based outline of KCRM issues	
Part 2	A Roadmap for Implementing Knowledge-enabled Customer Relationship Management	
4	Aligning and strategy and technology	1
5	Audit and analysis of knowledge and relationship assets	2
6	Building an implementation team	3
7	Blueprinting the technology infrastructure	4
8	Results-driven incremental deployment of the system	5
9	Leadership, cultural change, and rewards systems needed to make KCRM work.	6
Part 3	Planning for Success	
10	Evaluation metrics, selecting measure of success, and refinement	7

Audit Existing Knowledge and Relationship Assets

Knowing where you want to go requires knowing where you already are. The audit and analysis step explains how current customer and channel relationships are analyzed, and how existing customer knowledge is evaluated. Audit and analysis provide guidance for directing KCRM resources in directions that hold the most promise.

Design a Team

In the third step, we see how an effective team is built. This team includes employees who create the relationship management strategy and those who build the technology. We identify conflicts that you should expect, methods used to resolve them, and common but often overlooked pitfalls.

Blueprint the Technology Infrastructure

We use a customer knowledge management technology framework to understand various pieces of technology used for KCRM. We will attempt to understand the functionality, role, and relative fit of each piece. A closer look at KCRM system architecture will provide a clearer picture of how these pieces fit together in an e-Business system in a manner that is well aligned with business strategy.

Deploy Using Results-Driven Incremental Methods

Rapidity, results, and time-to-market are key to implementation success in e-business. Traditional systems deployment methods offer none of these. Deployment must be broken into small independent increments; results of each drive the next increment. Such incremental approaches to deployment are described with examples along with problems associated with other popular development approaches that served us well until recently.

Lead, Manage Change, and Adjust Corporate Culture

Knowledge management and all its variants fail to produce results until organizational culture is made more open and sharing, strong leadership exists, and change and reward systems are aligned. The sixth step on our roadmap explores these issues: lessons learned from exemplary e-business successes and failure, leadership expectations and choice, and the touchstones for this transition.

Evaluate, Measure, Refine

You cannot control what you cannot measure. Customer relationships and knowledge assets are hard to measure; so are the effects of your KCRM initiative. The final stop on our journey explains various measures that worked well before the e-economy upsurge and reasons why they do not fare well now. We examine measures such as Bohn's Scores and the Balanced Scorecard that do work, and understand how they are used to incrementally refine knowledge-enabled customer relationship management strategy and technology.

The
Essential
Guide to
Knowledge Management

Part 1

Fundamentals

In this part...

Chapter 1: Introduction

- Understand why e-business is different.

- Relate e-business and knowledge assets.

- Understand what digital capital really means.

- Appreciate the significance of relationship assets and customer capital.

- Trace the evolutionary path to the digital economy.

- Understand the value proposition of knowledge management in e-business.

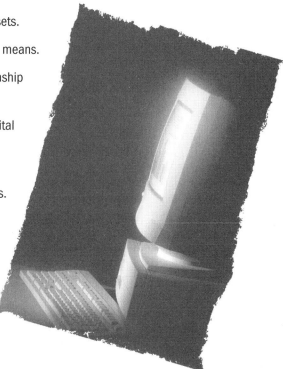

Chapter 2: Understanding E-Business, CRM, and KM

- Understand how e-business differs from traditional business.

- Comprehend the relationship between e-business and electronic commerce.

- Understand the fundamental ideas behind customer relationship management.

- Trace the transition from bits and bricks to click-and-mortar businesses.

- Understand the fundamental value proposition and key tenets of knowledge management.

- Identify the opportunities for knowledge management in e-business.

- Understand the fundamental ideas behind knowledge-enabled customer relationship management and its evolution.

Chapter 3: A Roadmap for Success

- Comprehend the significance of the KCRM roadmap.

- Understand how the KCRM roadmap links CRM and knowledge management.

- Understand various steps and the reasons for their parallel execution.

- Identify the three key phases, and the activities involved in each phase.

1 Introduction

In this chapter...

- Understand why e-business is different.

- Relate e-business and knowledge assets.

- Understand what digital capital really means.

- Appreciate the significance of relationship assets and customer capital.

- Trace the evolutionary path to the digital economy.

- Understand the value proposition of knowledge management in e-business.

Insurgents in e-business are using superior knowledge and strengths of their relationships to dramatically alter the traditional rules of business. As new e-businesses begin to alter longstanding industry structures and nimble newcomers leapfrog established leaders, incumbent businesses—both existing businesses and born-on-the-Web startups—wonder what can give them that endurable competitive edge. As businesses increasingly realize that knowledge (not capital or technology) is their only sustainable edge, customers their key assets, and channel relationships their fountainhead of adaptability, they are turning to knowledge management and customer relationship management with high hopes of weathering the complexity, uncertainty, unnatural time scales, unexpected competitor innovations, shifting markets, and ambiguity that surround them.

We have been perfectly schooled to think the wrong way. An introductory accounting text used in leading American business schools, for example, teaches us that "the value of an intangible asset such as a patent equals the fees paid to acquire it." Priceline.com's reverse auction patent should then be worth approximately $1,500. No wonder that when we see market valuations of the ticketing agency Priceline.com (market valuation, $6.5 billion), florist 1-800-Flowers ($400 million); application service provider Apponline.com ($65 million), online jeweler Ashford.com ($125 million), automobile infomediary AutoWeb.com ($65 million), and technology retailer Buy.com ($700 million), our first reaction is disbelief. Blame the Internet stock bubble and shrug it off as irrational exuberance. But they still won't go away.

Tech Talk

E-Business: Internet-facilitated integration of processes, applications, and information systems to facilitate rapid collaboration, coordination, and relationship formation across traditional organizational boundaries. Electronic commerce is a subset of e-business.

E-business is creating the New Economy's distribution model; the art, however, lies in bringing business judgment to that model. The ability of an electronic business to differentiate itself is heavily influenced by its ability to translate its innovative business strategy to online capabilities. Although relationships and knowledge are the key assets of the digital economy, the rewards are elusively reserved not for those who have the most knowledge but for those who actually use that knowledge to rethink, recast, and even cannibalize their own businesses. Is there a formula for success in the e-business-driven digital economy? Unfortunately, like snowflakes, no two businesses are alike. A formula-like approach that spells wonders in one business might be a deadhead in another.

As e-businesses move from once-rewarded customer acquisition to now-rewarded customer retention and loyalty, you might be thinking about implementing customer relationship management (CRM), knowledge management (KM), and channel relationship management—processes that bring together your suppliers, distributors, service providers, infrastructural partners, business allies, and customers. What are the key drivers, the right approach, and *the* method for implementation? How does e-business knowledge differ from that in traditional businesses? How did we get here and how does your firm get there? What role does technology play? How do we know that this is not yet another fix-it-all technology that actually delivers zilch? These are some of the questions that this book answers.

KNOWLEDGE MANAGEMENT, E-BUSINESS, AND CRM . . . .

Many failures in stable business stem from attempting to combine mainstream strategy with disruptive technology strategy. Although the potential of e-business has led many a firm to join the stampede toward building systems to support it, applying mainstream approaches and assumptions to these initiatives should raise a big red flag.

Tech Talk

Knowledge Management: Management of business, customer, and process knowledge and its application for adding value and competitively differentiating product and service offerings.

E-business is one such disruptive juncture. The transformative influence of e-business cannot be ignored by *any* business, because computing, financial services, retailing, and communications are all becoming e-business driven. Figure 1-1 shows the pervasiveness of its impact, which is only expected to increase in the near future.

E-business systems promise to deliver the much sought after competitive edge that businesses have looked for but never found in intranets and extranets, enterprise resource planning (ERP) systems, and electronic data interchange (EDI).

Table 1-1 Emergence of Business Drivers, 1960–2000

Era	Emergent Forces
1960s	New products
1970s	Low-cost manufacturing
1980s	Total quality management
1990s	Customer relationships and one-to-one marketing
2000s	Knowledge-enabled relationship management and e-business

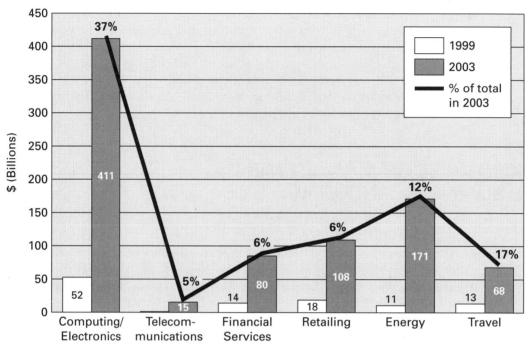

Figure 1-1
The predicted growth of e-business leaves no industry untouched.
Source: Business Week, October 4, 1999.

To comprehend the relationship between knowledge management and customer relationship management in e-business, it is necessary to take a closer look at what is truly new ("New-New") in the new economy and what is simply old in new clothing ("Old-New"). Table 1-1 lists the key forces that have driven businesses from the 1960s to the present. However, first we must see how the New Economy is being given a facelift by the e-business phenomenon.

Tech Talk

Customer Relationship Management: The process of managing relationships with existing customers to maximize their loyalty, increase revenues from them, and retain them while selectively attracting new customers.

THE NEW ECONOMY'S NEW FACE . . . .

Electronic commerce—using the Web to sell products and services to customers—is just the tip of the e-business iceberg. The Web and its e-business "consequences" are reshaping the face of the New Economy. E-Business is about managing your entire business, coordinating increasingly complex processes and activities, and weaving a complex web of collaborations facilitated by the Web. The Web provides the medium for building *nearly* perfect markets. The key ingredient of near perfect markets is perfect information and perfect knowledge of what has occurred and will occur in the marketspace. In *Digital Capital* (Harvard Business School Press, 2000), Don Tapscott and his collaborators suggest that the currency of the New Economy is not hard capital but knowledge and relationship capital. It is that capital that this book is concerned with. Let us briefly examine eight *New-New* trends that are transforming the face of businesses in unprecedented ways.

Knowledge Centricity

Francis Bacon was perhaps right in equating knowledge and power several hundred years back, but if he were around today, his words would have brought him more unshaken approval than astonishment. In the digital economy, *everything* is knowledge based. Nonphysical goods (news, software, music) and services (entertainment, consulting, design, distribution, shipping) depend on knowledge for their production and distribution, and physical goods (medicine, electronics, books, computers, vacuum cleaners, airplanes) have knowledge embedded in their design, production, and delivery. Knowledge and relationship assets (which includes brand recognition) of e-businesses such as Amazon.com, Buy.com, and eBay have led to their high market valuations. The complexity of e-businesses makes it too easy for knowledge to be fragmented, extremely difficult to locate and share, and therefore inconsistent, redundant, and ignored throughout the decisions that propel the company. To remain sustainably competitive, they must effectively and efficiently create, locate, capture, and share their organization's knowledge, and *most importantly,* rapidly bring it to bear on problems and emergent opportunities.

Increasing Returns and Network Effects

In e-business settings, knowledge-based offerings demonstrate *increasing returns*: Once the first unit is produced at a significant cost, additional units can be produced at near-zero incremental cost. In e-business, many products and services also demonstrate what economists call *network effects*: The more widely they are used, the high-

· ·

PATHS TO LEARNING

In *Paths to Learning*, Alfred Chandler traced two knowledge-intensive industries—personal computers and biotechnology—that emerged in the 1980s. The PC industry blossomed by giving away its secrets, with the singular exception of Apple which guarded its designs only to lose out. The biotechnology firms on the other hand still exist, but unlike the multi-billion-dollar PC industry, most of these companies have never turned a profit despite all their patents and legal forms of protection. The only way to protect your business knowledge is to apply, reuse, update, evolve, and outdate it too fast for competition to be able to copy it.

er their value becomes. Network effects and increasing returns have led to the rise of simple yet revolutionary business models such as those of eBay ("the classifieds killer"), the MP3 music format (the music industry's biggest nightmare), comparison shopping (such as Pricewatch.com, Cnet.com, Shopper.com, and mySimon.com), rebirth of the iMac, and the Linux phenomenon. These business models very suddenly and challengingly threaten the very existence of stable lines of business without the slightest forewarning.

As increasing returns and network effects begin to dominate business models, economies of scope and economies of networks supercede economies of scale—a shift that most old-age business have trouble grasping. Increasing returns are increasingly path dependent: Other businesses necessarily have a hard time coming up to speed with a competitor that has started utilizing increasing returns assets relatively early on.

Accelerated Clockspeed

In the Internet-driven economy, rapidity of unpredictable change predominates. Clinging to old ways often causes severe mismatches of internal and external pace. Change cannot be controlled; instead, it can be led. To cope with such unpredictable changes, managers cannot afford to pace themselves any slower than Internet time. Businesses must have real-time access mechanisms to apply knowledge across the value chain and integrate it to interpret and respond to business changes—technological, environmental, regulatory, or customer related. This requires coordination, knowledge sharing, and collaboration, and organizational and technical mechanisms that support speedy adaptation.

Transparency, Information Symmetry, and Knowledge Asymmetry

Customers have access to near perfect information through the Web. As business processes and activities become increasingly transparent, and as information asymmetries (such as those that once allowed travel agents and stockbrokers to enjoy healthy margins) disappear, information by itself no longer provides any advantage to businesses. Differences in the levels of which businesses assimilate knowledge and actually mobilize it—knowledge management asymmetries—then differentiate firms. As a business' knowledge becomes increasingly networked with others', it can create a win-win situation for all organizations involved because networked knowledge is more potent than aloof knowledge. Although e-business relationships are bathed in knowledge, the fine line between collaboratively sharable and competitive, strategic knowledge must be drawn meticulously.

Low Switching Costs, Lock-Ins, and Price Discovery

The outlays needed to acquire customers are considerably higher for e-businesses. In the brick-and-mortar business world, customers were often loyal by necessity, not by choice. Convenient store locations, information asymmetries, and agreeable terms often let businesses get away with mediocrity, inconsistency, and less than thrilling levels of service. Profits in e-business—even survival—may be elusive goals unless these customers stick around long enough and repeatedly buy from you. "Your competitor is a click away" is almost a cliché. Just as the costs of switching from one long-distance service provider are relatively low for consumers, switching suppliers for many commodity-like products are low and falling further. The key reasons for low switching costs are: (1) perfect information availability and (2) commodification of products (wherein they become undifferentiated, substitutable commodities).

Switching costs lowered by the Web in business-to-consumer (B2C), business-to-business (B2B), and consumer-to-consumer (C2C) transactions eventually commoditize any and all undifferentiated product and service offerings. Relationship building prevents such commodification by differentiating it from other similar products or services, and through intimate customer knowledge that creates lock-ins. Lock-ins increase switching costs: Time, money, and energy expended by buyers in schooling a new seller all about their needs and preferences might not remain worth it. In e-businesses, loyalty-driving lock-in—the glue of e-business—is the ultimate objective. Thanks to the Web, price fixing is being replaced by joint price discovery by buyers and sellers. When the price is right—not necessarily the lowest—lock-ins can be sustained, and customers retained. Creating such lock-ins requires thorough knowledge of a business' customer base and of the interdependent business processes that serve them.

Modular Innovation and Recombinations

Knowledge management has focused on preventing imitations, but with e-business, the additional threat of substitution comes in. MP3 player manufacturers do not need to make a better CD player; they simply substitute it. Dialpad.com does not offer more services than Sprint or MCI; it replaces it. eBay does the same for your neighborhood yard sales and local newspaper classifieds, eSteel for steel trading consortiums, and the list goes on. One of the substitute New Economy business models is the E-hub (like eSteel.com, Chemdex, and Ariba Networks); another threatens to substitute the entire packaged software development industry (application service providers, or ASPs, that rent software applications through the Internet).

In e-business, it is essential to stay tuned to other businesses that can potentially eliminate the need for your business' offerings by providing a substitute. Substitution rarely requires amazing new technology; often old technology combined in a new novel way can create a substitute offering. Of course, the old worry of looking out for competitors and copycats still exists. Resource recombinations help assemble new packages of existing capabilities and reconfigure existing products to meet emerging market needs in real time. This concept is called modular innovation. In addition to knowledge-facilitated novel recombinations, an e-business needs knowledge to adapt its business model for each successive round of competition.

Tech Talk

Modular Innovation: Innovation and breakthroughs that are achieved by recombining and reconfiguring existing technologies in novel ways.

Rapid and Ad Hoc Alliances

As unpredictable opportunities for value creation emerge, e-businesses must be able to see these windows of opportunity and fill them through what management guru Peter Drucker calls *purposeful opportunism*. Effective response to changes in the e-business environment requires efficient response mechanisms. Knowledge workers, their productivity, and the scope of their relationships are the most valuable capability determinants of adaptability within an e-business. Collaborative competition ("co-opetition") is now the norm as reliance on partners and competitors for the rapid formation of ad hoc alliances to deliver such response increases. In e-business, ad hoc alliances are formed rapidly and opportunistically. For example, affiliate programs—electronic commerce based on interorganizational relationships—on the Internet generated about $5 billion, or 10 percent of all U.S. online electronic commerce spending in 1999 alone.

Old sources of advantage based on proprietary knowledge are rendered irrelevant by the rapidity of knowledge obsolesce. New knowledge must be integrated on an as-needed basis through the formation, dissolution, and reformation of nonpermanent collaboratives in which partners and members necessarily come and go. In these collaboratives, process transparency, not combative attitude, prevails. Time-to-market and organized abandonment of business concepts that might have served well *in the past* are cardinal.

Products as Experiences

Products and services are increasingly being defined as experiences rather than their tangible selves. Associated services have become more important determinants of value than the product itself. Businesses are also increasingly codeveloping products with their customers. Dell, Apple, and Gateway are good examples from the computer industry. Levis has done the same with custom-fitted jeans; Ford is planning to do the same with cars as another Japanese high-end bicycle manufacturer does to deliver customized bicycles. More than anywhere else, businesses that interact with their customers through the Web must define the experience to the customers' needs and wants. Such customization needs intimate customer knowledge and a continuing relationship. The role of the firm is then not that of a car manufacturer, PC market, clothier, or bookseller; it is one of a knowledge integrator.

The shift is not easy: It needs a different organizational culture, reward systems, and motivators across the channel, and seamless integration across the supply-chain. As control is redistributed, organizational boundaries blurred, and collaborative partnerships formed and dissolved in real-time, search, transfer, coordination, and collaboration cost economics become strikingly different from those found in the Old Economy. Businesses that do not recognize these subtleties will self-destroy their margins by commodifying their offerings.

HOW WE GOT HERE:
THE LONG-WINDED ROAD . . . .

How did we get to the juncture where access to other businesses' competencies and knowledge becomes crucial? Why have businesses had to begin listening to customer, and made them cocreators of their products rather than nonconversing masses of statistically similar buyers? Why have active dialog and customer communities created mega e-businesses like eBay and Ratingwonders.com?

THE HAMMER THAT ROCKS THE CRADLE

Knowledge and relationship management work optimally only if they are established as an integrated business model rather than as a set of independent capabilities. Alignment of business and Information Technology (IT) goals, senior management support, middle management motivation are the keys to integration success. Unfortunately, technology is the hammer to which almost every problem looks like a nail. Most often, problems result from systems perspective-driven investments that precede customer strategy formulation. Conversely, customer relationship management is not about technology; it is about knowing your customers. It is about retaining the right set of customers, selectively attracting new customers, and guiltlessly getting rid of unworthy customers. The value of a customer is not that of one transaction, but about the customer's lifetime value (net present value (NPV) based on estimates of the customer's relationship duration).

Tech Talk

Knowledge-Enabled Customer Relationship Management (KCRM): Managing customer knowledge to generate value-creating lock-ins and channel knowledge to strengthen relationships and collaborative effectiveness. Knowledge-enabled CRM is more of a business model/strategy than a technology-focused solution.

The answer lies in looking at the past, for those who forget the past are condemned to repeat it. To illustrate this, Table 1-2 shows how marketing evolved from the 1970s to the present.

We examine this evolution in further detail in Chapter 2. For the moment, let us take a closer look at the two key imperatives in e-business as we evolve through the columns of Table 1-2.

THE NEW-NEW IMPERATIVES

As business processes become increasingly knowledge intensive, transaction costs decline, and new relationships are defined opportunistically, the focus of attention shifts to core capabilities of the firm—the few things it can do well. In any type of e-business, the challenge begins once customers are onboard: retaining them, expanding their business, and keeping them coming back for more. Such competitive strength building loy-

Table 1-2 Evolution of Knowledge-Enabled CRM

Dimension	Target Marketing	CRM	KCRM
Time frame	Late 1970s	Mid to Late 1990s	2000s
Horizon[1]	One-shot	Sequential	Ongoing/lifetime
Output	Offer	Information	Predictive knowledge
Customer	Average statistic	Individual statistic	Value cocreator
Customer role	Passive	Passive	Active part of fabric
Channels	Mail/phone	Multiple touchpoints	Simultaneous touchpoints
Scope	Marketing	Front-office	Enterprise
Collaboration	Marketing/sales	Cross-functional	Cross-institutional
Data	Purchases	Contacts	Relationships
Updates	Monthly	Daily	Real time
Reaction time	Billing cycle	Transaction	Proactive, instantaneous
Goal	Efficiency	Revenue enhancement	Sustained relationship

[1] *Horizon of relationships.*

alty comes from (1) integrating and turning customer and channel knowledge into action and (2) forging strong relationships with customers and channel partners.

Customer Knowledge Integration

As customers increasingly contribute knowledge to businesses that they transact with, it is still the business' job to be able to assimilate and integrate this knowledge. Firms that can convert knowledge in the heads of their employees and customers (human capital) into actual capabilities (structural capital) and relationships (relationship capital) are the ones that will lead the way.

Knowledge management is a potent competitive tool for an ever more brutally competitive age of shrinking margins, shorter product development times, and fickle customers *if and only if* you are willing to listen to customers rather than just talk. Moreover, you must be willing and able to change your behavior toward an individual customer based on what you know about *that* customer.

Customers on the Web are price rational, but not price obsessed. Why do 70 percent of Amazon.com customers return to pay more when many of them know of other places on the Web where they can find the same item for less? If you cannot pinpoint reasons for your own customers or business partners to do the same, you are most likely not integrating subtle tacit knowledge into your business processes well enough. In-depth knowledge of your customers can allow you to engage in dynamic pricing (called *price discrimination* in economics) where you price your offerings based on what the customer is willing to pay.

Relationship Management in E-Business

The Web is a marketer's dream for relationship building for three reasons: (1) inexpensive, individual addresability, (2) two-way exchanges between buyers and sellers that supercede the broadcast strategy of traditional marketing, and (3) its instantaneous, real-time nature. Taking advantage of this medium, however, requires businesses to get out of the illusive trance of rigor and accuracy that is associated with collecting lots of customer data and leads businesses to falsely believe that the ensuing data-based decisions will be good, accurate, objective, and rational.

In their analysis of e-loyalty (*Harvard Business Review*, July-August 2000), Reichheld and Schefter noted that increasing customer retention rates by 5 percent typically increases profits by 25 to 95 percent. Engaging in an indiscriminate frenzy of customer acquisitions and obsessing over the raw number of unique visitors, page hits, and sales revenue are not the nirvana of e-business. Neither is trying to be all things to all people by accommodating all levels of service requirements, price points, and brand pull.

The biggest strength of the Web is its ability to forge communities (as demonstrated by the early success of AOL chat rooms). However, little is understood about how trust built in e-business-centric communities can be transferred to the companies that host them. Nevertheless, examples of companies that have succeeded at this abound: eBay, Dell, AnandTech, and Amazon to name a few. The key lies in broadening and deepening relationships over time, gaining the loyalty of your most profitable customers and maximizing their business, and selectively acquiring the *right* type of new customers. Referring to the new co-opetitive nature of collaboration, one executive described this as moving away from the idea of the lone corporate wolf hunting for new business to that of hunting as a wolf pack.

Value Proposition

Knowledge-enabled customer relationship management promises to help build several core capabilities in e-business. Specifically KCRM allows e-businesses to:

- *Apply existing knowledge.* Increase the *application* of information that flows through e-business transactions to personalize future interactions facilitates real-time response to events occurring over vast networks by using transaction-level triggers. Establish an ongoing dialogue with your customers. Leverage the Web as a direct interaction medium that lets them pull the answers that they need, and when they want them. Highly paid knowledge workers can spend less time looking for information needed to make streamlined and expedited decisions; instead, they have more time to share, leverage, and apply their tacit knowledge.

- *Predict and infer.* Use customer history (historical behavior monitoring) to infer and predict new needs (tactical behavior monitoring), and target cross-sell and up-sell pitches through the right channel. Interpret changes in customer behavior, provide real-time reasoning, deduce generalizations, selectively discard old customer knowledge, and change customer-related behavior accordingly. Target your marketing efforts based on your knowledge of customers' preferences, behavioral patterns, and history.

- *Coordinate.* Coordinate sales, service, and support across all customer touchpoints and channels and present a single, unified face—not the typical blame-transferring one—to customers. The ability to attract and retain customers is directly related to customer perceptions; these are managed through a hierarchy of complex internal and external communication and knowledge-sharing patterns. An integrated, enterprise-wide view of the customer helps present a single face to the customer and builds a 360-degree view of her value.

- *Build preemption strategies.* Anticipate the needs of customers, sometimes even before they realize what they want. Preempt customer defections by leaving no excuse for not exhilarating them.

- *Present one face.* It is commonly said, "On the Internet, no one knows that you're a dog." Likewise, a fragmented, patchy, distributed business that comes across the same way will lose face, however customer oriented it may be. On the other hand, even a small e-business that presents a unified, consistent, and knowledgeable face will make a positive impression. On the Internet, no one knows or cares that you were once a great company.

- *Integrate external knowledge.* As ad hoc teams are built in real time, external knowledge is integrated to avoid costly errors instead of getting lost in the information glut. As customers and noncustomers visit any channel, clickstream analysis and treatment differentiation approaches help analyze their potential needs and methods for fulfilling them.

Tech Talk

Clickstream Analysis: Analysis of a series of mouse clicks from a customer's computer when she is visiting a Website to discern behavioral patterns. These patterns may, for example, reveal that she puts an expensive dress in her shopping cart every time she visits the site but never checks out with it.

Companies are expected to spend an estimated $90 billion on CRM initiatives in 2003, according to IDC Worldwide. This is considered staggering growth compared to the $40 billion spent in 1999, and an indicator of how keen companies are to "do something about" customer retention and relationship management.

The Devil Is in the Details

Many early e-businesses have found the promise of cheap and easy customer service through the Web to be hollow. Traditional businesses lured by the promise of the Web are the ones that are most flirting with disaster, as they are unable to singly recognize the customers who came on foot, those who came through the Web, and those who call their catalog business. The severity of this problem is somewhat less pronounced in born-on-the-Web businesses that do not carry a legacy from their brick-and-mortar days. Just as a person's character is characterized by what he does when he is not being watched, an online customer's loyalty is judged by whether she buys from you without the coupons and other last ditch customer acquisition attempts by soon-to-fail e-businesses. Loyal relationships are not built by pouring more fuel down the black hole of technology but by integrating, managing, and applying deep knowledge of customers, markets, and business partners. The starting point is a vision for getting closer to your customers and channel partners using sales, service, marketing, and knowledge-centric relationships that increase the *exchange of value* and *value of exchanges* between your company and them. The chapters that follow will help you understand how the devil hidden in the details of implementing KCRM can be systematically slayed, and how e-business vision can be translated into reality.

In the next chapter, we examine the three facets of e-business, customer relationship management, and knowledge management to understand how knowledge-enabled customer relationship management emerges at their intersection. This provides the foundation for the chapters that follow.

TEST YOUR UNDERSTANDING . . . .

1. What is so new about the New Economy? How is the New Economy different from the Digital Economy, if at all?

2. If e-business is so great, and over 60 percent of the U.S. population had Internet access by 2001, why are some early adopters having a hard time even staying in business? How does e-business differ from electronic commerce?

3. What is knowledge management? Why should e-businesses care about knowledge management any more than their brick-and-mortar counterparts did?

4. Why did Windows becomes the de facto standard for personal computing if Apple has been consistently several years ahead of Microsoft, as is commonly believed? (The cost differential cannot be considered a valid argument because Apple computers typically outlast Windows machines by several years and iMacs can be had for as little as $700.)

5. What is the significance of network effects and increasing return economics in the e-business era? What do they imply for knowledge management?

6. We discussed that price fixing has been replaced by price discovery. If that is true, are price tags on those nifty little hand-held computers at your neighborhood Office Depot meaningless, and can the customer and the store manager collectively "discover" a fair price?

7. How did mass-marketing pitches evolve into customer knowledge management from the 1960s to the 2000s?

8. What are the two imperatives in e-business? Should technology novelty be counted as one of them?

9. If your business manages to retain just an additional 5 percent of its customers, how much can it expect its revenues to increase? Why not 5 percent? Do economics of increasing returns have anything to do with this figure?

10. What is purposeful opportunism and what does knowledge management have to do with it?

2 Understanding E-Business, CRM, and KM

In this chapter...

- Understand how e-business differs from traditional business.

- Comprehend the relationship between e-business and electronic commerce.

- Understand the fundamental ideas behind customer relationship management.

- Trace the transition from bricks to click-and-mortar business.

- Understand the fundamental value proposition and key tenets of knowledge management.

- Identify the opportunities for knowledge management in e-business.

- Understand the fundamental ideas behind knowledge-enabled customer relationship management and its evolution.

The future may be exciting, but it is also ambiguous, complex, and often unpredictable. Traditional assets that differentiated businesses no longer hold stead in e-business; instead, knowledge and relationships represent the currency of such businesses. The ability of e-businesses to differentiate is heavily influenced by their ability to translate their innovative business strategy to online capabilities.

In this chapter, we survey the new digital landscape to identify key differences between e-businesses and traditional businesses. We see how e-business and electronic commerce are related, and how traditional marketing stratagems begin to fall apart in this environment. We then explore the fundamental ideas behind customer relationship management (CRM) and examine how we arrived there from mass marketing and one-to-one marketing-like approaches. Then, we take a closer look at knowledge management (KM) and its role in e-business settings. Finally, we examine the fundamentals of how knowledge management and customer relationship management are integrated—a concept described herein as knowledge-enabled customer relationship management (KCRM). The complementarities of the two will make it clear why customer-focused knowledge management is a potent tool in e-business.

THE NEW DIGITAL LANDSCAPE . . . .

Emergence of e-business—only a small part of which is electronic commerce—is changing the face of commerce. Revenues for e-businesses grew at three times the growth rate of the economy between 1998 and 1999 as the Internet economy ballooned to $850 billion in 2000. Business-to-consumer (B2C) electronic commerce alone exceeded banking, aerospace, and drug industries *combined*.

Death of the 4 Ps

The holy grail of marketing that once consisted of the 4 Ps—product, price, place, and promotion—is not built around relationships and customer knowledge. In e-business, these four Ps have been replaced by their digital successors (see Table 2-1).

Whether a physical product (such as a toothbrush or a car) or an intangible product (such as a digital product, information, or service), customer satisfaction and loyalty now depend on the quality of customer *experience* associated with your offerings. As Joe Pine suggests in *The Experience Economy* (Harvard Business School Press, 1999), it all boils down to pre- and post-sales customer experience.

Table 2-1 Death of the Old Ps of Marketing

The Old Ps	Their Digital Successors
Products	Customer experience, customized products, and individualized services
Price	Dynamic markets and intelligent agent-based dynamic, even individualized, pricing
Place	Digital marketspace that is not associated with any specific physical location
Promotion	Two-way interaction, mass customization, and customer relationships

Building Digital Capital

Don Tapscott, in his book *Digital Capital* (Harvard Business School Press, 2000), suggests that the new currency of e-business consists of networked knowledge and relationship capital. Unlike brick-and-mortar brands that were built through media blitzes, e-brands are solely a function of relationship capital. Amazon.com, Outpost.com, E*Trade, eBay, and Buy.com have brand value not because they are well known for their full-page advertisements in *The New York Times* but because they have a huge base of customers that trust and repeatedly buy products and services from these businesses (relationship capital). To succeed in electronic business, firms must build their digital capital. To build digital capital, relationships and knowledge must be integrated into business strategy. The focus of this book on using knowledge management to build customer relationships in e-business settings translates to the accumulation of precisely such digital capital.

If the health of a business depends on customer relationships, then B2C e-businesses might have a little problem. According to Forrester Research, 67 percent of first-time buyers empty their shopping carts. B2B electronic commerce sites lost $3.2 billion in potential sales in 1999 because of inadequate customer service provided to potential clients—double the 1998 figure. Moreover, customer service is just one relatively minor dimension of relationship management.

GETTING DOWN TO E-BUSINESS . . . .

Customer centricity has become the hallmark of today's businesses. Many businesses are stuck in the customer-centric mindset of the 1990s; however, few that have peeked beyond the knowledge-technology discontinuity will come to dominate their lines of business. Those few, as Peppers and Rogers would describe it, "have seen the 1-to-1 future and have come back to prepare for it."

Much knowledge is created at the interfaces of an e-business. The interface between customers and an e-business—sometimes called the *marketface*—is one such interface. E-businesses must therefore incorporate the ability to give customers individually relevant products and services while providing them the opportunity to offer feedback to improve the site's ability to meet their continuing needs. Savvy e-businesses are using knowledge-driven personalization to create digital stores that treat each customer as though she was their only one. Online systems for tracking knowledge of customer preferences (such as through analysis of clickstream data) can help your company recover the kind of customer loyalty that used to be common in the Old Economy. Other interfaces exist at the blurred boundaries between a business and its partner firms.

Getting Real About Virtual Commerce

Several unique strengths of electronic markets remain untapped until e-businesses actually attempt to capitalize on the perfection of these markets. Selling is a complex, information-intensive (sometimes, knowledge-intensive) process that requires the salesperson to act as an expert problem solver. Once customers are on board, the battle is to retain them, expand their leads, and to keep them coming back for more.

Tech Talk

Customer Acquisition Cost: Amount of money spent in acquiring a typical new customer. In e-businesses, this cost runs as high as $700.

Channel Strategy: Allows organizations to increase profitability by ensuring that the most effective channel is used to distribute various products and services to customers.

The ability to attract and retain customers is directly related to customer perceptions; these are managed through a hierarchy of complex internal and external communication and knowledge-sharing patterns. To begin tapping into the actual potential of e-business, firms must:

1. Coordinate sales, service, and support across all customer touchpoints and channels and facilitate real-time response to events occurring over large networks by using transaction-level triggers.

2. Increase *application* of information that flows through e-business transactions to personalize future interactions. Information about any given customer must be able to travel to any other touchpoint and across any

combination of channels that may be needed to conclude a transaction with the customer *never* having to begin anew. Multichannel customer interaction support is needed for this. To do this, they must leverage existing data warehouses, mine knowledge, and use it to personalize customer experiences, target promotions, analyze strategic aftereffects, and dump unworthy (those whose lifetime value exceeds the cost of retaining them), never pleased customers!

3. Interpret changes in customer behavior, provide real-time reasoning, deduce generalizations, selectively discard old customer knowledge, and change customer-related behavior accordingly. They must use customer history (historical behavior monitoring) to infer and predict new needs (tactical behavior monitoring), and target cross-sell and up-sell pitches through the right channel.

4. Present a single, unified face to customers and not the blame-transferring one that characterizes many e-businesses. The goal is to build an integrated, enterprise-wide view of the customer, integrate all front-office functions involving customer contact, and present a single face to the customer.

5. Avoid suboptimal product or service quality by facilitating the smooth flow, sharing, and application of actionable information and tacit knowledge throughout the e-business. Costly errors resulting from repeated mistakes must be avoided.

CUSTOMER RELATIONSHIP MANAGEMENT . . . . . .

Customer relationship management (CRM) is a combination of business processes and technology that seeks to understand a company's customers from multiple perspectives to competitively differentiate a company's products and services. Customer relationship management represents a concerted effort to improve customer identification, conversion, acquisition, and retention. The focus of CRM is to improve levels of customer satisfaction, boost customer loyalty, and increase revenues from *existing* customers in the face of stiff competition, globalization, high customer turnover, and growing customer acquisition costs.

The potential of CRM in dot-com businesses is higher than that in traditional businesses because switching costs as well as transaction costs are lower in such environments. One-to-one relationships that predominated businesses in the 1950s have returned—this time with new technology-driven vigor. For what it cost the 1950s market to track a single customer, today's CRM technology allows tracking of millions of

· ·

HASBRO'S SOLUTION FOR UNEXPECTED WINDFALLS

MicroProse, one of the world's leading developers and publishers of entertainment software, is the wholly owned subsidiary of Hasbro, Inc. The company produces some of the industry's best-selling computer games, including such titles as M1 Tank Platoon II™ and Star Trek.™

During the Christmas season of 1996, when sales of some of its game titles suddenly surged, the company realized that it was about to face a surge of post-holiday support calls. MicroProse's reliance on traditional phone support left too many customers waiting on hold, and the number of people who abandoned their calls without getting through grew. Fearing for its future customer base, the company placed support information on its Website in the form of a series of frequently asked questions (FAQs) but saw no noticeable reduction in its help desk volume.

The company rethought the FAQ approach and built an interactive troubleshooting system that would appeal more to its customers—something that was interesting and engaging. Customers could rapidly answer a series of questions on the Web and go through a decision tree that helped them diagnose their problem. The system paid for itself in two months, and the average hold time of the help lines fell by about 34 percent. MicroProse learned that self-service could be done well, and in a value-adding manner for its market.

customers, *individually*. Knowledge gained from CRM techniques can allow a business to efficiently create new delivery channels, capture massive amounts of actionable data from existing customers and use that knowledge to create a customized experience focused on customers' need in real time. CRM marks a definite shift from mass marketing as illustrated in a cross-comparison in Table 2-2.

It is indeed important to provide customers a single face across technologies and media. Why should the same customer be treated differently whether on a Website, in a brick-and-mortar store, or on a toll free phone order line? Promoting and selling a product and associated intangibles—convenience, savings, and personalized service—on the Web and not delivering that complete package is much like breaking a promise. Fail to deliver just one of the three components, and you might lose that customer forever.

Remember that customer relationship management is a business strategy, not a suite of software products. Though vendors—software and service—would have you believe that they offer end-to-end customer relationship management solutions, nothing—economies of scale, broad reach, or fancy software—can compensate for strategic inelegance.

Table 2-2 From Mass Marketing and Customer Relationship Management

Mass Marketing	Customer Relationship Management
Sell one product to many customers	Sell many products to one customer
Differentiate products	Differentiate customers
Acquire a constant stream of new customers	Acquire a constant stream of new business from existing customers
Focus on product features	Focus on customer value
Discontinuous customer interaction	Continuous customer interaction
Customer research	Customer participation
Physical collaboration with suppliers	Knowledge collaboration with suppliers
Short-term focus	Long-term focus
Economies of scale	Economies of scope

REFLECT.COM: PROCTER & GAMBLE'S NEW-NEW THING

Procter & Gamble is a 164-year-old, $40 billion consumer products giant. As the company's sales growth halved from 1996 to 1999, CEO Durk Jager started to look at approaches to revitalize the conservative, slow-moving company into an Internet-savvy, red-tape-free, agile business. E-Business, B2C electronic commerce, and Web-based supply chain management are a fundamental part of that approach.

P&G's new electronic commerce venture, called Reflect.com, was started in Silicon Valley, far from the cultural shackles of its Cincinnati headquarters and its own leading brands including Max Factor and Cover Girl. The value proposition was to deliver individualized beauty-care products, ordered over the Web, and custom-made for each individual consumer. A lipstick ordered through Reflect.com, for example, comes with the shopper's name printed on it. Attempting to leverage P&G's extensive manufacturing, supply chain, R&D, and marketing muscle, the electronic commerce store even lets the shopper pick the packaging material. The bottom line is to create a unique experience for the customer, one that she will remember well enough to repeatedly return. Although the company had secured $50 million in venture funding by mid-2000, the success of its business model was still to be seen.

Fundamentals of Customer Relationships

Marketing has long been a broadcast discipline grounded in practices and norms developed for selling mass-produced products to broad, homogeneous markets and market segments. CRM takes an opposing approach that advocates building a business' customer portfolio through interaction, relationships, networks, and communities of loyal adherents, and through a long-term, transaction-unspecific view. CRM takes a collaborative approach rather than an adversarial approach that has traditionally dominated marketing.

CRM is grounded in the age-old concept of relationship marketing; that is, establishing a learning relationship—one that gets smarter with each interaction—with each customer, starting with the most valuable ones. CRM is an integrated sales, marketing, and service strategy that builds on coordinated action and helps establish collaborative relationships with customers on a long-term basis. As customers assimilate technology, especially in electronic commerce relationships, their expectations about service, support, and dependable service have increased. With the foothold that CRM technology and processes are gaining in small and mid-sized businesses, these businesses can hope to have the level of customer service that only their competitors with deep pockets could afford until recently. Customer relationship management depends on determining the lifetime value of a customer to classify him on a scale of good to bad. The concept underlying this scheme, the CRM lifecycle, and its suitability in various types of businesses are discussed in the following sections.

Lifetime Value of Customers

CRM necessitates viewing a customer not as a one-time transaction but as a series of transactions over time. The focus then shifts from maximizing a single sale to maximizing a single customer's lifetime value to your company. Don Peppers and Martha Rogers point out in *The One to One Future* that it costs companies five times as much to get a new customer as it does to keep an existing one. Companies in the pre-Web era tended to lose about 25 percent of their customers every year. This number has risen drastically since electronic commerce went mainstream. Reducing customer loss by 5 percent can often translate to adding as much as 100 percent to your company's revenues.

The Good, Bad, and Ugly

On the customer front, customer relationship management depends on classifying customers as being good or bad. Defining good and bad customers is the tricky part—one that is accomplished by marketing shrewdness and technology *together*. Some rela-

KCRM IN THE MORTGAGE BUSINESS

Fifty percent of prospective homebuyers use the Web to educate themselves about the home-buying process, and a growing number are shopping online for mortgages and loans, according to Weston Edwards and Associates, of Laguna Beach, California. This trend implies that the online mortgage business will grow to cover almost 10 percent of the business by 2003—a whopping $92 billion. Lendingtree.com, E-loan.com, iOwn.com, and QuickenLoan.com are some of the e-businesses eyeing that market. The basic value proposition of these businesses is their ability to aggregate many buyers and sellers in one place; shoppers can review, compare, and apply within hours. Businesses such as iOwn.com that are doing well in this segment are those that participate in the entire lifecycle and provide a complete end-to-end package from searching, buying, remodeling, maybe even reselling. Old-New principles of taking a lifetime view of each customer is necessary here, as is elsewhere.

tionships are valuable, many more than others. A company's most valuable relationships and most profitable business define their best customers. A corollary to identifying your best customers and rewarding them is identifying the worst ones and getting rid of them! These customers are described as having negative value—they cost more in time and money expended in satisfying them than they will be worth to your company over their lifetime. All is fair in capitalism and competition.

The subtle distinction between the good and the bad is vital because you might as well make little green paper airplanes out of hundred dollar bills and save yourself the effort spent trying to lure potential customers who never will buy your product or those who will never return. Companies that learn to use KM and CRM methods to recognize that can stop investing resources on these potential noncustomers. On the other hand, it is equally critical that you identify potentially loyal customers and ensure that they choose your products and services even more often. Through customer KM, smarter companies have been able to identify the unmet—sometimes unrelated—needs of this second set of customers and fulfill them by diversifying into newer lines of business.

With this end in mind, we will examine how customers can be classified into three broad categories: most valuable, most growable, and below zero (those that must be gotten rid of), in Chapter 5.

The Four Tenets of CRM

Four fundamental ideas explain the value proposition of customer relationship management: Using existing relationships to maximize revenue, using customer knowledge to consistently deliver excellent service, developing repeatable sales processes, and delivering value and developing customer loyalty.

1. *Use existing relationships to maximize revenue.* CRM focuses on establishing stronger relationships with existing customers, retaining "good" customers, and weeding out "bad" customers. The lifetime value of a customer defines his or her value to your business, and maximizing relationships between your business and customers with high lifetime values through up-selling and cross-selling through CRM can push average revenue per existing customer. With CRM, customers' lifetime value can be maximized by retaining them at previously impossible retention levels. At the same time, acquisition costs for existing customers are leveled down to almost zero for new sales of complementary or new products that your company sells.

2. *Use customer knowledge to consistently deliver excellent service.* Effective CRM should surprise your customers with how well your company knows them. It must help overcome the often-observed frustration that customers have in repeating the same information to different departments. When knowledge about an individual customer aggregates over time and allows your company to deliver personalized service, it increases switching costs for the customer. This lock-in arises from the customer having to explain his needs over again to a prospective seller.

Tech Talk

Switching costs: Financial *and nonfinancial* costs incurred by a customer in taking her business elsewhere.

Lock-in: Deliberately increasing switching costs that a customer must incur to take her business elsewhere. In electronic commerce terms, sticky sites that a customer has put time and energy into customizing, increase switching costs.

3. *Develop repeatable sales processes.* CRM facilitates integration of customer knowledge through supporting technology and allows companies to use knowledge of past transactions to effectively sell to both

new and existing customers. Effectively integrating knowledge management and CRM means that your customers can expect to have consistent, dependable, and accurate answers to their questions in every interaction with your company. A long-term customer-centric CRM perspective facilitates usage of accumulated knowledge about the customer for building a more intimate, value-added relationship.

4. Deliver value and develop customer loyalty: Loyalty can be stimulated by proactively using collected information to resolve issues before they become problems. Further, by showing the customer that you know her, and offering products and services that already consider her needs, you can help establish dependence on your offerings over time.

....

CUSTOMER RELATIONSHIP MANAGEMENT TERMINOLOGY

Segmentation: Subdivision of customer populations into finer groups defined by their characteristics.

Customer profitability: Measurement and ranking of customers based on their long-term profitability calculated by measuring accumulated customer revenue less operational costs and acquisition costs.

Customer retention: Measuring how likely the customer is not to churn, and engage in repeat transactions with your business without switching to a competitor (churning).

Response analysis: Measurement of the effectiveness of a customized campaign or promotion within a specific customer segment.

Even before the Web was publicly available, satisfied customers did more good to a business than those who replaced them (see Table 2-3). The secret to customer-driven business success lies in keeping existing customers rather than blindly going all out to get new ones.

Electronic commerce has increased customer expectations for instant gratification. No longer does one have to drive to the other end of town if she is displeased with your store; your biggest competitors are just two mouse clicks away. Customer dissatisfaction ripples as one unhappy customer tells several others. In the digital marketspace, *word of mouse* gets around faster and more pervasively than does word of mouth. Mistakes cost more, and their fatalities can destroy businesses faster than in

Table 2-3 Satisfied and Dissatisfied Customers—A Comparison

Dissatisfied Customers	Satisfied Customers
Only 4% of dissatisfied customers complain	Customer retention costs one-sixth of acquisition
75%–90% of unhappy customers won't be back	Satisfied customers are willing to pay more
Each dissatisfied customer tells nine more	Each happy customer will tell five other potential customers

Source: Data collected by U.S. Office of Consumer Affairs in 1992, and reported by Jon Anton in Customer Relationship Management, Prentice Hall, Englewood Cliffs, 1996.

traditional business settings; ValueAmerica.com, Staples.com, and Buy.com have histories that are plagued by consumers who literally mobbed the stores when word got around the Net about faulty Christmas season discount coupons that would allow customers to purchase goods worth hundreds of dollars without spending a penny.

The CRM Lifecycle

Customers—whether consumers or businesses—do not merely want more choices. "They want exactly what they want—when, where, and how they want it," Pine, Peppers, and Rogers wrote in their 1995 *Harvard Business Review* article. In turbulent and fragmented markets, applying a mass-marketing or mass-production mentality only turns customers off by bombarding them with too many choices. Marketing drivel must go beyond mass customization and instead focus on *individualization* based on sustainable two-way learning relationships. To build such relationships, it is necessary to understand the three phases of customer relationship management: acquisition, enhancement, and retention, as shown in Figure 2-1.

Although all three phases are interrelated, not many companies are able to do all three as well. It therefore becomes essential to choose one activity as the primary, initial focus of your CRM initiative. This choice is important because technology infrastructure-related investments are guided and shaped by it. Choosing a primary focus does not mean that the other two be neglected. We will understand how these phases (Table 2-4) can be supported as we move through the later chapters of this book.

Is CRM Right for All Businesses?

While customer relationship management is often considered a strategic imperative, not all customer interactions need to be personalized. The need for personalizing interactions and determining the value of customer relationship management depends on

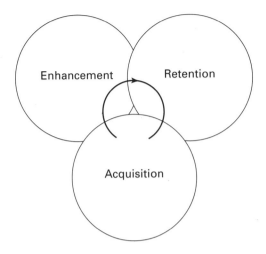

Figure 2-1
Three phases of customer relationship management.

the nature of products and services sold by your company, and on the level of dispersion among various customers' needs. Figure 2-2 shows how customer relationship management is a strategy most fitting businesses that have highly valued customers with diverse needs. In any of the other three quadrants, the cost of managing customer knowledge-based relationships might not be necessarily worth the value derived.

A leading U.S. airline, for example, recognizes that 6 percent of its customers represent 24 percent of all miles flown, and 37 percent of its revenues. This airline's initial customer relationship building efforts must therefore focus on this small segment of most-valuable customers. While focusing on these customers is a significant underpinning behind CRM, recognizing customers who represent a majority of its future income stream is also critical.

Table 2-4 Three Key Phases of CRM

CRM Phase	Key Activities
Acquisition	Differentiate product/service according to customer needs
	Offer unmatched convenience through customer knowledge
	Back with excellent service and support and proactive response
Enhancement	Cross-sell and up-sell products
	Increase sales per customer
Retention	Gain customer knowledge to build service adaptability
	Deliver new products that meet current customers' needs
	Employee incentives to retain customers

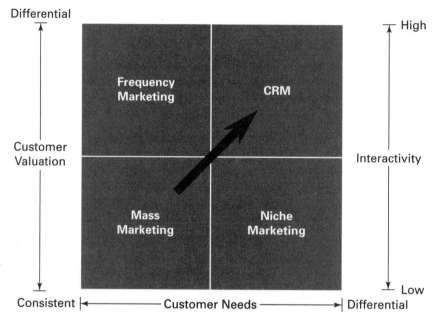

Figure 2-2
Customer valuation, interactivity, and the need for relationship management.

RETURN OF THE CORNER PIZZERIA?

The mega mergers and national chains of the 1970s left a noticeable trail. Barbershops became national chains like Great Clips and corner pizzerias became international chains like Pizza Hut and Papa Johns. All this only made it increasingly impossible to develop and maintain individual relationships between customers and businesses. Welcome to the world of electronic commerce, even that last ray of geographic vicinity is gone; the bookstore in your living room computer might have a warehouse on the opposite coast, and the complex supply chain through which your goods get delivered makes it impossible that you personally interact with anyone at all in the business chain except for the UPS delivery guy! Aha, just when you thought that cost-competitiveness and process transparency eliminate most competitive differentiators, you realize that the medium is rebuilding the corner pizzeria-like relationships again. Welcome to the New-New world of the Old-New.

From Bits and Bricks to Clicks-and-Mortar

Many stable businesses that have attempted to transition to the Web have learned that new technology that is blindly applied to an old organization results only in an expensive old organization. E-business requires a fundamentally new approach to business—one that is built on the foundations of knowledge and relationships. Building relationships requires a unified, comprehensive view of each individual customer (see Figure 2-3) that is analyzed in real time ("Internet Speed") and that is actually brought to bear upon customer interactions throughout the enterprise. It should not matter where, how, or through which channel a customer visits the business. Think of a local office supply store such as Staples or Office Depot: The store should be able to recognize you, remember your preferences, and customize its behavior toward you based on your history across its brick and mortar, catalog, and Web channels.

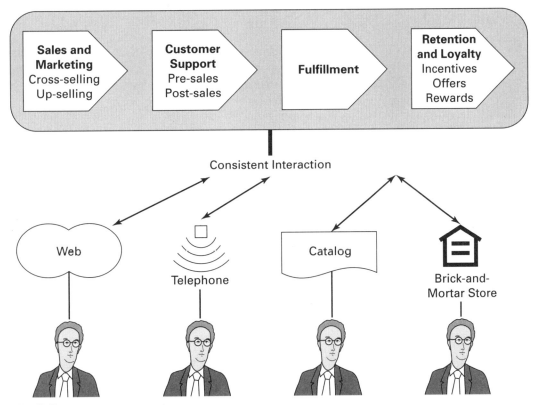

Fig 2-3
Consistency of interaction across all channels is key.

Questions like "But don't you all work for the same company?" from brick-and-mortar turned click-and-mortar store customers are a warning signal. Your business' inability to share customer information across internal spheres of influence can be detrimental to the quality of customer interaction and communication, and in turn degrades the customer experience and loyalty. Service and support representatives who cannot provide intelligent and accurate answers to customers' questions make their businesses come across as being incompetent and uncaring. Understanding and optimizing the entire customer lifecycle, from prospect to lead customer, require integrating data from front- and back-office systems and across all customer touchpoints, electronic and traditional.

Most companies do not have the necessary levels of integration between functional departments (such as sales and service systems) or across channels (Web and in-store accounts) to collaboratively support electronic transactions. In a challenging world of e-business, you need to respond to increasing customer demands and constantly changing technology and market needs; relationship management technology support infrastructure must allow you to be more responsive to existing customers, reduce customer acquisition costs, and provide a consistent level of service within each customer cluster *based on its value to your business.*

To build digital capital, your business cannot be stuck in its old ways of doing things, especially if it is a brick-and-mortar business transitioning to the "e" medium. The bits and the bricks cannot be separate, disconnected entities. For born-on-the-Web businesses, there is no such legacy to deal with.

KNOWLEDGE MANAGEMENT . . . .

Knowledge management is the process of managing organizational knowledge for creating business value and sustaining competitive advantage through the creation, communication, and application of knowledge gained from customer interactions to maximize business growth and value. In the context of CRM, knowledge management focuses on creating and delivering innovative products or services; managing and enhancing relationships with existing and new customers, partners, and suppliers; and improving customer-related work practices and processes.

Businesses that have tried to gain sustainable competitive advantage through new and innovative technology have eventually been copied. Many businesses have given lip service to the concept of knowledge management using oxymorons such as expert systems, core competencies, best practices, learning organizations, and corporate memory and have tried to continue relying on their capital, labor, natural resources, and innovations—all of which have been displaced by knowledge. In dynamic electronic markets characterized by uncertainty, new technologies, multiplying global competitors, and accelerated product and service obsolesce, businesses that consistently create new knowledge, quickly disseminate it and embody it in their new products and services are the ones that lead the way.

The ever-growing business centrality of the customer makes it even more crucial to be able to harvest customer knowledge as action to develop stable, long-term relationships with existing customers, knowing, understanding, and serving their needs, and consistently applying new customer knowledge to accurately and rapidly reshape your business' offerings. Delighting the customer means asking the right questions without losing control of costs or quality. Businesses that do not embrace a stance on customer-centric knowledge management will soon fall too far behind to be able to catch up.

Defining Knowledge

Knowledge is defined as a fluid mix of framed, contextual experience, values, situated information, expertise, and grounded intuition that provides the framework for evaluating, understanding, and incorporating new experiences and information. Such knowledge becomes not only embedded in documents or repositories but also in organizational routines, processes, practices, and norms. For the purpose of this book, we will deal with knowledge as it relates to customers and markets.

Knowledge, Market Value, and Prosperity

In a knowledge-based digital economy, a business' intangible assets carry more weight than last year's balance sheet or income statement. These intangibles primarily include their (1) knowledge capital and (2) relationship capital. Examples of such intangible assets include:

- Brand recognition
- Industry-driving vision and ground-breaking business strategy
- Patents and technological or process breakthroughs
- Customer relationships and customer loyalty
- Innovative business ideas
- Anticipated future products
- Recognized history of past achievements

Amazon, eBay, America Online, eFax.com, E*Trade, and Schwab are some excellent e-businesses that have excelled at building such intangible assets. These intangibles account for tens, even hundreds of billions, of dollars in differences between their capital assets (land, building, computers, and other property) and their market valuation (*the* measure of value that investors and markets associate with a company). Unfortunately, few companies have succeeded in simultaneously maximizing *both* their knowledge capital and relationship capital.

....

Intellectual Capital Versus Knowledge

Intellectual capital (IC) is an asset such as knowledge, collective expertise, good will, brand value, or a patent that cannot be measured by traditional accounting methods but can be used by a company to its advantage. Skilled people, their competencies, market positions, good will, recognition, achievements, patents, contacts, support, collaborators, market innovation leadership, a repeat customer base, and reputation represent various facets of IC.

Knowledge is actionable information—deeper, richer, and more expansive. It is available when and where needed to make the right decisions, and in the right context. It is valid information endowed with meaning, context, and purpose that bring it to habitually bear upon decisions. Knowledge is a subset of intellectual capital.

If knowledge and relationships are the digital currency of e-business, employee walkouts often cause a business to lose some of this capital, often to competitors that those employees join. In *The Loyalty Effect*, Fred Reichheld and Tom Teal (Harvard Business School Press, 1996) warn that knowledge attrition is a severe problem in many businesses as up to half of a business' knowledge is lost over a period of 5 to 10 years through employee, customer, and investor turnover. The key notion behind knowledge management is to safeguard and maximize the value derived from tacit knowledge—knowledge that is in the mind and cannot be expressed—held by employees, and indeed, customers and partners as well. While KM is partly a technology problem and partly a business-strategy issue, it is too easy to confuse the relative significance of one and attempt to solve a nontechnology problem with an expensive piece of technology.

Comprehending Knowledge

To understand what knowledge management implies, it is necessary to get a grip on what knowledge means in the context of a customer. The fundamental mistake that companies repeatedly make is that of equating information and knowledge. Table 2-5 contrasts information and knowledge. This distinction can be taken one step further to categorize some knowledge as wisdom (i.e., the state of knowing which knowledge to apply to solve a given problem).

Table 2-5 Differentiating Information from Knowledge

Information	Knowledge
Processed data	Actionable information
Simply gives us the facts	Allows making predictions, casual associations, or predictive decisions
Clear, crisp, structured, and simplistic	Muddy, fuzzy, partly unstructured
Easily expressed in written form	Intuitive, hard to communicate, and difficult to express in words and illustrations
Obtained by condensing, correcting, contextualizing, and calculating data	Lies in connections, conversations between people, experience-based intuition, and people's ability to compare situations, problems, and solutions
Devoid of owner dependencies	Depends on the owner
Handled well by information systems	Needs informal channels
Key resource in making sense of large volumes of data	Key resource in intelligent decision making, forecasting, design, planning, diagnosis, and intuitively judging
Evolves from data; formalized in databases, books, manuals, and documents	Formed in and shared among collective minds; evolves with experience, successes, failures, and learning over time
Formalized, captured, and explicated; can easily be packaged into a reusable form	Often emerges in minds of people through their experiences

· ·

THE FLOWERS IN MY GARDEN.COM

Austin, Texas-based Garden.com is a B2C gardening supply store and gardening enthusiast community hub. The company posted $3.2 million in revenues—still a scratch on the surface of a $47 billion market. Even though 48 percent of online users are gardeners according to The National Gardening Association's estimates, no two gardens are the same. To drive revenues, online gardening experiences must be personalized to *each* gardener's own garden.

Recognizing this as an opportunity rife for personalization, Garden.com has built several features into its Website to entice users to register and stick around. Over a million users have registered, and another 600,000 subscribe to a bimonthly e-mail bulletin, *Bloom Times*, that reminds shoppers about various facets of gardening based on their location, interests, and preferences. Although the site up-sells offerings, it also *down-sells* when a potential shopper tries to buy a flower bulb at the wrong time of the year or for an unsuitable region of the country. Trust can indeed be a significant relationship builder, and Garden.com is building it well.

The company creates lock-ins by having users enter various details of their own garden into the system. Once these details are available, potential shoppers can use the Landscape Planner feature, which picks plants suited for the member's region of the country, unique yard shape, and conditions. These plants can then be dragged and dropped (using a Java-based interface) to different spots on a diagram of the yard's layout to design a personalized garden.

Knowledge can be either explicit or tacit. Explicit knowledge can be stored in databases, codified in books and manuals, and expressed in some written form. Tacit knowledge, on the other hand, is inexpressible.

Tacit knowledge represents what we know but cannot express in its full form. For example, you may know how to drive, but you cannot teach someone else how to drive by explaining it in an e-mail, and they cannot learn simply by reading a driving manual. Seeing the robot Number Five learn how to drive a truck in *Short Circuit* is not the simple reality of business. Tacit and explicit knowledge are compared in Table 2-6.

Knowledge management creates value by actively leveraging the know-how, experience, and judgment resident within and outside an organization.

Components and Characteristics of Knowledge

Intuition, ground truth, judgment, experience, values, assumptions, beliefs, and intelligence are various components of knowledge (see Table 2-7). These largely exist in tacit form and can be occasionally codified in systems, software, and documents.

Three characteristics of knowledge provide insight into its management: (1) its experiential nature, (2) its collaborative nature, and (3) reciprocity.

Table 2-6 Tacit Versus Explicit Knowledge.

Characteristic	Tacit	Explicit
Nature	Personal, context specific	Can be codified and explicated
Formalization	Difficult to formalize, record, encode, or articulate	Can be codified and transmitted in a systematic and formal language
Development process	Trial and error encountered in practice	Explication of tacit understanding and interpretation of information
Location	People's minds	Documents, databases, Web pages, e-mails, charts, etc
Conversion processes	Converted to explicit through externalization that is often driven by metaphors and analogy	Converted back to tacit through understanding and absorption
IT support	Hard to manage, share, or support with IT	Well supported by existing IT
Medium needed	Needs a rich communication medium	Can be transferred through conventional electronic channels

1. *Experiential knowledge is stored as scripts.* Knowledge is largely derived from experience. Being able to transfer knowledge implies that a part of experiential knowledge—scripts, intuition, rules of thumb, heuristics, and methods—get transferred to the recipient as well.

2. *Knowledge is essentially collaborative and falters with a data-hoarding mentality.* New knowledge is created, in part, through the collaborative processes that employees pursue as a part of their work. The threat to such enabling collaboration comes from the "more is better" data-hoarding mentality inherited from data processing and data management eras.

3. *Success of a knowledge management system depends on reciprocity.* Knowledge management depends on knowledge sharing, reciprocity, and a supporting culture. Reciprocity drives people's willingness to share knowledge and such reciprocity can be introduced only through appropriate reward systems and corporate culture change.

Table 2-7: Components of Knowledge and Tacit/Explicit Nature of Existence

Component	Description	T	E
Assumptions	About markets, customers, the business environment, consumer preferences, competition Need for discovering, recording, and maintaining these assumptions over time	√	√
Judgment	Allows knowledge to rise beyond an opinion when it reexamines itself and refines every time it is applied and acted upon	√	
Experience	Provides a historical perspective Connects past happenings with present scenarios Helps determine shortcuts to previously encountered problems	√	√
Scripts	Facilitate mental pattern matching Guide thinking and rule out previously rejected/failed option paths	√	
Rules of thumb/heuristics	Experientially approximate solutions for efficient analysis of present situations	√	√
Norms and values	Determine the basis for commitment to selected solutions	√	
Beliefs	Often ingrained in corporate culture; usually influenced by founders^φ	√	√
Skills	Tacitly held abilities honed over time	√	√

^φ *E.g., "having fun" at Southwest Airlines, "an ambient experience" at Starbucks, and creating "insanely great" (such as the iMac and iBook) products at Apple.*

KM's Value Proposition

Businesses can reap an immense payoff when a knowledge management solution makes it easier for employers to reach out to employees, customers, and partners who share common problems or have experiences to share—a key candidate being customer relations and support departments. The value proposition of KM in the context of the 10 challenges faced by businesses, and more so by e-businesses, is described in Table 2-8.

Table 2-8: Understanding the Value Proposition of Knowledge Management

Challenge	Value Proposition
Better, faster, and cheaper	Shorter time-to-market, quality maximization, and cost minimization creates a three-way pull that can force business to move in contradictory directions. KM leverages your business' core competencies to provide the launch pad for their new product and service offerings
Different requirements for success	Product success drivers are getting increasingly hard to pin down as Ford's Taurus, 3Com's PalmPilot, Apple's iMac and iBook, and their many unsuccessful clones exemplify
Process competition	Process, not the ingredients used to deliver a product or service to the consumer, differentiates successful e-businesses. KM helps you develop and refine these processes in ways that allow their application long after an existing contract or product line has been archived or discontinued. Dropping old ways of doing things altogether or challenging the fundamental ways in which the company does business is made possible by KM
Market volatility	Market instability necessitates organized abandonment so your business can reshape its products and services and proactively exit declining product lines
Opportunity spotting	Knowledge-enabled businesses can anticipate changes in customer preferences—an evolving social trend, a new management practice, a nascent technology, rival innovations, or economic development in a potential foreign market. KM tracks and maintains knowledge regarding the validity of assumptions about markets, customers, and business environments before critical decisions are made based on flawed ones
Collective expertise	KM supports collaborative knowledge sharing among employees, teams, and communities to help them collaboratively make accurate decisions faster—and act on those decisions to create more economic value for your business
Knowledge attrition and loss	Tacit knowledge, skills, competencies, understanding, and insight are mobile. KM can prevent knowledge loss commonly associated with employee departure
Inimitability	Creating new knowledge provides process competence and an inimitable hard-to-copy competitive advantage
Knowledge embedding	Embedding knowledge in products, services, and processes helps deliver higher-quality, individualized offerings that can lock in customers
Distributed intelligence	Transferring existing knowledge into other parts, departments, and locations of the company, especially when it is virtually distributed. With methods such as profiling, information that might be relevant in near-term decisions can reach the right people ahead of time

Weaving the Web of Knowledge

The Web, for the first time, has provided a medium through which a two-way conversation can occur and a long-term relationship be built. What was once a dream of the one-to-one relationship is now a viable possibility, though still not a given. In such relationships, customers teach the company what they want; thanks to e-business technologies, such teaching can often be accomplished rather transparently, without the customers realizing that they are even doing it. Technology is not the savior; intranets, discussion list tools, collaborative systems, and object-oriented database systems are not KM systems, but mere components of a KM solution for which there is no single, canned approach. Technology must enable a business to hear what the *customers* are saying, not what the business wants to hear. In their book *Information Rules*, Hal Varian and Carl Shapiro describe this concept as a *lock-in*—a dependency so strong that customers are even willing to pay more just to keep buying from the same supplier.

LANDSEND.COM: THE EARLY ARRIVAL

In Internet time, three months equal a lifetime. Some businesses have arrived past the notion of the lone corporate hero and at the knowledge management juncture ahead of others; others must get there soon or they might not get there at all. Strategy and culture come first, technology comes second; reverse them and you are in trouble. Lands' End, the Wisconsin-based direct merchandiser, is one of those that arrived early. In a move from their catalog to a Web storefront, Lands' End (www.landsend.com) introduced two collaborative services for its customers: (1) Lands End Live and (2) Shop with a Friend.

Lands' End Live uses hundreds of well-trained customer support representatives who man the retailer's Website to answer questions from customers live over the Web. Although conventional wisdom would say that shoppers prefer the telephone for asking questions about a product, four out of five Lands' End customers actually preferred chat.

Shop with a Friend similarly allows two customers to shop together as though they were shopping at the same physical store. The technology synchronizes two browsers so that two remotely located parents can shop for, say, swimwear for their kids together.

Lands' End also introduced another feature called The Personal Model, a virtual image of the customer built from a series of questions (build, shoulder width, hips, bust, skin tone, etc.). Customers can then select clothing from the catalog and try different combinations on their own virtual model.

E-businesses have been hoping to create such lock-ins for a long time, desperately spending ridiculous amounts of money on new customer acquisition. Unfortunately, there is no such thing as a lock-in if the customer begins to expect freebies such as discount coupons before they return. Although the stock markets had been rewarding Web-based businesses for the sheer size of their individual customer bases until late 1999, the focus has since shifted to measuring how many of those customers actually return. Customer loyalty and retention now differentiate an e-business from its competitors.

Tech Talk

Strategic Innovation: Strategic innovation occurs when a company identifies gaps in its industry's positioning map and decides to fill them, and the gaps grow into mass markets. Gaps might imply new emerging customer segments that competition might have neglected, new and emerging needs of old customers, or just new ways of delivering products and services.

KNOWLEDGE-ENABLED CUSTOMER RELATIONSHIP MANAGEMENT . . . .

Knowledge management principles applied to e-business relationship management are described in the rest of this book as knowledge-enabled customer relationship management. Knowledge management and customer relationship management have like goals and are closely related to the health of any business. In a 1999 survey of managers by IDC, an analyst group, increasing profits and revenues, followed by expertise retention and then customer retention and satisfaction were cited as top reasons for managing knowledge. Figure 2-4 illustrates what KCRM exactly means. Knowledge-enabled customer relationship management lies at the intersection of knowledge management, collaborative relationship management (with customers *and* partners), and e-business.

Knowledge management lets you challenge what you know, and redesign and reconfigure existing products and services to radically transform their value proposition to meet new customer needs. Integrating knowledge management practice into relationship management processes ensures that your business will recognize triggers of change in your customer base (satisfaction levels, new market segments, and attrition), competition (new entrants, declining market share, profits), and the external business environment (substitute products and services, discontinuous innovation, new market openings). Integrating knowledge management and CRM gives business-

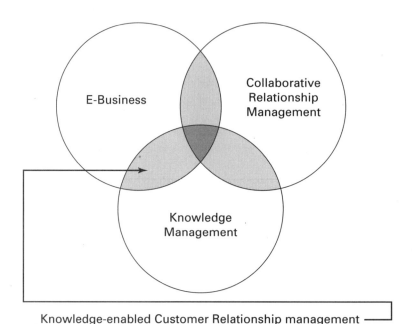

Knowledge-enabled Customer Relationship management

Figure 2-4
KCRM lies at the intersection of knowledge management and relationship management in e-business.

es the depth of customer information, analysis, and intimacy that they need to truly understand customers' needs.

Strategic knowledge management allows your business to be *purposefully opportunistic*—recognize and act on market gaps and opportunities as they emerge. As todays' innovative knowledge degrades to the core knowledge of tomorrow, your business must keep pace to maintain knowledge at a level that exceeds that of its competitors. This necessitates a comprehensive knowledge management strategy that takes into account your company's history, culture, experience, goals, realities, and problems. This process indeed involves the transformation of human capital into applied knowledge within customer-interaction processes and decisions. KCRM is the art of transforming knowledge of your customers into a sustainable source of value for your customers and your business, and a mechanism for building lasting relationships with them. Knowledge-enabled CRM is little different from the old-time systems in small towns where the barber knew everyone by name. The so-called customer database was in his head, and business intelligence came from his tacit understanding of the customer. In between these good old times and the present came the era of mass production, which drastically changed the scale of production. Specifically in the context of e-business, this involves the end-to-end value chain, which also includes your suppliers, business partners, and ally firms.

Evolution of KCRM

As we move from simple, transaction-oriented marketing processes such as order fulfillment and inventory management toward knowledge-oriented, multidimensional, integrated activities like relationship management (see Figure 2-5), coordination requirements and operational dependence on other business processes increase exponentially. Integration of knowledge management then begins to play a key role in determining the efficiency and efficacy of business processes. As Figure 2-5 describes, with increasing levels of process complexity and knowledge intensity, knowledge-oriented business processes replace activity- and transaction-oriented business processes that preceded them.

As the level of interactivity between businesses and their customers increases, we move away from approaches such as data mining (which is rarely real-time) and interactive marketing to knowledge-enabled and real-time customer relationship management processes (see Figure 2-6).

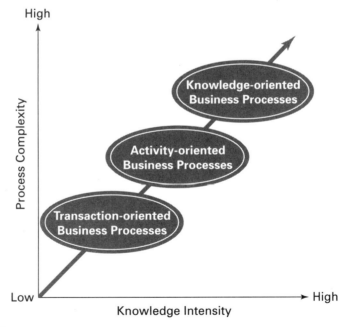

Figure 2-5
The evolution of knowledge-oriented business processes is motivated by process complexity and knowledge intensity.

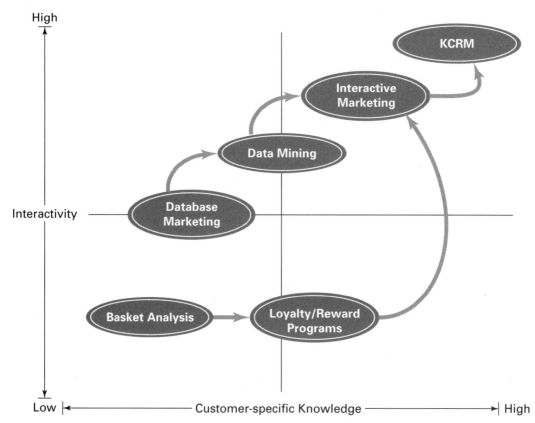

Figure 2-6
High levels of interactivity and knowledge intensity demand new approaches to customer knowledge management.

Customer loyalty programs such as the many frequent flyer airline clubs or frequent shopper cards given away by grocery stores provide valuable insight into the spending habits of major target customer groups. Unfortunately, as I reported in another book, *The Knowledge Management Toolkit* (Prentice Hall, 2000), only two percent of grocery store scanner data that is collected ever is analyzed.

Understanding the Customer Knowledge Value Chain

To believe that CRM—or any of its faddish mutants such as e-CRM (CRM in an "e" environment) and PRM (partner relationship management)—can be implemented without *all* relevant knowledge about your customers is a perfect invitation for disas-

WHAT MAKES A CUSTOMER LOYAL?

Customer loyalty is founded on the satisfaction with the total experience with your company. A loyal customer will want to purchase incremental offerings, products, and services often without exploring comparable competitor offerings. In e-business, the *word of mouse* that often moves faster than word of mouth will be in your favor if you consistently meet these three needs:

1. Knowledge—of the customer's past dealings with your company, of market and industry trends, of your own products, its features, and benefits
2. Anticipation of future needs
3. Superior communication across all experiential phases of each transaction

To be able to retain customers, your business must meet these needs better than any competitor. If one employee conveys limited knowledge, poor anticipation of customer needs, and unsatisfactory communications, he or she stereotypes the entire organization in that customer's perception.

ter. The starting point in implementing KCRM in a business is to gain a complete understanding of customers, their needs, and preferences, and the processes that support fulfillment of those needs. Processes in the front office are unsuited for this because they are often unstructured, nontransactional, highly distributed among functional divisions of the business, and difficult to standardize. Furthermore, merely gathering information is not enough—businesses must be able to analyze it, convert it into knowledge, and act upon it in a timely manner that influences customer purchases and relationships. Effectiveness of these front-office processes is influenced by the supply of accurate knowledge about markets, customers, and products. As businesses add new channels for customer interaction—only one of which is the Web—gaining a 360-degree view of the customer requires real-time integration of customer information and its contextualization. As companies increasingly shift their focus toward e-business, the old-age value chain (sequence of value-adding activities) transforms as illustrated in Figure 2-7.

With this shift coupled with customer centricity, capital intensity reduces and knowledge intensity increases. Maintaining a large inventory, for example, becomes cost prohibitive because it translates into a higher cost for the final product. All tradi-

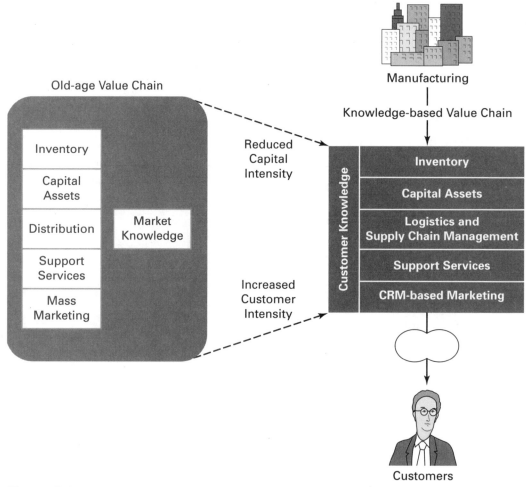

Figure 2-7
Customer intensity takes precedence over capital intensity as businesses transition toward New Economy business models.

tional supply-chain management functions and investments are then increasingly driven by customer knowledge.

Business must become asset poor and knowledge rich to viably compete in this new environment. As Figure 2-8 illustrates, even though the attributes of customer relationships that determine their overall perceptions are arguably similar in e-business settings, the processes required to deliver those are very different. Sales, service, delivery, and support in a typical B2C electronic commerce store are highly distributed functions. Your book order at Buy.com might be placed on a server in Washington

DEREGULATION AND CUSTOMER RENEWAL: THE CASE OF HONG KONG'S T&T

Hong Kong's telephone density is among the highest in the world with 70 telephones for every 100 people. The introduction of deregulation-induced competition raised the level of service, lowered prices, and delivered more options to telephone users in Hong Kong. By 1997, 3.4 million exchange lines were serving 4.5 million telephones. T&T, a major telephony provider in Hong Kong needed to compete on quality of service, a goal that was hindered by a complicated and difficult-to-use support and service system. With most processes handled manually, customer service was locked in a slow and cumbersome procedure. Support staff often had to go through more than 10 time-consuming, error-inducing screens to create a file for a new client. Accounting functions and service orders took place independently of each other with no mechanisms for tracking or analysis of consolidated customer history. Recently, the company began an initiative to build new systems that would allow support staff to integratively address customer support issues, increase loyalty, and retain their business. The company began by putting into place a Web-facilitated system that provided a unified view of each customer, his or her history, and integrated his or her interactions across all channels of contact.

State, perhaps fulfilled by Ingram, shipped from a warehouse in Tennessee, and delivered by UPS to your Atlanta address. Customer support might be provided by Buy.com's staff in California. If the book was delivered soggy, I as a customer will blame no one else but Buy.com ("They took my money and sent me a soggy book!"). Making a customer happy now takes a lot more than a pleasant store clerk at a Borders bookstore around the corner. Coordination and collaboration become key. Low prices could tempt a customer once, but not forever, if it translates to compromise on service quality.

Relationship management in an e-business context cannot be limited to customers alone. The new transparent collaboration-driven e-business model also necessitates collaborative sharing of significant amounts of sensitive information among your company and its suppliers. The ability to successfully communicate determines the strength of relationships among business units and customers and, in turn, a critical competency needed to sustain customer relationships. The customer sees your company as a black box: He asks a question, it is answered; he orders a product, it is delivered. No excuses of internal noncoordination will work anymore.

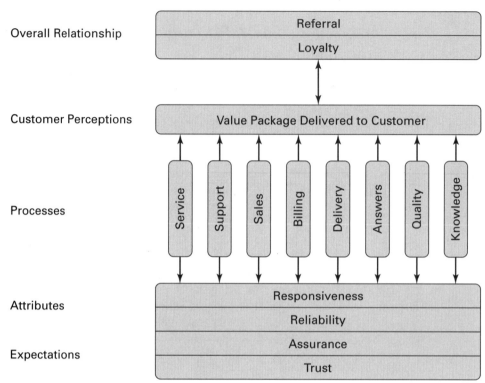

Figure 2-8
The relationship value chain is influenced by a multitude of processes.

SELF-HELP IN A NETWORK OF PERFECT STRANGERS

> Self-service, often considered a cost-cutting measure, can be a significant value adder in e-business as Dell, Amazon, eBay, and Half.com evidence in their ability to bring small-town rules in global networks of perfect strangers.

Unfortunately, customer data is scattered across a range of stove-piped operational systems and must be aggregated instantaneously; both vendors and suppliers must be able to share information across the channel at lightning speeds. Table 2-9 shows just three business activities in a retail consumer product-related B2C transaction. As products and the nature of transactions become increasingly complex, both

Table 2-9: A Typical B2C Consumer Product Transaction

	Marketing	Sales	Service and Support
Product/service delivery	Product management Lifecycle management Segmentation Promotion Cross-selling Up-selling	Sales planning Sale analysis Sales force management Web support management	Service planning Defect reporting Technical support
Business process coordination	Sales coordination Promotion design Promotion delivery Profile linking Market research	Web order placement Call process management Order confirmation Activity reporting	Service coordination Scheduling Channel integration
Transaction management and knowledge creation	Profiling Service "assembly" Product configuration Knowledge application Cross-sell offer generation Business-rules management	Clickstream analysis Account management Customer profile analysis Data mining Knowledge application	Warranty claim management Contractual issues Complaint resolution

information coordination hurdles and opportunities for customer knowledge management increase.

For most e-businesses, customer retention is the hardest part—one that can be assisted by knowledge management. New knowledge management tools to source, collect, combine, sift, and analyze a wealth of data and convert it into actionable information are crucial facilitators for marketing (processes that address identification of prospective customers and classification and differentiation of existing customers along the continuum from most valuable to below zero), sales (to existing and new customers), and support (pre- and post-sales) functions.

Knowledge-Based Individualization

Managing customer knowledge and applying it to strengthen relationships are not about maximizing profits or the size of the customer base alone but about maximizing the *value* and *loyalty* of your existing customer base. In few words, it means that you as a business are willing to change your ways with a customer based on what she tells you about herself and what else you know about her. This implies identifying, tracking, and interacting with an individual customer and then reconfiguring your product or service to precisely meet the needs of *that* customer. Every interaction must improve your company's ability to fit your product or service to that customer's current and future needs.

> **Tech Talk**
>
> **Individualization: Designing and delivering a product or service package in response to the customer's needs—explicated or predicted.**

Nevertheless, there is a big slip between the cup and the lip. Asking your customer interaction representatives to be polite and friendly is one thing, but it is quite another thing to be able to identify, track, learn from, and interact with each customer on an individual basis *and then* individualize and configure your product or service package to meet each customer's specific needs. Delivering such individualization— and delivering it better than any competitor—is what differentiates e-businesses. Traditional store perks such as valet parking, ambient surroundings, premier location, late hours, or catchy paintings on your store walls do not have any equivalents in the digital world. Besides a reliable and easy-to-use site, electronic businesses have little to boast about other than their relationships with happy and loyal customers.

A DIFFERENT MEANING OF RELATIVITY

> Remember the tale of two friends who went camping? Later that night when both were fast asleep, a lion appeared outside their tent. One of them started to put on his sneakers. Astonished, the other one asked him why he thought that he could outrun the lion. The first one replied, "I only have to outrun you."
>
> Likewise, in e-business, capabilities are *relative* to those of your key competitors. The objective of KCRM is not that of perfectionism but that of managing relationships and knowledge better than your competitors.

In a relatively complex digital business environment, this necessitates seamless integration of business processes across internal departments and functional divisions, customers, suppliers, and business partners. Integration means that a customer feels that he is dealing with a single organization, not disparate departments. Excuses that have long worked in brick-and-mortar stores ("But that is not my department," or "Sorry, I cannot find you in my system") are rarely acceptable in electronic business-es. It's not your customer's job to know who to call in your organization for assistance; it's your job to transparently route your customer to employees who can and will answer his questions, no matter how the customer approaches your organization.

Thinking Beyond Customer Segments

Tomorrow's leading e-businesses must use what has been learned about individual customers—not just microsegments—to determine product and service configura-tions, promotion tactics, pricing and service levels; understand evolving needs; predict behavior; maximize share of the customer (not just market share), and select the right interaction and sales channel mix (i.e., channel strategy).

E-business success is increasingly measured not only through improved quality of customer information but also through increased customer retention, sustained loy-alty, and better-than-industry-average quality of customer relationships. Operational efficiency is expected and is rarely sufficient to distinguish one business from another, especially when competing e-businesses demonstrate it. Changes to business process-es, organizational structure, people, and culture must accompany e-business strategy formulation. Customer relationship management effectiveness must therefore be mea-sured using a comprehensive set of metrics that benchmark both financial and nonfi-nancial outcomes—a hard transition from the return-on-investment driven mentality for many managers that is addressed in Chapter 10.

Building Learning Relationships

Building customer loyalty heavily depends on the strength of the learning involved in the business' relationships with its customers. A learning relationship is one that gets smarter with each successive interaction. Eventually, the relationship becomes so strong that the cost of rebuilding it with another competitor makes it prohibitive for the customer to switch. That is when you know that you have created a lock-in. However, lock-ins must be sustained, and that is where customer knowledge manage-ment comes in.

Learning relationships can be built with customers in any industry and in any line of business. However, it is not always worth the cost. The cost of building a long-term relationship must be weighed against the lifetime value of the customer, not just her immediate revenue stream (a concept that is elegantly elaborated by Martha Rogers and Don Peppers in *Enterprise One-to-One*). Generally, complex products and services that are (1) *customer* knowledge intensive, (2) big-ticket items, or (3) highly specialized are the best candidates for building such relationships. That would not include burgers at Burger King but does include financial services, consulting, banking, and even car maintenance. Digital goods—information services, online products, e-services, music, and Web-based applications—unequivocally fall in the highly customizable group.

The Three-Phase Customer Knowledge Cycle

The actual process of knowledge management involves three broad phases that often run in parallel: (1) acquisition, (2) sharing, and (3) utilization, as illustrated in the context of the customer in Figure 2-9. Development and creation of insights, skills, and relationships (knowledge acquisition), when disseminated and shared (knowledge sharing) are followed by integration of learning, insights, and experiential knowledge and bringing it to bear upon current decisions (knowledge utilization).

Customer knowledge management technology must help create a dynamic web of intelligence to support an ongoing, concerted effort to improve customer identification, conversion, acquisition, and retention, and to deliver personalized services. E-businesses need analytic applications that can integrate customer information across all customer touchpoints—traditional sales channels, online sites, phone and Web-based support channels, print and online media, and other channels. Knowledge management technologies can offer high levels of personalization, automated rule-base categorization, and strategic decision support without the expense of maintaining individual relationships. KCRM solutions therefore provide the foundation for relationship and knowledge management platforms that are:

1. *Rapid*: Fast time to market, responsive, and real time
2. *Robust*: Tightly integrated, scalable, flexible, adaptable, and semi-intelligent
3. *Reliable*: Accurate, fast execution of key business activities (such as answering customer queries or providing a quote) facilitated by the sharing of best practices across locations and functional divisions within your business and with your channel partners

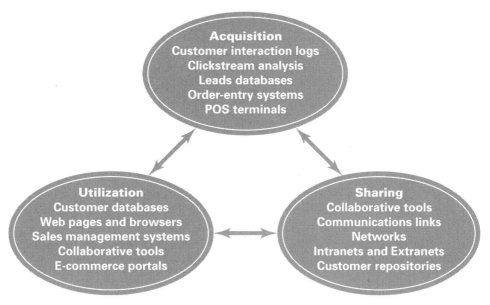

Figure 2-9
The three-phase customer knowledge cycle.

Knowledge-based strategy must be integrated into the fabric of your business to produce worthwhile results. This necessitates a leap from grass roots to enterprise-wide adoption with clearly laid out financial metric linkages. In other words, the process of implementing customer knowledge focus needs process, people, and technology issues to be simultaneously addressed. In the chapters that follow, we examine how strategy and technology collectively address these customer knowledge integration phases.

SELLING TO AN UNWILLING CUSTOMER

Consider the hypothetical scenario of Gertrude, who has been thinking about the Blueberry iMac for many months now. She has seen it in her local computer store and spent many Sunday mornings there, trying to convince herself that she does not really like it all that much. However, every time she comes back home, she is convinced that she would like to have one to replace her old Windows PC. She has been looking for a deal on eBay, but has figured out that those computers sell too close to their retail price there to justify buying a used one. Although she does not have an explicit price in mind, she does have an implicit price, knowing that a brand-new unit sells for $999. After adding taxes, she has a mental figure of about $1,100 that she cannot justify. Although she goes to her local computer store, the sales representatives there are too busy to note that she is a good prospect. What the brick-and-mortar store could not do happened at TheBigAppleStore.com, a site located on the opposite coast. She has visited this site several times and has used its "compare models" feature to compare various models. Last week, she even added the Blueberry iMac to her shopping cart and calculated shipping costs to her apartment address. Then, she abruptly left the site to go to NewYorkTimes.com.

TheBigAppleStore.com captured the entire session, offering key insights into her buying behavior. Gertrude had browsed many times without buying. Sales managers at TheBigAppleStore.com realized that Apple was introducing new models of the iMacs, and the one that Gertrude had been looking at would soon be discontinued. They send her an e-mail generated automatically by the CRM system and tell her that the $999 iMac has been marked down to $699, and that for a limited time it will be shipped free. Knowing that she had previously purchased a copy of Microsoft Works from this site—software that is only sold for the Windows platform—the system guesses that this might be her first Macintosh. Based on this knowledge, the CRM system attempts to cross-sell by offering her a $30 rebate on a combined purchase of the iMac and the top word processing program for that platform, Microsoft Word. Thrilled at the prospect of the deal, Gertrude is glad she waited. She snaps the deal while CRM-supported TheBigAppleStore.com gets the customer that the local computer superstore just missed.

Now, if TheBigAppleStore.com had integrated its CRM system better, it would have generated targeted offers of first-generation iMac refurbs that it carried, months back. Maybe Gertrude would have bought one then. In the meanwhile, if she had given in and purchased one at the local superstore, Gertrude would probably not want to buy another one for several years.

SUMMARY ....

Electronic business is changing the face of commerce. The Internet economy—valued at $850 billion in 2000—will be dominated by B2B transactions and relationships. The business-to-consumer electronic commerce alone, which is a small fraction of e-business, exceeded banking, aerospace, and drug industries *combined*. In 2000, B2B transactions accounted for most (77 percent, according to IDC) of worldwide electronic commerce. Knowledge and relationships gain an unprecedented level of significance in e-business.

- *The currency of the digital economy is largely intangible.* Relationships, collaborations, and levels of knowledge define the currency of the New Economy. Such intangibles account for huge differences in their capital assets (land, building, computers, and other property) and their market valuation (*the* measure of value that investors and markets associate with a company). E-businesses must be asset poor and knowledge rich.

- *Traditional marketing approaches fall apart in e-business.* The four touchstones of mass marketing—products, price, place, and promotion—were built in an era dominated by one-way broadcast marketing. Web-based marketing takes a different, collaborative approach dominated by knowledge and strengths of relationships with customers and business partners.

- *Customer relationship management focuses on a customer's lifetime value.* CRM is a combination of business processes and technology that seeks to understand a company's customers from multiple perspectives to deliver identification, conversion, acquisition, and retention. Contrary to popular belief, CRM is a business strategy, not a suite of software products.

- *Well-managed knowledge serves as a competitive differentiator in e-business.* Knowledge management is the process of managing organizational knowledge—explicit or tacit—for creating business value and sustaining competitive advantage through the creation, communication, and application of knowledge gained from customer interactions to maximize business growth and value. It focuses on creating and delivering innovative products or services; managing and enhancing relationships with existing and new customers, partners, and suppliers; and improving customer-related work practices and processes.

- *Knowledge acquisition, sharing, and utilization overlap.* Development and creation of insights, skills, and relationships (knowledge acquisition), when disseminated and shared (knowledge sharing) are followed by integration of learning, insights, and experiential knowledge and brining it to bear upon current decisions (knowledge utilization).

- *KM and CRM are complementary.* Knowledge-enabled customer relationship management lies at the intersection of knowledge management, collaborative relationship management (with customers and partners), and e-business. Knowledge management and CRM can be integrated to use customer knowledge and channel relationships to deliver excellent service; maximize retention, loyalty, and revenue from existing customers; and develop continually refined, repeatable sales processes. Secondarily, this combination can assist in customer acquisition, enhancement, and ad hoc alliance formation.

In the next chapter, we examine a roadmap along which each key activity set involved in applying knowledge management and relationship management collectively can be understood.

TEST YOUR UNDERSTANDING . . . .

1. What were the four Ps of marketing and why are they now believed to be dead? What have they been replaced by?

2. We discussed that Amazon.com, Outpost.com, E*Trade, eBay, and Buy.com have lots of digital capital. What is digital capital and can you think of some other businesses in the non-dot-com world that possess it?

3. We discussed how a transaction-based perspective of customers is a potion for disaster in e-business. If businesses should not care about transaction value, what else do they have to care about?

4. What are the four key tenets of customer relationship management?

5. How are knowledge, market valuation, and e-business prosperity interrelated?

6. How do knowledge and information differ? Is the distinction always crisp and unmistakable?

7. What are the eight components of knowledge? Think of your own job and list the ones that are accounted for in your daily work.

8. We discussed the notion of process-based competition. Does that mean that processes are more important than the quality of products?

9. What exactly is meant by knowledge-enabled customer relationship management? Where does it lie with respect to e-business, knowledge management, and relationship management?

10. Can you think of some traditional businesses that have used the principles of individualization before the e-business era? Do you think that they would now have to do the same differently?

3 A Roadmap for Success

In this chapter...

- Comprehend the significance of the KCRM roadmap.

- Understand how the KCRM roadmap links CRM and knowledge management.

- Understand various steps and the reasons for their parallel execution.

- Identify the three key phases, and the activities involved in each phase.

Implementing complex systems for knowledge management, e-business, or customer relationship management requires a plan that delivers hard-hitting business results. This chapter outlines that plan for knowledge-enabled customer relationship management that lies at the junction of the three above. Although it is described as a roadmap, the steps of the roadmap must not be considered sequential, linear activities but parallel areas that must be addressed. Think of the roadmap as a conceptually simplified way of explaining the seven key topics relating to KCRM, and a logical way of explaining how it relates to knowledge management and customer relationship management in general. The seven chapters that follow describe one step each along this roadmap.

THE KNOWLEDGE-ENABLED CUSTOMER RELATIONSHIP MANAGEMENT ROADMAP . . . . . .

For clarity of description, the process of knowledge-enabled customer relationship management is described as a roadmap (see Figure 3-1). Each of the seven chapters that follow describes one step each of this roadmap. Although these steps are shown in a sequential manner, they often overlap and run in parallel.

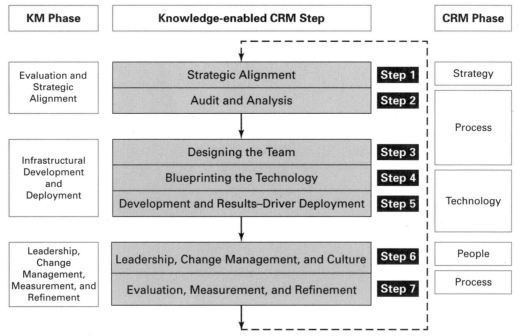

Figure 3-1
The KCRM roadmap.

The Road to the Map

We discussed in the last chapter that knowledge-enabled customer relationship management (KCRM) lies at the junction of knowledge management, e-business, and customer relationship management. In essence, it is the principles of knowledge management in the context of the customer applied in e-Business settings. It will be worth spending a moment to see the four dimensions of customer relationship management (CRM). CRM, as illustrated in Figure 3-2, consists of three simultaneous considerations that drive strategy: (1) people, business culture, and relationships, (2) processes, and (3) technology.

Figure 3-1 describes the seven broad steps involved in implementing KCRM. Because knowledge-enabled customer relationship management builds on knowledge management and customer relationship management, corresponding phases of KM and CRM are shown on either side of the KCRM roadmap. Remember, although these steps are described in a sequence, that is only for the sake of systematic presentation; in real life, these are often executed in parallel.

PHASE I: EVALUATION AND STRATEGIC ALIGNMENT . . . .

Implementing knowledge-enabled customer relationship management begins with strategically aligning business strategy and technology for supporting knowledge and relationship capital building. This involves two key activities: (1) evaluating and

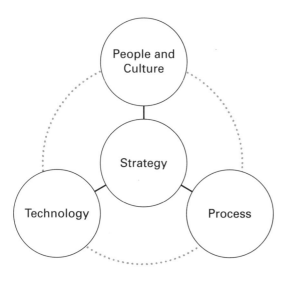

Figure 3-2
Linkages in traditional customer relationship management.

auditing customer knowledge and relationships, and (2) aligning various facets using the KCRM strategic framework. In knowledge management terms, these activities address strategic alignment issues; in customer relationship management terms, they address all strategy and some process issues. These cross-mappings are illustrated in Figure 3-1 and described next.

Step 1: Strategic Alignment

Knowledge-enabled customer relationship management must be aligned with e-business strategy to deliver results. The first step in implementing KCRM therefore aligns business and technology strategies. Long-term strategy must be based on a vision that must be decomposed into short-term, achievable wins. Four barriers to knowledge-enabled customer relationship management implementation must be recognized: The environment is shielded by an interpretation barrier, the context by an expression barrier, strategy by a specification barrier, and technology by an implementation barrier. Customer loyalty is determined by (1) your knowledge of their needs, (2) anticipation of future requirements, and (3) superior communication. Five key KCRM outcomes that depend on knowledge to enhance both customer and channel relationships include consistency, speed, accuracy, increased levels of satisfaction, and cost reduction. Three gaps—(1) strategic gaps, (2) knowledge gaps, and (3) relationship gaps—are analyzed and opportunities recognized using knowledge-mapping techniques. Depending on whether your business emerges as an innovator, market leader, competitive threat, straggler, or exit candidate, you can determine the cost of pursuing a certain market and decide on whether to invest in playing catch-up or focus on a different market segment. Strategy must be implemented after considering the 17 drivers of knowledge management (outlined in Chapter 4) and then by (1) articulating a company vision and strategic intent, (2) translating this strategic intent into actionable business strategy, and (3) laying out discrete and measurable goals that lead your business in the direction of realizing its vision. In this first step, you must

1. Understand the KCRM strategic framework
2. Identify the four barriers to alignment and strategies for removing them
3. See how knowledge emerges in B2B, B2C, and C2C e-businesses
4. Review the key outcomes of well-executed strategy
5. Understand how exploitation and exploration are balanced
6. Identify and analyze strategy, knowledge, and relationship gaps
7. Recognize the 17 success factors critical for strategic alignment

If such alignment is done right, Web self-service, collaborative communities, intelligent personalization, and knowledge-based adaptation provide individualization at mass-market cost-efficiency.

Step 2: Audit and Analysis

Audit and analysis—the second step on our roadmap—help determine the present state of your business' relationship and knowledge assets. Beginning with a description of key outcome expectations from an audit, we examine how resulting audit information is used to prioritize investments and to classify customers into clusters and segments based on their perceived lifetime value. The *Capability Classification* framework is used to document customer knowledge and relationship assets that can serve as a lighthouse for guiding the direction of further KCRM initiatives. In this step, you must

1. Understand the objectives and significance of a customer knowledge audit

2. Analyze the three phases and seven steps of the audit process

3. Determine a method of choice and select reference measures

4. Classify customers based on their lifetime value to your business

5. Use this information to differentially interact and deliver customized value packages to different customers

6. Understand how the Capability Classification framework is used to document intangible knowledge and relationship assets

7. Analyze audit outcomes to determine KCRM strategic imperatives

Audit and analysis are discussed in depth in Chapter 5.

PHASE II: INFRASTRUCTURAL DEVELOPMENT AND DEPLOYMENT . . . .

Implementation of knowledge-enabled customer relationship management involves the building of an implementation team, creating the technology infrastructure blueprint, and deploying the system using a results-driven, incremental approach. In knowledge management terms, these activities constitute infrastructure development and deployment stages; in customer relationship management terms, they represent all technology and some processes issues (see Figure 3-1). These aspects are described next.

Step 3: Designing the Team

Implementing KCRM is a necessarily collaborative process that spans both traditional departmental boundaries and organizational boundaries. The third step on our
roadmap is concerned with the process of assembling a boundary-spanning team for
KCRM implementation. Specifically, you must

1. Understand the implementation team design
2. Balance conflicting requirements for project design
3. Understand tasks and expertise involved in implementing KCRM
4. Balance managerial and technical composition
5. Understand the differences between pre- and post-chasm team
    members
6. Identify and prioritize risk factors using a risk assessment framework
7. Avoid common team formation pitfalls

Team design is discussed in detail in Chapter 6.

Step 4: Blueprinting the Technology

The fourth step on our roadmap involves understanding of the technology plan or the
blueprint. Technology's role in building KCRM systems is that of broadening reach,
enhancing the speed of knowledge transfer and real-time knowledge application,
enabling informed decision making, mapping sources of tacit knowledge, communicating and integrating diverse channels and touchpoints, and facilitating collaborative
success. Success in managing customer relationships and knowledge boils down not
to which customer relationship management software package you buy but to how
well you build, upkeep, integrate, and actually imbibe the accompanying business processes. Our focus in this book is not on actually building the technology but that of
understanding how it is blueprinted, how various requirements are balanced, and how
this blueprint is created with future adaptability in mind. Specifically, in this fourth
step, you must

1. Understand the design challenges of creating a KCRM technology
    blueprint
2. Compare the requirements against CRM objectives
3. Understand various pieces of the customer KM technology frame-
    work

4. Identify the collaborative platform for use in a Web-based environment
5. See examples of customer knowledge systems used in B2C, C2C, and B2B e-businesses
6. Analyze the relative fit of various key business intelligence methods in e-business settings
7. Understand various pieces of the KCRM technology architecture
8. Examine various long-term design considerations, including the build-or-buy choice

This encompasses suppliers, partners, and even competitors that the system must help acquire, retain, enhance, and maximize their relationships with. Interoperability among internal and external Web information systems, choice and suitability of tools for specific activities (such as artificial intelligence subsystems, intelligent data warehouses, genetic algorithm tools, neural networks, expert systems, case-based reasoning applications, rule bases, and intelligent agents) and e-business processes, various search and retrieval mechanisms (metasearching, hierarchical, tagged-attribute, combinatorial, and content searching) must be appropriately weighed.

Step 5: Development and Results-Driven Deployment

Need for investments will fall on deaf ears if you cannot show that these investments will come back as increased revenues, market share, and profits. The fifth step on our roadmap deals with strategies that ensure that KCRM systems are built with an eye on results—long and short term. Implementation of a customer knowledge strategy depends on a detailed breakdown of the vision into discrete steps that are accompanied by milestones that act as markers for operationalizing the vision. Overengineering, poor communications and coordination processes, lack of cumulative characteristics, relegated releases with the highest potential payoffs, and ignored human issues are commonly observed problems in the deployment phase.

Tech Talk

Results-Driven Incrementalism: Deployment method that divides a complex, expensive project into smaller pieces; each piece is implemented based on the results obtained from implementing the preceding one.

You must specifically examine the following issues:

1. Understand what it takes to deploy KCRM systems successfully.
2. Understand the role of prototyping and pilot testing.

3. Recognize the limitations of traditional big-bang deployment methods.

4. Understand how results-driven incrementalism (RDI) overcomes these problems.

5. Create incremental, cumulative business releases.

6. Recognize potential pitfalls in using RDI and avoidance strategies.

7. *Deployment must encompass technology and nontechnology issues.* Training, reward systems, and integration of business processes and systems must be explicitly considered during the deployment phase.

8. *Decomposability facilitates modularity.* Complex systems must be decomposed into chunks—technology modules that fit together and can be implemented together as a single whole—to allow results-driven systems that solve current, not past problems.

9. RDI overcomes these problems.

Balancing technology and nontechnology issues, modularity and flexibility, results-driven incremental approaches to development (incremental but cumulative results through system-level chunking in the form of business releases) are described in detail in Chapter 8.

PHASE III: LEADERSHIP, CHANGE MANAGEMENT, MEASUREMENT, AND REFINEMENT . . . .

Strong leadership, cultural adjustment at an organizational level, and change management are needed to integrate KCRM, and knowledge management in general, into the fabric of a business' work processes and culture. Actual results and performance impacts of KCRM must then be measured using customized nontraditional measures and metrics that can guide further refinement. In knowledge management terms, this set of activities constitutes management, metrics, and refinement. Similarly, in customer relationship management terms, these activities address all people issues and some process-related issues, as illustrated in Figure 3-1. These are discussed next.

Step 6: Leadership, Change Management, and Culture

Technology can bring the horse to water, but to make him drink, technology use must be made attractive to frontline employees. Successful KCRM initiatives need fundamental readjustment of corporate culture, strong leadership, and financial and nonfinancial reward structures that together gain the hearts and minds of employees and *motivate* them to share knowledge across the e-business channel. Building a knowledge-sharing culture in your business begins with linking knowledge sharing to personal rewards for employees and partners, encouraging risk taking and educating, and addressing people before technology problems. Customer support representatives, marketing managers, corporate sponsors, senior management, KCRM proponents, early adopters and zealots, and cynics must all participate in this transformation process. In this sixth step, you must specifically

1. Understand the role of corporate culture and leadership
2. Understand championing roles and goals
3. Understand what makes for a good customer relationship visionary
4. See that your organizational culture can be transformed from a fear- to knowledge-sharing-based one
5. Determine the process of cultural transition to support KCRM
6. Reconfigure reward structures to encourage knowledge sharing and relationship building
7. Understand the key elements of change management using the five touchstones of change management

Successfully imbibing these norms in your organization's culture, practices, and work will provide the complementary assets that can help you build networks of accessible knowledge and lasting relationships with customers and channels partners—assets that provide inimitable advantage to traditional and e-businesses alike. Chapter 9 describes these aspects of KCRM in detail.

Step 7: Evaluation, Measurement, and Refinement

Traditional measurement methods clearly do not stand up in e-business. What is needed is a comprehensive set of measures that take into account long-term and short-term objectives, financial and nonfinancial measures, lagging and leading indicators, and internal and external perspectives. In the final step on our roadmap, we gain an understanding of the reasons for this failure and examine methods such as benchmarking, quality function deployment, and Balanced Scorecards which can be used instead. Specifically, you must

1. Understand the need for effective metrics.

2. Understand the limitations of traditional metrics such as return on investment, net present value, Tobin's q, and total cost of ownership

3. Understand how benchmarking and the Stages of Growth framework provide comparative measures

4. Understand the use of quality function deployment for evaluating KCRM success

5. Build a custom Balanced Scorecard for comprehensive evaluation and refinement

6. Understand and avoid the most common pitfalls in devising KCRM metrics

To evaluate a knowledge-enabled customer relationship management initiative accurately, both soft and hard aspects must be measured. These issues are described in detail in Chapter 10.

SUMMARY ....

The knowledge-enabled customer relationship management roadmap must not be confused with the series of sequential steps that must be executed. Instead, think of it as a set of activities that are put into seven broad buckets. Each bucket represents an aspect of the often-parallel tasks that are pertinent to managing customer knowledge and channel relationships in an e-business context. In the chapters that follow, most examples and illustrations are from Web-based businesses. However, many of the concepts described are applicable to traditional businesses that are now espousing the Web.

TEST YOUR UNDERSTANDING ....

1. What is the KCRM roadmap? What is its purpose?

2. What is the significance of strategic alignment? Is it more important for e-businesses than technology itself or can good technology compensate for its lack?

3. Why do we use the *Capability Classification Framework?* Why bother?

4. What are some of the key issues that you think must be considered when designing a knowledge-enabled customer relationship management implementation team?

5. Why is adaptability needed in the technology blueprinting process? Would it be safe to assume that the need for adaptability has decreased as the Web becomes increasingly popular?

6. What is interoperability and its significance in developing e-business systems? Why do you think that e-business both creates and solves many interoperability problems?

7. We spend some time discussing change, change management, reward systems, and leadership. Don't you think that a cool, state-of-the-art system should motivate just about everyone from your company's propeller head to your cleaning guy to actually use the system? Why don't people use these systems, especially when your company pays for them?

8. Do you believe that traditional ways of measuring "success" hold well in e-business? Think of a few common ways of measuring success in your own work and then think about them if you ran an electronic commerce site. Why do you think that they would or would not hold steady in both settings?

9. What are the four barriers that surround KCRM implementation? Do you think that honest, open collaboration and knowledge sharing in your own job might help overcome them?

10. Let us assume that you finish reading this book and implement everything from Step 1 through 7. What next? Should you go again to Step 1 or look harder for Step 8 and write to us about it? Should you even execute these steps in a perfect sequence or would it be safe to run a few of them in parallel?

PUTTING IT ALL TOGETHER: FUNDAMENTALS . . . .

Knowledge and relationship assets constitute *digital capital*—the key assets of the New-New economy. Although e-business provides the New Economy's distribution model, it can do no good until business judgment is applied to it. It costs a lot more to gain one more customer on the Web, and takes much less to lose another. Smart e-businesses know that customers and their knowledge of them are their key assets, and channel relationships their fountainhead of adaptability; these intangibles account for huge differences between their capital assets (land, building, computers, and other property) and their market valuation (*the* measure of value that investors and markets associate with a company). The mantra of traditional marketing—products, price, place, and promotion—is replaced by a single word: *loyalty*. E-businesses that will thrive in the future are those that recognize their best customers and retain their loyalty. That takes time, energy, and initiative. The key to customer loyalty lies in your business' knowledge about them, and its ability to use that knowledge to rethink, recast, and even cannibalize your own businesses.

Knowledge management with the sole focus of cultivating relationships with customers and channel partners is called knowledge-enabled customer relationship management (KCRM). KCRM lies at the intersection of knowledge management, collaborative relationship management, and e-business. This approach goes far beyond e-CRM or traditional CRM in managing and creating customer loyalty. Knowledge management and CRM can be integrated to use customer knowledge and channel relationships to deliver excellent service; to maximize retention, loyalty, and revenue from existing customers; and to develop continually refined, repeatable sales processes. KM focuses on creating and delivering innovative products or services; managing and enhancing relationships with existing and new customers, partners, and suppliers; and improving customer-related work practices and processes.

Loyal relationships are not built by pouring more fuel down the black hole of technology but by integrating, managing, and applying deep knowledge of customer, markets, and business partners. Loyalty is often generated in part by good will and experience, and in part through lock-ins. Think about Microsoft Word. You're probably a loyal user. Why? Because you like the product or because you have no choice. If your answer is both, then you're looking at the reason why Microsoft is so successful. In the e-business world, Amazon.com and eBay are close equivalents. The problem of managing knowledge in an "e" context is more pronounced in traditional businesses that have turned to the Web than it is in born-on-the-Web businesses that have no legacy.

Think about some companies that were supposed to be the superstars of tomorrow's e-business. Instead they bit the dust. CDNow.com and Boo.com were two such e-business that spent far too much on customer acquisition (CDNow.com is rumored to have spent as much as $700 to acquire each new customer). On the other hand, some small businesses have built relationship assets with their customers and unexpectedly thrived: RatingWonders.com, MyCoupons.com, Bluemountain.com, and Eudoramail.com.

There is no formula for implementing KCRM, because even the most similar businesses are different enough that a great formula from one will deliver zilch in the other. However, the KCRM roadmap described in Chapter 3 provides a guided and systematic approach to understanding seven key sets of activities involved in implementing KCRM strategies and systems.

Part 2

A Roadmap for Implementing KCRM

In this part...

Chapter 4: Aligning Strategy and Technology Choices

- Understand the KCRM strategic framework.

- Identify the four barriers to alignment and strategies for removing them.

- See how knowledge emerges in B2B, B2C, and C2C e-businesses.

- Review the key outcomes of well-executed strategy.

- Identify and analyze strategy, knowledge, and relationship gaps.

- Recognize the 17 success factors critical for strategic alignment.

Chapter 5: Audit and Analysis

- Understand the objectives and significance of a customer knowledge audit.

- Analyze the three phases and seven steps of the audit process.

- Determine a method of choice and select reference measures.

- Classify customers based on their lifetime value to your business.

- Use this information to differentially interact and deliver customized value packages to different customers.

- Understand how the Capability Classification framework is used to document intangible knowledge and relationship assets.

- Analyze audit outcomes to determine KCRM strategic imperatives.

Chapter 6: Building an Implementation Team

- Understand the implementation team design.

- Balance conflicting requirements for project design.

- Understand tasks and expertise involved in implementing KCRM.

- Understand the differences between pre- and postchasm team members.

- Avoid common team formation pitfalls.

Chapter 7: Blueprinting the Technology Infrastructure

- Understand the design challenges of creating a KCRM technology blueprint.

- Compare the requirements against customer relationship management objectives.

- Understand various pieces of the customer knowledge management technology framework.

- Identify the collaborative platform for use in a Web-based environment.

- See examples of customer knowledge systems used in B2C and B2B e-businesses.

- Analyze the relative fit of 10-key business intelligence methods in e-business settings.

- Understand various pieces of the KCRM technology architecture.

- Examine various long-term design considerations, including the build-or-buy choice.

Chapter 8: Results-Driven Development and Deployment

- Understand what it takes to deploy KCRM systems successfully.

- Understand the role of prototyping and pilot testing.

- Recognize the limitations of traditional big-bang deployment methods.

- Understand how results-driven incrementalism overcomes these problems.

- Create incremental, cumulative business releases.

- Recognize potential pitfalls in using RDI and avoidance strategies.

Chapter 9: Leadership, Change Management, and Corporate Culture

- Understand the role of corporate culture and leadership.

- Understand championing roles and goals.

- Understand what makes for a good customer relationship visionary.

- See how you can transform your organization's fear-based culture to a knowledge-sharing culture.

- Determine the process of cultural transition to support KCRM.

- Reconfigure reward structures to encourage knowledge sharing and relationship building.

- Understand the key elements of change management.

4 Aligning Strategy and Technology Choices

In this chapter...

- Understand the KCRM strategic framework.

- Identify the four barriers to alignment and strategies for removing them.

- See how knowledge emerges in B2B, B2C, and C2C e-businesses.

- Review the key outcomes of well-executed strategy.

- Identify and analyze strategy, knowledge, and relationship gaps.

- Recognize the 17 success factors critical for strategic alignment.

The hardest part in e-business is not that of knowing the right answers but that of asking the right questions. As the line between customer relationship management and e-business activity fades away, it becomes ever more important to seamlessly integrate customer knowledge across all channels, to present a consistent, knowledgeable, and responsive face to the customer. In highly distributed value chains that characterize e-business, strategy formulation must encompass business partners, allies, and organizational business units. Technology—only if applied strategically—allows businesses to redefine customer relationships. The potential for technology-facilitated customer relationships is most persuasive in e-business. In the B2C segment, banking (American Express Membership Banking, X.com, MBNA), financial services (E*Trade, Schwab), retail (Amazon.com), travel (Expedia, Priceline), and software (Beyond.com) have been revolutionized by hard-hitting combinations of knowledge management technology and relationship management strategies. Three-year plans become obsolete before they can be implemented; knowledge-based strategy must therefore operate in real time.

In this chapter, we examine the first step on the KCRM roadmap—aligning technology and business strategy. Using the four-pronged KCRM strategy framework, we identify four sets of barriers to such alignment. Then, we take a close look at each dimension of the framework, see how gaps are analyzed and opportunities recognized using knowledge maps, and look at how this alignment is achieved.

GETTING PAST THE INNOVATOR'S DILEMMA . . . . .

In *The Innovator's Dilemma*, Clayton Christensen suggested that good companies go bad when they try to apply yesterday's successful strategies in today's business environment. There is often a tendency to fine-tune current processes instead of promoting radical changes in many e-businesses. Although no industry segment is left unscathed by the emergence of e-business, this is a especially critical recognition in e-businesses. Market strategy must be defined from outside in, not inside out—that is, it is centered on customer needs instead of product features. Technology never provided anyone a competitive edge that lasted even in the Old World of business; it surely does little in the New Economy. The playing field is leveled when competitors roll out the similar operational applications and automate the same processes in the front office. Companies must then move from efficiency to effectiveness and from technological sophistication to continual competitive differentiation. Relying too heavily on computer-based systems is ineffective, and relying too heavily on humans is inefficient. Where is the balance then? Strategic planning systems are of little respite: Systems do not think, and when used for more than the facilitation of human thinking, they can actually prevent thinking. Competing in an "e" environment needs a radically different approach—one that builds relationship webs and knowledge capital.

Integrating, analyzing, and applying customer transactions and data from across the enterprise create a customer-centric view for the organization. This requires an understanding of the entire customer lifecycle beginning with the prospective customer, to lead to new customers; it also necessitates data integration from front and back office system and online and offline customer touchpoints. This requires the ability to see a market gap, evaluate it, and rapidly move to fill it—if your business processes the requisite knowledge and relationship capital to do that.

The promise of integrating knowledge management and customer relationship management in the form of knowledge-enabled customer relationship management is attractive in an online context for several new capabilities that can be brought in:

- Building long-term, profitable relationships with customers, and maximizing their business with your firm (i.e., share of the customer)
- Sharing best practices and lessons learned without having to relearn by repeating the same mistakes across different locations
- Understanding and applying the "who, what, where, why, how, and when" of each customer's actions and behavior (patterns, behavior, clickstream data, feedback) and using that knowledge to change your business' behavior toward that customer
- Integrating a myriad of channels in real time to build a highly knowledge-intensive unified view of each customer
- Removing the process bottlenecks in sales and customer support processes
- Analyzing abandoned shopping cart behavior through profiling and customized dynamic pricing
- Charging customers prices based on their willingness to pay rather than on predetermined profit margins
- Adding value and up/cross-selling complementary products, services, and information
- Personalized touch combined with the efficiencies of mass marketing to deliver new product and service bundles that the *customer* values

KCRM, especially in e-business settings, is about balancing strategic certainty against time-to-market. Building knowledge-enabled customer relationships requires robust, scalable, responsive (clickstream data alone takes up several gigs per day), flexible, and adaptable technology as well as coordination across bits and bricks.

THE KCRM STRATEGIC FRAMEWORK . . . .

Customer knowledge and relationship management can be analyzed using the customer KCRM strategic framework described in Figure 4-1. Four dimensions—business environment, the strategic context of your customer knowledge management project, knowledge-enabled customer relationship management strategy, and technology pathways—can be analyzed using this framework. By simultaneously tracking internal and external events and priorities, and incorporating change, this framework provides a robust and adaptable way for analyzing KCRM strategy. Each of these is discussed in detail in the following sections.

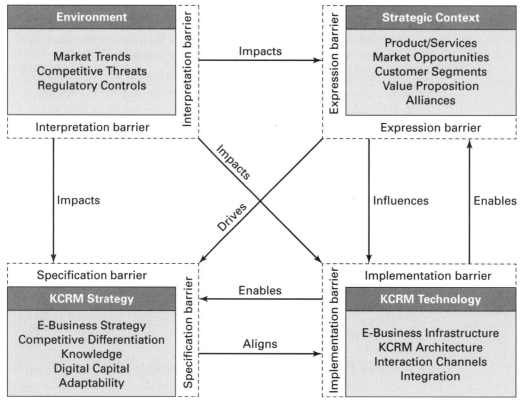

Figure 4-1
The KCRM strategic framework.

Four Barriers to KCRM Actualization

The KCRM strategic framework has four dimensions: (1) environment, (2) strategic context, (3) KCRM strategy, and (4) KCRM technology. Using this framework for KCRM strategy development ensures that customer knowledge management strategy and technology choices are attuned to both business environment and your business' strategy. Each dimension is surrounded by barriers as shown in Figure 4-1. Analyzing the environment is impeded by the ability to interpret what the changes in business environment mean for your business. The context of your knowledge management strategy in general, and customer knowledge management in specific, is impeded by an expression barrier—the inability to express the influence of the business environment in explicitly worded strategic needs. Similarly, KCRM strategy is slowed down by a specification barrier—the inability to specific what technology is needed to leverage customer knowledge and build customer relationships. In addition to customer relationships, supplier and business partner relationships must also be addressed in e-business settings. Finally, KCRM technology deployment is inhibited by an implementation barrier. The implementation barrier might be caused by a lack of any or all of the following: technical skills, analysis skills, know-how, incompatible infrastructure, time pressures, or unfeasible technology solutions. In e-business settings, it might also be influenced by inequities between your business and its partner firms.

Outcome Indicators of Effective KCRM Strategy Formulation

The objective of implementing a KCRM strategy is to enhance and apply a business' digital capital, that is, its relationships and knowledge. The outcomes supported by KCRM include assimilation and deployment of digital capital that provides your business a source of sustainable competitiveness. The preconditions for this are its value, rarity, and inimitability. Although technology provides temporary advantage, any technology can be imitated given enough time and resources. Furthermore, effective KCRM should help build synergy among the supply and demand side of your business, reduce the level of complexity in interpreting and adapting to change in the external environment (such as new market trends, competitive substitutes, etc.), and help maintain a balance between strategy and technology investments, as described in the following sections. As businesses embrace the Web, these factors increase its agility in a cut-throat and unpredictable environment.

Valuable, Rare, and Inimitable Digital Capital

Knowledge strategy begins with a business vision, a penultimate long-term strategic intent. Effective KCRM must result in networked knowledge and relationship capital (collectively called e-business digital capital) that is valuable, rare, and hard to imitate. Strategy formulation must therefore *first* focus on valuable knowledge with relatively short term payoffs. Second, identify sources of knowledge that your competitors do not possess but those that could potentially create a competitive advantage. Industry benchmarks and public documents can often lead to such insights. Forget technology-based advantages in the market. The playing field is leveled when competitors roll out similar operational applications and automate the same processes. As more competitors adopt the same set of technologies or their substitutes, any competitive benefits provided by them will deteriorate as shown in Figure 4-2.

When attempting to build digital capital that is hard to replicate, also make sure that it is hard to substitute. When your business is trying to choose between two focal knowledge areas, it is better to err in the favor of one for which no straightforward substitutes exist.

Synergy

Synergy—the *Holy Grail* of e-business—is a goal that is pursued more often than it is achieved. Successful KCRM strategy brings synergy among multiple departments, business units, customers, and your business partners to produce better customer-driv-

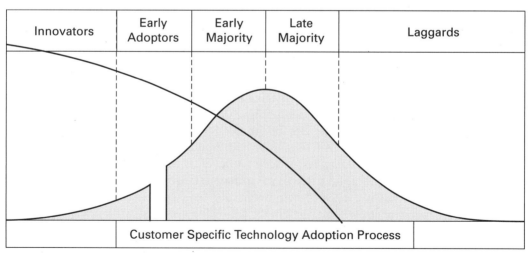

Figure 4-2
Competitive advantage bestowed by any technology declines with its increased use.

en outcomes than they could as a nonsynergistic sum of their parts. Achieving synergy is indicated, among other things, by the collective ability to recognize threats and emerging opportunities and acting on that recognition. When business units dispute alternative solutions and approaches instead of their turf, e-business strategy becomes more proactive and responsive to changes occurring in either of the four KCRM framework dimensions.

Complexity

Four types of complexities influence the operations of e-businesses (see Table 4-1). Effective management of customer knowledge can help your business reduce the severity of all four and specifically address logistical and organizational complexity.

Table 4-1 A Taxonomy of Complexities in Business Processes

Type of Complexity	Cause
Logistical complexity	High volume of transactions, projects, categories, and tasks
Technological complexity	Inherent nature of the systems and technologies that the user needs to interact with both at a product and service level and at a process level
Organizational complexity	Congregation of multiple organizations and departments into one group, cross-functional and cross-organizational relationships, new procedures that employees are expected to adhere to, changed structures of interaction
Environmental complexity	Rate of change in business markets, regions, and industries

Balance

Managing customer knowledge is much like rope walking: On one side is technology and on the other, business strategy. Balancing the two is necessary to prevent a fall. The two must be aligned—a purpose that well-executed KCRM strategy fulfills. Business goals, not technological feasibility, must drive technology design. To make the horse drink the water, technologies for customer knowledge management must be accompanied by cultural change and new compensation and reward systems (Chapter 9), and driven by results (Chapter 8), and the deliverance of promises (Chapter 10). The much talked about but frequently ignored alignment of technology and business strategy for customer knowledge management should be *the* starting point.

··

THE CHICKEN AND THE EGG PUZZLE

> If customer knowledge drives strategy and strategy drives knowledge management, what comes first? Developing a strategy for customer knowledge management derives from customer knowledge; once this knowledge is refined and corrected, it is used to define strategy, which in turn provides the direction for focusing customer knowledge assimilation and integration strategies and technology enablers. Businesses must capture both hard data and soft insights. Depending solely on market data and numbers might be efficient, but it does not always prove effective in capturing the subtle insights that lead to new lines of expansion or hint at impending market changes. Hard data is aggregated and lacks qualitative richness that may mistakenly lead managers to see patterns in perfectly random data.

Let us begin with the first of four blocks in the strategy framework to understand how the business environment influences KCRM strategy alignment.

ANALYZING THE BUSINESS ENVIRONMENT ·····

The external business environment impacts your company's strategic context, its products, services, markets, customers, and allocation of resources, and in turn its knowledge-enabled customer relationship management strategy. Because technical opportunities, market gaps, competitive threats, and regulatory controls emerge in the environment, the criticality of being attuned to it cannot be overemphasized. We first take a look at how knowledge is created in e-business settings and how it affects market positioning. Using a simple market positioning matrix, we will see how gaps in the market, internal knowledge, and relationships are analyzed and correlated. By analyzing 17 key drivers of knowledge management, we can get a better handle on using knowledge maps that help determine the balance between the levels of exploration and exploitation of its intangible assets that a business should engage in.

Knowledge Evolution in E-business Settings

The four goals of customer relationship management—identification, differentiation, interaction, and customization—have evolved since the introduction of electronic commerce, and now further so with the evolution of e-business. Deployment of associated enabling technologies has become increasingly focused on improving effectiveness *and* efficiency rather than efficiency alone. As various information technologies are integrated, systems for managing business processes in Web settings go far beyond traditional electronic commerce. Figure 4-3 maps the levels of knowledge involved in customer relationship management processes and in building relationship capital in e-business settings across the four phases of traditional CRM.

Several relationship-building tools and technologies have gained a loyal following among businesses because of their ability to enhance one or more of the four customer relationship management capabilities. As businesses integrate knowledge management and e-business processes increasingly tightly, strategic knowledge integration approaches begin to differentiate Web-centric firms, their cost efficiencies, their operational efficiencies, and their effectiveness in addressing and capturing their target markets. By comparing your own business to Figure 4-3, you can determine the level at which your own business perhaps operates. This, in turn, will indicate the level of customer knowledge that your business currently deals with (high, intermediate, or low).

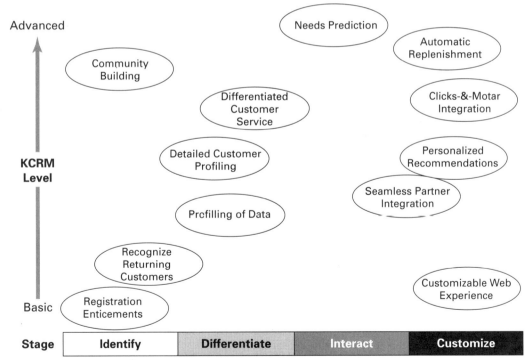

Figure 4-3
Stages of the customer relationship management process and knowledge intensity associated with different approaches.

Market Positioning

Positioning choices of e-businesses depend on the attractiveness of the market segments that they plan to compete in, and on their ability to compete in those segments. Figure 4-4 shows how varying levels of profitability and the existence of market need gaps change the attractiveness of given market segments.

The strategic positioning choices that your company makes regarding technology, markets, products, services, and processes have a direct impact on the knowledge, skills, and competencies that it needs to compete in its intended markets. Of the four quadrants, market segments in which the potential for profitability and the size of market gaps are the highest are the most attractive (ones that should be *attacked*). Similarly, for market segments in which profitability is low in spite of large need gaps, a business should stay clear unless it has a technology or business edge that cannot be easily replicated.

Indeed, some businesses might choose to take an approach different from the one illustrated in a given segment. It can choose to do so because it might possess some unique intangibles that make it more attractive to compete in a segment in which other competitors might not want to. These distinguishing assets are usually knowledge- or path-dependent relationships. Instead of interpreting approaches that appear in the four quadrants, think of your own business and analyze where it falls within this matrix.

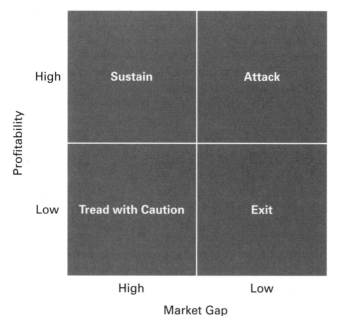

Figure 4-4
The market position matrix links four possible approaches.

··

MICROSOFT AND MACINTOSH SOFTWARE: MATRIX POSITIONING

Although Microsoft's Windows operating system is a direct competitor of Apple's MacOS, Microsoft has been a leading developer of Mac software. As the Web gained prominence in the software industry, Microsoft incorporated a personal information management (PIM) software application, Outlook, into its Office suite of programs. Although several vendors including Palm Computing, the developer of PalmOS, developed PIM applications for the Mac platform, Microsoft chose to develop a new PIM application for the Mac platform as part of its already popular Office suite, Mac Office 2001. Although the market gap was small, Microsoft could afford to do so because it already possessed a path-dependent relationship developed through earlier versions of Office applications with Mac users.

Tech Talk

Path dependence: A unique history of events that led to a certain capability or outcome. If competitors want to develop the same capability, they must go "through the same path" or sequence of events. There is no way to short-circuit that path to build the same capability. The higher the level of path dependence of a capability, the higher the level of difficulty involved in copying or replicating it.

Gap Analysis

KCRM strategy formulation depends on three types of gaps: (1) strategic gaps, (2) knowledge gaps, and (3) relationship gaps, as described in Figure 4-5.

1. *Strategic gap.* The gap between what your business must do and what it can feasibly do in order to fill existing market gaps.

2. *Knowledge gap.* The gap between what your business must know and what it actually knows about its customers and business partners who belong to its e-business supply chain. This gap also indicates the degree of the knowledge-doing gap—that is, the difference between what your business actually knows and the level to which it brings that knowledge to bear on routine decision-making processes.

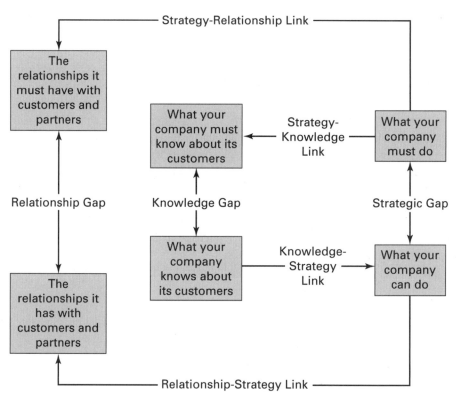

Figure 4-5
Linking strategic, knowledge, and relationship gaps.

3. *Relationship gap.* The gap between the strength of relationships that your business must have in order to fill the existing target market gaps and the relationship capital that it actually has. This gap is an indicator of customer loyalty, strategic partnerships with suppliers, and alliances with other business units and businesses.

Tech Talk

Gap Analysis: The process of analyzing what is and what should be in terms of strategy, markets, knowledge assets, and relationship assets. Evaluating these gaps provides the business with an accurate picture of market segments that it can viably compete in.

Knowledge management and relationship management strategy are linked to your e-business strategy through this set of bidirectional linkages. KCRM strategy implementation then involves the process of identifying the best approaches for bridging these gaps.

Exploit or Explore?

The degree to which your business exploits its existing knowledge and relationships for short-term gains is known as its exploitation level. However, exploitation must also be accompanied by exploration of new business possibilities of internal and externally assimilated knowledge and creation of new knowledge through various mechanisms and interaction channels. Exploitation implies the intent to focus on deriving financial and productivity gains from knowledge that already exists, both inside and outside, your company. Exploration implies the intent of your company to develop knowledge that helps it create new niches for its products and services. This intent has profound implications for the design of both the knowledge management strategy and system: Exploration alone cannot be supportively pursued or financially sustained for too long without having a negative impact on the company's bottom-line results.

Being an innovator is of little use if your business is not an exploiter. Exploitation of knowledge must often precede exploration. Correspondingly, your customer knowledge management strategy must support exploitation of your business' digital capital before it focuses on exploration. Microsoft is an excellent example of such a business that began with exploitation of QDOS (a small-time operating system acquired from another Seattle developer that was used to create MS-DOS) and eventually moved toward exploration. This combinatorial strategy bode well for the company's late entry into the Internet-centric computing market.

A business must simultaneously engage in knowledge exploitation and exploration. The delicate balance between the two must be struck through careful articulation and refinement of your business' strategy.

Tech Talk

Exploitation: The extent to which a business uses its existing knowledge and relationship assets to create short-term gains.

Exploration: The degree to which a business engages in creating new knowledge and building relationships with a long-term focus.

Mapping Knowledge Assets

Strategic categorization of knowledge is best done when you can categorize knowledge in three broad clusters—innovative, advanced, and core—as described in Table 4-2. Knowledge that is innovative eventually becomes more commonplace as it is absorbed by competitors over time. In this process, it deteriorates to the level of advanced knowledge and eventually becomes core knowledge—knowledge that *every* player in the same market possesses. Knowledge is not static; what is innovative knowledge today will become the core knowledge of tomorrow.

Table 4-2 Innovative Knowledge and Advanced Knowledge Eventually Become Core

Level	Description
Core knowledge	Basic knowledge required just to play the game
	Knowledge that creates a barrier for entry of new companies
	Provides zero competitive differentiation
Advanced knowledge	Provides competitive differentiation through application
	Enables head-on competition with competitors in the same market, addressing the same set of customers
	Makes your company competitively viable
Innovative knowledge	Provides clear competitive differentiation
	Allows the business to lead its entire industry
	Allows a company to change the rules of the game

Based on an adaptation from Michael Zack's description of knowledge strategy formulation. See Zack, M., "Developing a Knowledge Strategy, " *California Management Review*, 41(3), 1999, 125–145.

Knowledge management investments need both foresight and hindsight coupled with careful planning and long-term and short-term analysis. Systematic analysis requires comparative analysis—a process that compares your business' knowledge assets with other direct and indirect competitors. The Zack knowledge-mapping grid shown in Figure 4-6 is used to perform such mapping.

Create one such grid for each competitor and place your own company along one axis and your competition along the other. Categorize knowledge possessed by the two as core, advanced, or innovative and determine the point of intersection. The point of intersection on this grid will help you determine how your own business stands in comparison to each competitor. Depending on whether your business emerges as an innovator, market leader, competitive threat, straggler, or an exit candidate, you can determine whether the cost of pursuing a certain market and the investment needed to catch up is worth the differential. Knowing your business' relative position on this grid will help you are (1) decide on whether to invest in playing catch-up or focus on a different market segment instead, (2) focus your business' own customer knowledge management strategy, and (3) target investments in a defensible manner.

Knowledge mapping can also be a useful exercise in comparing your own internal business units and departments and for analyzing your company against industry averages. Knowledge maps provide a snapshot of your business markets and industry at a given time. They must be updated to account for market shifts, innovation, and new entrants from other market segments.

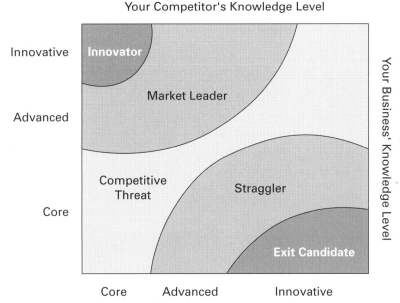

Figure 4-6
Knowledge maps provide conceptually simple but powerful high-level comparisons with competitors.

Drivers of Knowledge Management

The knowledge-based, Web-connected business environment is one that favors knowledge-rich but asset-poor organizational structures. It is important to relate these to the context of your own business by understanding the drivers of knowledge centricity in the "e" economy. Seventeen drivers account for the knowledge-economy-based, technological, structural, process-focused, and increasing returns economic characteristics of the e-business environment.

Tech Talk

> **Functional Convergence: Convergence of knowledge workers from different areas of specialization and across traditional departments such as marketing, sales, finance, and manufacturing. To bring together collective expertise, employees work in parallel to complete assignments that span traditional departmental and diverse organizational boundaries.**

These are summarized along with their symptoms (to help determine their existence in your own line of business) and the threats (and possible solutions) in Table 4-3.

Table 4-3 The 17 Drivers of Knowledge Management

Driver	Problem Symptoms	Threats Addressable by KM Solutions
Knowledge-Concentric Drivers		
Knowledge recognition failure	Companies don't know what they already know.	Reinventing old wheels.
Smart knowledge distribution	Employees can't find critical existing knowledge in time.	Inconsistent performance across locations.
	Lessons are learned but not shared.	Expertise localization.
		Repeated failures.
	No knowledge gained from failures; failures are soon forgotten.	Erosion of customer base.
	Expertise is not shared.	Competitors innovate at a faster rate.
Tacit knowledge walkouts	Employee departure causes loss of key clients, suppliers, best practices, and even revenue.	Critical tacit knowledge is closely held by a few key individuals; capabilities are movable to competitors.
	Departure of some employees reduces collective firmwide competency.	KM provides processes to retain tacit knowledge through informal methods and pointers.
Knowledge hoarding	Individual employees closely guard knowledge and insights; fear of job security exists.	Arguments flare over turf, not approaches.
	Collaboration is only namesake.	Collaborative knowledge sharing needs strong motivators.
Unlearning	Assumptions, rules of thumb, heuristics, and processes associated with business processes are unreliable or outdated	Unlearning is not systematically incorporated; knowledge is not revalidated.
		Old practices, methods, and processes continue to be inappropriately applied.
Technology Drivers		
Technology provides temporary advantage	Technological innovation and adoption fails to sustain competitive advantage.	Technology acts as an entry-precursor and core-capability leveler, not a sustainable competitive differentiator.
		Knowledge management provides a robust differentiator.

Table 4-3 The 17 Drivers of Knowledge Management (cont.)

Driver	Problem Symptoms	Threats Addressable by KM Solutions
Technology drivers (cont.)		
Compressed product and process lifecycles	Market information, service, and physical product lifecycles have significantly shortened→ compressing the available window for recouping development expenses. Frequent changes in the software, communication protocols, and computing hardware and software.	Complex and often irreversible design decisions need to be made fast and accurately; knowledge management can facilitate this. KCRM develops process competence resulting in time-to-market and cost reduction.
Link between knowledge, relationship capital, market strategy, and information technology	Information technology is confused with information, and CRM technology with customer knowledge. Business and IT strategy are "not on the same page."	Business needs and strategy must not drive technology investments. Customer knowledge and relationship-building needs must drive customer interaction and relationship management technology choices.
Organizational Structure-Based Drivers		
Functional convergence	Complex dependencies among and between different functional areas necessitate inputs and cooperation from different divisions to accomplish joint objectives. Collective expertise is needed. Brainstorming, strategy planning, competitive response, proactive positioning need collaboration, often across multiple functional areas, departments, and companies with differing notions, values, and beliefs. Employees work in parallel to complete assignments spanning traditional boundaries and functional areas. Complex products require melding of knowledge from diverse disciplinary perspectives.	Team members lack understanding of the critical process factors for areas other than their own. KCRM facilitates seamless integration of business divisions and collaborative firms. KM encourages conversation and discussion that precede collaboration and effective sharing of knowledge. Cultural enablers facilitate cooperation across design, engineering, packaging, manufacturing and marketing that is critical for innovation. KCRM presents a unified, competent, and consistent organizational face to the customer.

Table 4-3 The Seventeen Drivers of Knowledge Management (cont.)

Driver	Problem Symptoms	Threats Addressable by KM Solutions
Organizational Structure-Based Drivers (cont.)		
Convergence of products and services	Products and services are increasingly bundled. Blurred boundaries between products/services.	Perceived market value of products might vary depending on how the bundling is done KM provides a continually refined process-focused reference point for future bundling decisions.
New organizational structures	Ad hoc project-centered team structures bringing together the best of their talent and expertise. Expertise gained during development of a product or service is not readily available to subsequent project teams. Skills developed during the collaboration process lost and redistributed.	Knowledge integration across business units helps in reducing process complexity. Relationship building based on customer knowledge reduces logistical complexity in interacting with your business.
Deregulation and globalization	Virtual collaboration and global remote teaming occurs among highly distributed teams and partnering firms.	Intensified competition from deregulated marketplaces can lead to the loss of competitiveness without appropriate partnering.
Process Focused Drivers		
Expensive, repeated mistakes and reinvention of solutions	Businesses are disconcerted by reinventing solutions and repeating mistakes because they could not identify or transfer best practices and experiential knowledge across locations or projects. Businesses incur unnecessary expense to relearn the same lessons.	Knowledge is neither being effectively retained nor shared. KM support can help your business realize what it already knows.
Proactive opportunity-seeking behavior	Inability to integrate external knowledge with internal expertise Inability to recognize the forces that will shape your future markets	Knowledge management provides an opportunity to anticipate such change, realize that it's coming, and lead it. Knowledge management, by integrating otherwise-dispersed knowledge, lets you apply your company's collective knowledge to turn business turbulence into opportunity.

Table 4-3 The Seventeen Drivers of Knowledge Management (cont.)

Driver	Problem Symptoms	Threats Addressable by KM Solutions
Process Focused Drivers (cont.)		
Responsiveness	As competitors become increasingly responsive to customer needs, companies must match the effort, using the right application of knowledge within the proper structures and processes.	Ability to proactively anticipate and respond to market trends. Use aggregated knowledge to control complex, multi-participant business processes.
Economic Drivers		
Increasing returns	Physical assets—both production-oriented and technological—lose value as they are used.	Sustainability of knowledge-based competitive advantage comes from knowing more about the same things than your competitors. Customer knowledge generates superordinary returns to scale—creating a self-reinforcing cycle. Multiple users can simultaneously benefit from knowledge assets and increase its value as they add to, adapt, enhance, enrich, and validate it. Bulk of the fixed cost in knowledge-intensive products and services usually lies in their creation rather than in manufacturing or distribution. Once such knowledge-intensive products have been created, their initial development cost can be spread out across mounting volumes.
Differentiation	Traditional capital assets or technology no longer suffices as a competitive differentiator in the e-business era	Building and deploying digital capital in the form of knowledge and relationship capital provide a sustainable source of competitive differentiation.

Adapted from A. Tiwana, *The Knowledge Management Toolkit*, Prentice Hall, 2000 and A. Tiwana, "Custom KM: Implementing the Right Strategy in Your Organization," *Cutter IT Journal/American Programmer*, November 1999.

UNDERSTANDING THE CONTEXT . . . .

Strategic context has an *expression barrier* surrounding it, as shown in Figure 4-1. This barrier is breached by (1) articulating a company vision and strategic intent, (2) translating this strategic intent into actionable business strategy, and (3) laying out discrete and measurable goals that lead your business to realize that strategy. While this barrier makes the task of implementing KCRM arduous, it also makes it inimitable by shielding (making ambiguous) its context and details.

> **Tech Talk**
>
> **Expression Barrier: Inability to articulate the strategic context of relationship-building strategy as influenced by product and service offerings, market opportunities, target customer segments, and relationships across the value chain of the business.**

In the following sections, we begin by looking at how such knowledge aggregation mechanisms are built using the Web. We examine various types of e-business hubs such as commerce hubs, customer hubs, corporate hubs, and finally knowledge hubs (or k-hubs). K-hubs are the ones that provide a central point for knowledge-enabled relationship building processes, and often subsume the other three types to varying degrees. Then we analyze three factors that are key to building a loyal base of customers, and how knowledge can be aggregated and applied during those activities. Finally, we analyze how the strategic context is interpreted and applied, and use an example.

E-Business and Web-Hub Strategies

Knowledge management systems could once be built with or without purely Web-based front ends. The pervasiveness of the Web coupled with mobility offered by wireless application protocol (WAP)–based mobile devices have narrowed that choice solely to the Web. A portal is essentially a Web-based front end for a collaborative system such as a knowledge management system (KMS). These portals act as digital hubs for facilitating various kinds of transactions and business activities. Beginning with customer hubs (or portals) that electronic commerce took off from, businesses have increasingly diversified to other kinds such as commerce hubs and corporate hubs. Table 4-4 compares these portals/hubs along six different dimensions.

Although variations based on the themes of commerce, corporate, and customer hubs might already exist in your own business, the one that we are focusing on is the k-hub. A careful examination of the table will reveal that the k-hub is a digital, customer-focused knowledge management hub that incorporates features from the other

Table 4-4 A Comparison of E-business Hubs

Context/Type	K-Hub	Commerce Hub	Corporate Hub	Customer Hub
Intent	Digital knowledge-based marketspace that integrates e-business, e-commerce, supply chain management, and relationship management to build long-term customer, relationship, and knowledge capital (digital capital)	Electronic hub for online transactions of goods and services, and optimization of procurement and supply chains	Enterprise knowledge management portal that integrates departmental coordination information in real time; knowledge sharing and discussions; Web presence for customer information gathering	E-commerce front end that allows customers to buy products and service online
Users	Customers, partners, and internal staff	Customers, partners, and internal staff	Internal staff, prospective and existing customers	Customers
Content	Customer and process knowledge, competitive intelligence, market segmentation, predictive anticipation, collaborative work, coproduced knowledge (with customers)	Digital catalogs, rating systems, Web self-service, account management, discussions, individualized target marketing, and customer profiling integrated with real-time multichannel integration	Annual reports, product and service manuals, resource pointers, skill directories, and company news	Electronic product and service catalogs, support information (FAQs, e-mail addresses and telephone numbers), manuals and product brochureware, account management, delivery tracking

Table 4-4 A Comparison of e-business Hubs (cont.)

Context/Type	K-Hub	Commerce Hub	Corporate Hub	Customer Hub
Applications	Dynamic pricing, business intelligence, knowledge management, supply-chain management, B2B and B2C integration, data Web-house, informal communication channels, e-communities, multichannel real-time information integration and distribution.	Exchanges, auctions, B2C and B2B trading, account management, inter-organizational process tracking, and real-time inventory management.	Internal communications, scheduling, reports, skill databases, and department specific applications, product and service information (brochureware).	B2C electronic commerce systems, transaction and payment processing systems, CRM packaged suites, order tracking and status, order history, Web-based querying, and real-time inventory information.
Platform	Interenterprise	Internet and extranet	Intranet/enterprise	Internet
Scope	Expansive	Specialized	Generalized	Specialized
Examples	Amazon.com	Chemdex.com eSteel.com Freemarkets.com Sciquest.com CommerceOne.com	Corporate intranet- and extranet-based KM systems	Outpost.com Buy.com iTools.apple.com

three types and integrates as KMS. The focus of the k-hub is to provide an aggregated point of activity where internal business processes, partner coordination, and customer integration can occur. The objective is to build, apply, and maximize the benefits realized from your business' digital capital—networked knowledge assets and relationship capital. KCRM systems strategy therefore goes beyond the basic notion of knowledge management in that it is focused only on customer-related activities and knowledge and on business relationship management. The k-hub therefore subsumes or seamlessly integrates the intranet and extranet as well as any other legacy interorganizational systems (such as electronic data interchange, EDI, and specialized enterprise resource planning, ERP); the k-hub is therefore largely synonymous with the KCRM system as discussed in the following chapters.

Three Keys to Customer Loyalty

Building customer loyalty begins with your business delivering three things valued by the customer: (1) knowledge, (2) anticipation of future requirements, and (3) superior communication. Consistently delivering on these three facets can help build a knowledge-based relationship with the customer, eventually leading to the possibility of creating a lock-in. The more a supplier knows the way her customers have configured, used, and integrated her company's products, the better understanding she will have to suggest value-enhancing services and up-sells. Such knowledge can be gained directly from the customer. In the context of e-businesses, such knowledge can be gleaned indirectly and transparently over the course of normal business activities. Table 4-5 shows examples of knowledge that can be gained between business processes (as shown on the intersections on the grid).

Table 4-5 Opportunities for Knowledge Assimilation in Pre-, In-, and Post-sales Processes

Business Process	Product Development	Marketing	Sales	Order Processing	Service	Quality Management
Product Development		Market specifications				Iterative improvements through feedback
Marketing	Market segmentation					
Sales		Customer profiles; customer data		Contract specifications	Contractual up-selling	
Order Processing			Logistics			
Service			Emergent customer needs			
Quality Management					Best practices; problem resolution	

Profitability analysis, for example, requires customer transaction detail—current and historical, integrated with product/service and financial records. Knowledge management activities can be seamlessly integrated with e-business transactions as they increasingly occur transparently and simultaneously. Identifying these business processes can reveal several points in e-business systems at which customer knowledge can be acquired:

1. Web interface used for electronic commerce transactions
2. Interorganizational e-business systems, ERP systems, and supply-chain management systems
3. Order management system
4. Trouble ticketing system
5. Call center
6. Digital help-desk (chat rooms, company-sponsored forums, etc.)

The Web puts tremendous consumer-related information into the hands of businesses, especially electronic commerce businesses. Each transaction generates a transaction record in a log file. For example, cookies—text files that a remote server puts on a visitor's machine—can help track the navigation path of a customer, and keep track of his repeat visits irrespective of whether they resulted in actual purchases. Several such sources of transparently acquirable information that can be intelligently aggregated to produce customer-specific knowledge are described in Table 4-6.

Table 4-6 *Transparent Acquisition of Customer Information on the Web*

Information Collected	Content
Transfer log	Every browser-server transaction is time stamped and recorded
HostField	Host server making the request
AuthUser	Authenticated user name if provided
TimeStamp	Date and time of visit
HTTP Request	GET call from visiting browser
Status Code	Success, redirect, Server Error, or Failure record
Error Log	Record of site/server error instances
Referred Log	URL of referring server
Agent Log	Name and version number of visitor's browser

HOW THE COUPON STOLE CHRISTMAS

Acquisition costs for new customers on the Web can be much higher than those in the brick-and-mortar world. B2C electronic commerce businesses are spending an average of $100 to acquire a new customer— many B2C e-businesses are spending upwards of $500 to acquire each new customer—Donna Hoffman and Ton Novak noted in their June 2000 *Harvard Business Review* article. If a business can be sure of high margins or repeat purchases, that would make economic sense. It would make little sense, however, if a customer visits an online supply store and spends $4.50 for a printer, a briefcase, and a bag of coffee after redeeming an $80 new customer coupon and a $50 rebate on the printer, and then never returns.

If the average acquisition value exceeds the average lifetime value of a customer, it's plain suicidal in e-business. Christmas of 1999 marked a watershed year in the history of electronic commerce when online sales exceeded brick-and-mortar holiday sales. It also marked a phase when "e-tailers" went overboard in their desperation to attract new customers. Many B2C businesses have resorted to freebies to attract customers. During the 1999 Christmas season, Buy.com shipped the first $20 worth of merchandise for free, Drugstore.com up to $45, and BarnesandNoble.com up to $10 for every new customer. If those figures plus some overheads represent the average acquisition cost for new customers, they are probably fine. But most of these customers did not return. Web businesses do not always have accurate measures to determine how many of those customers end up being one-time customers and how many actually return. Money was lost ("But who's supposed to make money in electronic commerce?") and many went out of business in the first quarter of 2000. Finally, customer relationships—not numbers—rose to the top.

The ability to identify customers accurately indeed represents the first step toward customizing their experience. Because telephone numbers and credit card numbers do not always represent a single person, and street addresses cannot be directly matched as text strings, a combination of these identifiers are usually the best option for identifying individual customers.

Integrating Demand Chain Knowledge

Customer-driven businesses are influenced by the so-called *demand chains* that are manifested in their rigorous understanding of marketspace dynamics, evolving business models, and relationships. Knowledge about markets, competitors, customers, business processes, problems, and business unit best practices feeds these demand chains and must be integrated into a knowledge-enabled customer relationship management strategy. Table 4-7 provides examples of such knowledge sources and categories.

Table 4-7 Knowledge Sources and Categories

Category	Examples
Markets	Market trends, news, development, and analysis
Competitors	Competitor strategies, competing products and substitutes, and competitive intelligence
Customers	Customer markets, processes, interaction, and operational data.
Orders	Past and present orders, employees, and departments involved in their execution, delivery status, and follow-on interaction
Contracts	Contract formulation and implications
Products and services	Configurations, improvement specifications, product information, service referrals
Problems	Past complaints, present unresolved complaints, issues, and sources of customer dissatisfaction
Best practices	Best practices for sales generation, maximizing share of the customer, and problem solving (may span multiple locations)

To facilitate customer knowledge management, identify various aspects of customer relationships and customer-driven knowledge that must be managed. Articulate the reasons and rationale, processes, indicators of management success, and their bottom line impact. Then, list technology tools that might facilitate each aspect. Collect responses from a varying mix of stakeholders (preferably members of the KCRM team, as described in detail in Chapter 6). KCRM strategy designers must be closely linked to the actual areas of expertise and competency that a business possesses while collectively addressing the fundamental question of how it adds current and future value/agility/responsiveness to the business strategy. An appropriate mix of skill sets for one such company appears in Table 4-8.

Table 4-8 Skills and Team Composition of a Strategy Formulation Group

Core Capability	Business Skills Needed	Technical Skills Needed	Interpersonal Skills Needed	Focus Time Frame	Strategy Motivation	Structure Motivation	Technology Motivation	Customer Focus
E-business strategizing	High	Medium	High	Present and future	✓	✓		✓
Business systems analysis	High	Medium	Medium	Future	✓			✓
E-business architecture planning	Low	High	Medium	Future			✓	
Vendor selection	High	Medium	High	Present and future	✓	✓		
Customer Relationship management	Medium	Low	High	Present and future	✓			✓
Technology implementation	Low	High	Low	Present			✓	

Based on an adaptation from I. Feeny and J. Wilcocks, Core IS Capabilities for Exploiting Information Technology. *Sloan Management Review*, Spring (1998), 9–21 and A. Tiwana, *The Knowledge Management Toolkit*, Prentice Hall, 2000, p. 189.

An overly simplified example of such an identification outcome is shown in Table 4-9.

Use this as a template for creating one for your own business.

Table 4-9 Customer Knowledge Needs Analysis—A Sample Case

Aspect	Outcomes	Technology enablement
What is managed?	Knowledge creation and reuse; increased knowledge half-life	Systems life cycle and communication networks' reach and scope
Why manage it?	Deliver knowledge to consumers, provide historical basis to enable rigorous decision-making, increase decision and choice efficiency, and sustain competitive edge	Implement reliable and high-quality hardware, software, and communication systems
How do we manage it?	Integrated, cross-functional approach Include the entire extended enterprise, i.e., suppliers, consumers, consultants, vendors, and buyers	Integrate existing systems, control costs, increase process efficiency, document, and reuse, not reinvent; learn from mistakes
Metrics and success criteria	Tangible financial and intangible digital capital gains; improved performance, competitiveness, timeliness; higher benchmark performance	Working, well-utilized, and growing knowledge management system that encourages contributive reciprocity
Bottom-line effects	Improved financial performance and customer retention	Interenterprise integration

STRATEGIC TECHNOLOGY . . . .

One of the first technological choices that must be made begins with the determination of the focus of your customer knowledge management approach. There are two alternatives: codification and personalization, which respectively support an explicit and tacit knowledge bias. While matching strategy and technology, the outcomes must be kept in mind. Looking at the outcomes instead of getting caught up in the process facilitates adaptation as the project progresses. Seven key outcomes that depend on knowledge to enhance both customer and channel relationships include improving quality, consistency, speed, cost reduction, employee satisfaction, customer satisfaction and accuracy—each without excessively compromising on any other. These are described in Table 4-10.

Tech Talk

Codification: A knowledge management approach that focuses on storing explicit knowledge in a database or expert system for later search, retrieval, and reuse. This is best suited in environments where problems of a similar nature repeatedly surface.

Personalization: A knowledge management approach that facilitates communication and tacit knowledge sharing, and that deemphasizes trying to capture knowledge in a formalized format.

Table 4-10 Six Outcomes that Strategic Technology must Facilitate

Outcome	Description
Improving quality	High-quality technical expertise and best practices for use by front-line staff
Consistency	Consistent provision of accurate solutions for similar problems
Speed	Early problem solving without escalation
Reducing costs	Self-service approach implemented through online knowledge bases
Employee satisfaction	Ability of front-line staff to solve problems collaboratively
Customer satisfaction	Fast and accurate answers for customers
Accuracy	Knowledge can keep pace with changing product and service attributes

In the sections that follow, we begin by taking a closer look at codification and personalization, and their suitability in different settings; we examine various trade-offs that must be made in achieving these outcomes; we also examine examples of several relationship-building approaches that are unique to the Web, and finally review a checklist of critical success factors for KCRM strategy design.

Codification and personalization are two semi-exclusive approaches to managing customer knowledge. Codification is more focused on technology that enables storage, indexing, retrieval, and reuse; it is better suited to businesses that encounter similar problems over again and make similar decisions and choices repeatedly. This strategy would be appropriate in activities such as technical support, credit verification and credit rating, and troubleshooting. Personalization is focused on connecting knowledge workers (employees, business partners, even customers) through networks *of people* and is better suited to businesses that face *one-off,* unique problems that depend more on tacit knowledge, experience, and expertise than on codified knowledge that may exist in databases and expert systems. Both approaches *must* be present in the knowledge orientation of the firm, but not with equal weightage. If a company decides to use codification as its primary strategy, it should direct about 80 percent of its efforts toward codification and the remaining 20 percent toward personalization. Table 4-11 compares these two strategies for customer knowledge management based on a set of diagnostic questions.

Table 4-11 A Comparison of Codification and Personalization Strategies

Business Strategy Question	Codification	Personalization
How do you service your customers?	Provide high-quality, reliable, fast, and cost-effective services and products.	Provide highly customized services and products.
To what extent does your business reuse past problem-solving experience and knowledge?	You reuse past cases and customer response incidents to guide problem solving in future situations.	Every problem has a high chance of being a "one-off" and unique and highly creative solutions are often called for to address unanticipated problems.
What is the costing model used by your business?	Price-based, volume-driven competition.	Expertise-based pricing accompanied by high product and service prices.
Do your customers perceive your products and service easily substitutable?	Yes.	No.
What is the level of customer lock-in?	Low.	High.
What is your ideal share of the customer's business?	Low to medium.	High.
What are your firm's typical profit margins?	Low profit margins that necessitate revenue maximization.	High profit margins.

Table 4-11 A Comparison of Codification and Personalization Strategies (cont.)

Business Strategy Question	Codification	Personalization
What is your business' dependence on tacit knowledge of employees?	Relatively low.	Relatively high.
What role does IT play in managing relationships with customers, and in internal collaboration and external partnering?	IT is considered a key enabler; business dependence on customer databases and pattern mining tools is high; past cases are used for future problem solving.	Communication between distributed employees and experts is the primary use of IT tools.
How many channels of interaction and points of contact do your customers have?	Many.	Few.
How highly automated can customer querying ideally be?	Highly automated through Web and interactive voice response systems.	High levels of automation are not appropriate for our business.
How are employees rewarded?	Employees are rewarded for documenting problems encountered and solutions developed in customer-interaction support databases and knowledge bases.	Employees are rewarded for directly sharing their knowledge with colleagues and for assisting colleagues in other locations and divisions with problem solving.
How is customer-related knowledge exchanged and transferred?	Employees refer to a document or best practices database that stores, distributes, and collects codified knowledge.	Knowledge is transferred person to person; tacit knowledge, insight, experience, and intuition sharing are encouraged.
Do your rely on economies of scale or economies of scope?	Economies of scale lie in the effective reuse of existing knowledge and experience and applying them to solve new problems and complete new projects.	Economies rest in the sum total of expertise available within the company; experts in various areas of specialization are considered indispensable.
What are your business' team structures like?	Large teams; most members are junior-level employees; a few project managers lead them.	Junior employees are not an inordinate proportion of a typical team's total membership.

Based on A. Tiwana, *The Knowledge Management Toolkit,* Prentice Hall, Upper Saddle River, NJ 1999, 151-152.

Examples of Relationship Management Processes

Examples of the activities that must be managed to build customer relationship capital and knowledge, and the technology tools that facilitate them across the four stages of customer relationship management, are described in Table 4-12.

Table 4-12: Relationship Management Stages and KCRM Enablers

Stage	Relationship Management	KCRM Infrastructural Enablers
Identify	Aggregate customer information across all touchpoints. Verify and update customer information.	Real-time integration of interaction channels and touchpoints largely enabled by the Web.
Differentiate	Identify your most expensive customers. Define your ideal customer base (most valued customers, most growable customers, below-zero customers). Identify customers who buy a lot, but buy a little from you. Identify customers who buy infrequently. Identify customers who gave your business the most feedback in the past year.	Aggregation of explicit customer knowledge across all channels and tacit knowledge in employees' heads throughout the business. Identification of patterns in data—both explicit and observed (e.g., clickstream data).
Interact	Enable delightful interactions through all available channels. Develop customer-specific knowledge of preferred interaction channels. Interpret clickstream data collected through Web-based interactions.	Application of up-to-date customer preferences and historical knowledge to differentiate service levels appropriate for MVC, MGC, and BZC categorization. Real-time analyses of customer behavior across all touchpoints.
Customize	Personalize, customize, and individualize based on customer-specific knowledge. Maintain customer knowledge and share it widely across your enterprise. Balance transparent knowledge capture and privacy rights.	Customize Customization and service individualization based on directly provided and indirectly acquired knowledge about the customer. Integration of customer-provided insights into e-business strategy.

Customer profiling requires a broad range of data related to each customer, much of which might already be collected—but underutilized—by your organization. Ensure that existing customer knowledge is integrated into customer relationship management processes and activities right from the start. Explicit customer knowledge can be applied to support various relationship-enhancing processes. Table 4-13 provides a description of how such explicit knowledge can be readily applied in the B2C electronic commerce context.

Table 4-13 Making Explicit Customer Knowledge Versatile

Activity	Description
Identification	Identifies general domains of your business that given customer knowledge applies to
Segmenting	Identifies target user segments and classifies them into (1) broad and (2) few mutually exclusive groups
Mass customization	Tailors content to suit each audience segment (such as technical support and government sales), preferably through collaborative filtering mechanisms and choice-enabling software
Format selection	Selects appropriate format that is suited for the bandwidth through which it will be delivered; uses indexes, groupings, site maps, mind maps, and concept trees for easy retrieval and navigation
Testing	Uses user feedback on perceived usefulness and possible improvements

Richness or Reach

Developing rich interactions with customers and facilitating collaborative problem solving and discussion always come at a cost. The richer the interaction channel, the higher is the bandwidth cost. With the Web, the bandwidth available to the *average* customer in your target market must be taken into account. Figure 4-7 shows where some real-time customer interaction technologies fall on the richness-reach spectrum.

These exemplars exclude asynchronous channels such as e-mail. Live chat is perhaps one of the least expensive, resource-humble, and bandwidth-efficient channels for facilitating real-time interaction. As richer channels are added, faster networks and more computing power are needed both on client- and host-side systems. When you are trying to decide on the types of interaction channels to implement, especially on the Web, this balance must be maintained based on *current* customer and partner technological levels and types of interactions.

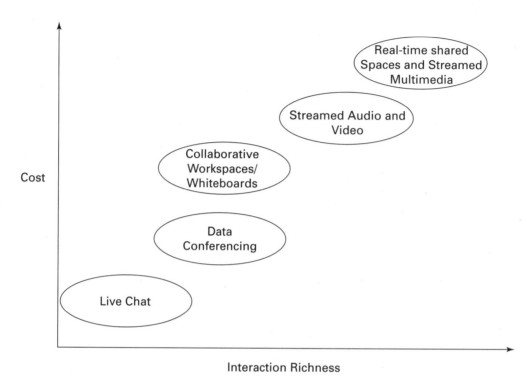

Figure 4-7
Tradeoffs between interaction richness and reach in various Web-based interaction channels must be accounted for in the design strategy stage.

Examples of Web-Only Relationship Tactics

Several relationship-building tactics are eminently suited to the Web environment, even though they have long existed without the Web. Value-added self-service is one such approach. Although self-service approaches have existed in almost all lines of business often as a cost reduction measure (e.g., fast food chains and package delivery services), their ability to create lock-ins by adding increasing value to the product/service package is profound in Web settings. Collaborative communities, adaptive real-time cross-selling, and intelligent personalization of services and products (especially in the case of purely digital products) are some other such tactics that are described in the following sections.

Encouraging Web Self-Service

Irrespective of whether your company decides to focus on the codification or personalization approach to customer knowledge management, the Web provides an unprecedented medium for self-service. If used in moderation, numerous rote tasks can be made more efficient *and* effective if put into the hands of customers. FedEx, one of the earliest companies to take advantage of the Web, provides an excellent example of such value-adding self-service. FedEx distributes its PowerShip software (see Figure 4-8) free of charge to all customers for the asking (a Web-based version is

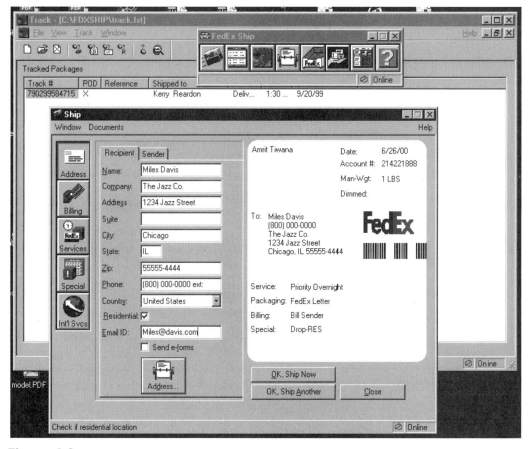

Figure 4-8
FedEx PowerShip provides a value-added self-service mechanism for individual and business customers and eventually creates a lock-in.

also available). Customers can electronically schedule shipments, maintain address books, manage accounts, track packages, order supplies, track supply orders, and print shipping labels on FedEx-provided label stock.

Interestingly, though FedEx makes its customers do all the work, the value-added by the service still keeps them happy! Not only are customers willing to pay higher prices than other competitors such as UPS; they are also locked in once they begin using the software and invest time and effort in keying in recipient addresses into the electronic address book. If a competitor introduced exactly the same type of software and the same set of streamlined package pickup processes, it might still be hard to convince customers to defect from FedEx due to the lock-in (which was precisely what happened when UPS introduced a similar package). Such self-service approaches can help deliver personalized service at mass-production cost-efficiency.

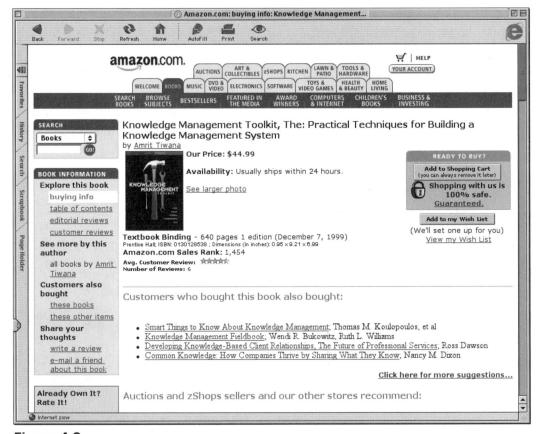

Figure 4-9
Analysis and aggregation of information gleaned from indirectly collaborative customer communities provide similarity-based recommendations for cross-sells.

Collaborative Communities

The Web also facilitates the formation of virtual communities at a relatively low cost. Amazon.com is an excellent example of such communities that can form around interest areas in the B2C context, much on the lines of UseNet groups in the C2C context. Such communities may be built either explicitly or implicitly. Figure 4-9 illustrates the case of a customer looking at a knowledge management book. Immediately below the actual listing, the customer can see what other customers with interests similar to hers actually purchased. By allowing customers to leave feedback and opinions on a particular product (reviews), Amazon.com creates an implicit community of buyers who share similar interests.

MP3.com and RatingWonders.com are other examples of such communities. Several other B2C businesses such as PriceWatch.com, Shopper.com, and mySimon.com act as *infomediaries* between businesses and consumers. A similar community-building approach has been used by several B2B trading hubs as well.

WHAT IS YOUR CUSTOMER WORTH?

CDNow.com, a once-major online music retailer, used a network of affiliates who posted links on their own sites to redirect potential customers. Even after paying off a percentage of each successful sale to these linkers, CDNow did better in reducing customer acquisition costs than it would through print, radio, and television advertising. However, with all its community support, it continued to be a loss leader: Customer acquisition spending was far too high compared to their lifetime value. Although many analysts argued that CDNow.com was like an Amazon.com, the company's attempts at building a brand in an unproven distribution channel were laid to rest when German media conglomerate Bertelsmann AG agreed to buy out the company for a $117 million pittance (at $3 per share). Often, a poorly executed business model (in this case, unreasonably high customer acquisition costs with margin expansion plans that worked, and an undying dependence on a purely commodity good) can negate any and all impact of supporting communities. It would be even more interesting to see online music retailers such as MP3.com and Emusic.com that sell MP3 music digitally (thereby avoiding the distribution overheads of CDNow.com) fare any better in the long run. In late 2000, Emusic.com was experimenting with an "all you can download" subscription-based model while dishing out free MP3 players that retailed well over $250, to its customers.

Adaptive Real-Time Cross-Selling

Cross-selling (i.e., offering related products at the time of sale) can be adaptively and intelligently managed in the Web environment. Figure 4-10 shows an example of a customer purchasing a digital camera. The system recognizes related items ("optional accessories") such as a digital camera case, a cable, and memory cards for digital pictures and offers them to the buyer as she gets ready to check out.

By being able to integrate past purchases, the system may reorder items that were most frequently purchased along with a given item, and offer them first. In addition, some Web businesses offer special bundle deals on such purchases. The key point here is that the Web provides a highly suited environment for cross-sell offers, and these can be made more effective by integrating aggregated knowledge gained from past buyers.

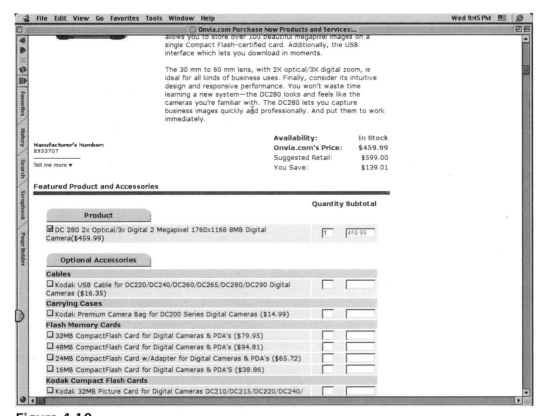

Figure 4-10
Cross-selling can be intelligently automated in B2C settings as shown in
Onvia.com's cross-sell offers with a digital camera shown above.

Intelligent Personalization

Technology tools such as intelligent agents apply artificial intelligence techniques for learning about consumer behavior through passive observation. Microsoft Word's assistants—though not always a pleasant example—are examples of such intelligent agents. As a customer interacts with a system, the agent (or set of agents) begins to deduce patterns in his behavior. Based on these deductions, agent-based tools can increasingly personalize offers for *that* user. This of course requires the agent's ability to individually identify each customer or visitor when the system is entirely Web-based. Even when such personalization is delivered using the most passive of technology, the level of dependence of the user can increase enough to make the site "sticky" (i.e., harder to leave for another one). Figure 4-11 shows how eBay delivers such information personalization based on registration information.

Figure 4-11
eBay's personalization aggregates customer-specific information without any intelligent back-end infrastructure.

By aggregating only relevant information from across several million listings, eBay provides an added value for the customer even without having to invest heavily in an intelligent-technology backend. Similarly, SonicNet personalizes delivery of digital products such as streamed music using customer-provided information collected at the registration stage (Figure 4-12).

As customer knowledge is increasingly integrated into interaction processes, the level of individualization delivered can be increased.

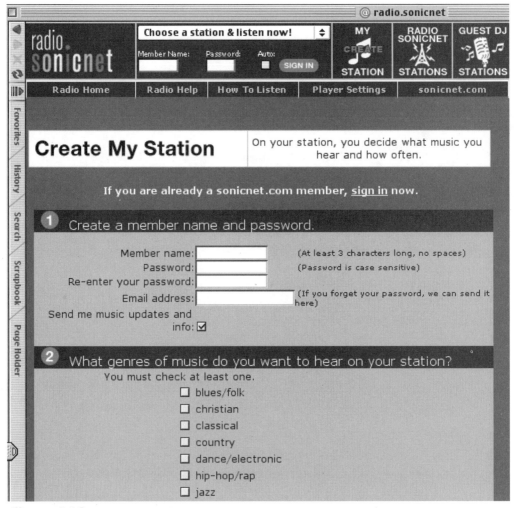

Figure 4-12
SonicNet uses barebones tag matching to personalize digital information products such as music.

Critical Success Factors

Seventeen critical success factors that determine the likelihood of success of a KCRM initiative are listed in Table 4-14. These have been extracted from research on several U.S. and foreign companies that have either been highly successful or encountered failure in knowledge-centric initiatives. Think of these as key lessons learned from these businesses—ones that you must keep in mind while planning your own initiative, especially while developing your KCRM strategy.

Table 4-14 Critical Success Factors and Their KCRM Technology Design Implications

What to Recognize	Implications for KCRM Technology Design
There is no "one right way"	What works well for one company often fails in another.
	Effective KCRM is situated in organizational context.
	Narrow down the scope of what you define as knowledge.
Need a process focus	Have a clearly defined business case.
	Identify key activities supported by your KCRM technology.
	Harmonize tools with actual business work processes.
Need initial metrics, however vague	No accurate or perfect measures of knowledge, knowledge work, and knowledge effectiveness exist.
	Use proxy measures such as patent counts, process innovation metrics, cycle time gains, and defect reduction.
	Plan to go deep rather than broad and start by picking a few well-executed initiatives.
	Managers may have to fall back on their business judgment and experience.
	Use knowledge maps.
	Limit unnecessary fiscal approximations to avoid tax liabilities.
Selling needs short-term impact demonstration	Continuing support depends on the demonstration of tangible and short-term results.
	Demonstrate tangible productivity gain along with proxy measures to demonstrate direct benefits to senior management.
	Accumulate some evidence to show that your project actually accumulates direct financial benefits if planned carefully at the outset.

Table 4-14 *Critical Success Factors and their KCRM Technology Design Implications (cont.)*

What to Recognize	Implications for KCRM Technology Design
Balance codification and personalization	Codification and personalization are not mutually exclusive.
	Pick one focal option, but divert 20 percent of resources to the opposite.
	One without the other is as fatal as pursuing both to equal degrees.
Create shared context beginning with existing customer knowledge	People with different functional, organizational, and divisional backgrounds often talk at different wavelength.
	Without shared context, people with different functional backgrounds, with different values, beliefs, assumptions and views are most likely to collide and immobilize consensus.
	Allow open, supportive, critical and reflective conversations between employees to help challenge, align, and establish a shared context.
	Begin by compiling expertise of key employees to give you a feel for who knows what throughout the organization.
	Begin with existing, underused knowledge assets before you address the softer and fuzzier aspects.
Eye on the future	Challenge assumptions about your markets and customers.
	Revalidate and invalidate existing assumptions.
Incentives	The supposed ability to be able to share knowledge will not break down employee determination to keep things to themselves.
	Build awareness and eagerness among employees on the value of creating, sharing, and using knowledge.
	Give incentives that are too attractive to be ignored.
	Provide cultural and reward system motivators, not just faster computers.
	Select incentives that are appropriate in the cultural context.
	Use employee knowledge contribution as an essential evaluation and promotion criteria.

Table 4-14 *Critical Success Factors and their KCRM Technology Design*
Implications (cont.)

What to Recognize	Implications for KCRM Technology Design
Ubiquitous and open access that still protects privacy	Most insightful suggestions might come from the most unexpected contributor.
	Do not restrict employees from contributing what they know and want to contribute.
	You may need to break language barriers to share across international offices.
	Should be accessible from any location and at anytime (maybe Web-based).
	Allow users to contribute insights and opinions anonymously without the fear of being reprimanded.
	Declare policies against anonymous abuse.
	Keep self-identification optional.
Resource maps help find tacit expertise	Excessive focus on formal knowledge leaves little room for informal, tacit, and socially embedded knowledge; make sure that tacit knowledge is included in your plans!
	Tacit knowledge problems will not wishfully "go away."
	Facilitate expression of perspectives, perceptions, values, and beliefs in KCRM systems.
	Provide pointers to internal and external experts in resource maps, expert directories, competency databases, and "corporate yellow pages."
Disseminate best and worst practices	Develop and maintain human networks that share current knowledge and create new knowledge in addition to IT networks.
	Share experiential customer-related knowledge regardless of proximity, through virtual collaboration and distributed decision making, often tapping into the original knowledge contributor's expertise.
	Identify and transfer both worst and best practices across far-flung units of the enterprise.

Table 4-14 *Critical Success Factors and their KCRM Technology Design Implications (cont.)*

What to Recognize	Implications for KCRM Technology Design
Ongoing senior management support	Senior managers are often concerned with the potential impact of KM and CRM initiatives on bottom-line results.
	Demonstrate in surrogate measures how the speed and quality of service to your clients will gain your initiative.
	Establish critical top management sponsorship with ongoing involvement during the design, development, implementation stages of your knowledge management system.
Informal and communicatively rich	A successful KCRM system supports the ways in which people naturally share information, and perform their tasks. Its use must be almost transparent, natural, hesitation free, and rarely formal.
	The system should support informal, rich communication and multiple ways of expressing ideas, thoughts, and communication. Context, meaning opinions, tone and biases should have a way to move through the system.
	The system should be well accepted in the community that will actually use it—including partner firm employees and customers—not just the community that creates it.
Package knowledge	Package and aggregate customer knowledge to make it insightful, relevant, and useful.
	Ask selected end users to evaluate the material and provide ideas for how to improve its content, value, quality, and style so that it increases the perceived credibility and value.
	Allow employees the time to package knowledge for further use.
Logically extend business processes	Build the system one logical component—matched with a specific business unit—at a time.
	Use results-driven implementation methods (Chapter 8).
	Partner with technology vendors who really get what you are trying to do.
	Let your customer relations folks, not just IT, have the final say on technology choices.
	Explore the long-term potential for IT suppliers to create win-win situations.

Table 4-14 *Critical Success Factors and their KCRM Technology Design Implications (cont.)*

What to Recognize	Implications for KCRM Technology Design
Make it intuitive	Most employees have little interest in dealing with cryptic and hard-to-use interfaces.
	Optimize KCRM systems for ease of use and ease of retrieval.
	Web browsers provide a familiar, intuitive interface option.
	Provide a feedback mechanism.
	Provide powerful search options (easily implemented on Web front ends).
	Provide resource maps that reflect your business' structure.
	Ask (but don't force) users to rate the usefulness of resources, documents, and content included; publish these results live.
Provide multiple delivery mechanisms	Balance, and let the user decide on the final delivery method:
	Pull versus push delivery of customer knowledge
	Just-in-time versus just-in-case
	Implement both options and make them user selectable.

SUMMARY ·

The KCRM strategic framework integrates four perspectives. Your business environment, strategic context, KCRM strategy, and technology can be harmonized and robustly adapted to changing needs using this framework. In aligning business strategy and KCRM technology, keep the following points discussed in this chapter in mind:

- *Four barriers impede knowledge-facilitated relationship building.* The environment is shielded by an interpretation barrier, the context by an expression barrier, strategy by a specification barrier, and technology by an implementation barrier.

- *Outcomes must be nonsubstitutable and inimitable.* Knowledge-enabled customer relationship management strategy should help build rare, valuable, and inimitable customer knowledge and relationships. It must also reduce the level of coordinative complexity and help maintain a balance between strategy and technology.

- *Effective KCRM must result in digital capital riches.* Knowledge and relationship capital together constitute the currency of the e-business environment. KCRM strategy must address building and deploying such intangible capital assets.

- *Opportunities are indicated by the three gaps.* Three types of gaps—strategic gaps, knowledge gaps, and relationship gaps—must be evaluated to judge the feasibility of pursuing given market segments.

- *Knowledge maps provide relative comparisons.* Depending on whether your business emerges as an innovator, market leader, competitive threat, straggler, or an exit candidate, you can determine whether the cost of pursuing a certain market and decide on whether to invest in playing catch-up or focus on a different market segment.

- *The expression barrier must be broken to implement KCRM strategy.* Strategy must be implemented after considering the seventeen drivers of knowledge management and then by: (1) articulating a company vision and strategic intent, (2) translating this strategic intent into actionable business strategy, and (3) laying out discrete and measurable goals that lead your business in the direction of realizing its vision.

- *Customer loyalty determinants must be consistently delivered.* Customer loyalty is determined by your knowledge of their needs, anticipation of future requirements, and superior communication. Seven key KCRM outcomes that depend on knowledge to enhance both customer and channel relationships include quality, consistency, speed, accuracy, increased levels of satisfaction, and cost reduction.

- *Balance exploitation and exploration.* The degree to which a business exploits its existing knowledge and relationships for short-term gains (exploitation level) and the extent to which it focuses on internal and externally assimilated or created knowledge, and on building new relationships must be balanced.

- *The Web makes new ways of relationship building feasible.* Self-service, collaborative communities, intelligent personalization, and knowledge-based adaptation provide individualization at mass-market cost-efficiency.

Aligning strategy and technology is a crucial but often ignored link that determines the eventual business benefits of any piece of technology. Knowledge-enabled customer relationship management is no exception.

TEST YOUR UNDERSTANDING · · · · · · · · · · · · · · · ·

1. What is the problem in three-year strategic plans in e-business? Why don't they work anymore?

2. What are we trying to do when we attempt to build a unified view of the customer?

3. What characteristics of digital capital make it valuable? Why can we not always manage these characteristics well?

4. Can you think of a business that you are associated with that is currently facing the Innovator's Dilemma that we discussed in this chapter? Why do you think this dilemma emerges and what can be done about it?

5. What are the three gaps that e-business must discover through gap analysis?

6. How do core, advanced, and innovative knowledge differ? Do these transform into each other over time? If they do, what can your business do about it?

7. What is a Web-hub? Can you think of common types of e-hubs that you have encountered in your own job?

8. Have you ever used online coupons to get discounts from websites? If you've never seen such coupons, point your browser to www.tech-bargains.com or mycoupons.com. Think of a B2C that runs coupons that cost it more than the lifetime value of an average customer? Do you think this is a recipe for disaster?

9. How do personalization and codification approaches to knowledge management differ? When is one better suited than the other is? Can they be pursued on an exclusive basis?

10. We identified several critical success factors for e-business strategy-KCRM technology alignment. Can you identify which of these do not exist in some of your favorite e-businesses? What do you think will happen because of each that is missing, provided nothing is done to fix its absence?

5 Audit and Analysis

In this chapter...

- Understand the objectives and significance of a customer knowledge audit.

- Analyze the three phases and seven steps of the audit process.

- Determine a method of choice and select reference measures.

- Classify customers based on their lifetime value to your business.

- Use this information to differentially interact and deliver customized value packages to different customers.

- Understand how the Capability Classification framework is used to document intangible knowledge and relationship assets.

- Analyze audit outcomes to determine KCRM strategic imperatives.

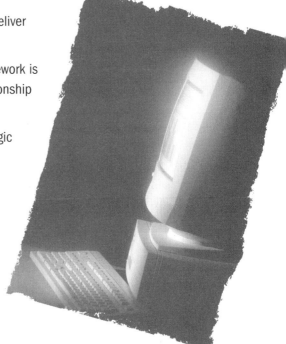

The second step on the KCRM roadmap involves auditing and analyzing existing customer knowledge to lay a foundation for prioritizing knowledge support mechanisms, strategic options, and technology investments. To support frontline decisions made by your sales and marketing staff, knowledge-enabled customer relationship management—at least at the outset—must be focused on a specific knowledge niche rather than trying to support all customer interaction processes.

Beginning with a description of key outcome expectations from an audit, we examine how resulting audit information is used to prioritize investments and to classify customers into clusters and segments based on their perceived lifetime value. In tracing a series of steps across the three audit phases, we see how the Capability Classification framework is used to document customer knowledge and relationship assets that can serve as a lighthouse for guiding the direction of further KCRM initiatives. Let us begin by understanding the objectives of a customer knowledge audit.

WHY AUDIT CUSTOMER KNOWLEDGE? . . . .

Knowledge of customer knowledge assets provides the basis for planning and implementing knowledge-enabled customer relationship management that is aligned with the strategic needs of your business. The audit process helps take into account both explicit and tacit knowledge of customers—present and potential. With a limited budget within which such projects are typically implemented, investments must be prioritized to retain focus on areas with the potential for maximum future growth, future payoff, and sustainable relationship advantages.

Customer and relationship knowledge does not just involve traditional aspects such as customer records, databases, and leads but also encompasses tacit aspects within your own business such as its rituals, processes, structure, communities, and people. Results from such an audit will help in the following key activities:

- Devising a knowledge-enabled CRM strategy (Chapter 4)
- Helping plan effective metrics (Chapter 10)
  - For knowledge management
  - For customer satisfaction
  - For measuring "share of the customer"
  - Planning product development and related financial allocations
  - Building competitive relationship capital
- Building an enterprisewide architecture for KCRM

- Developing an IT system to implement that architecture
- Leveraging your business' people assets and employee-owned tacit knowledge
- Control corporate ebbing in the form on competitive failure, earning shortfalls, employee dissatisfaction and customer defection, and financial overruns
- Catch-up with competitors who are currently ahead on the knowledge curve
- Provide a focus for company-wide learning
- Plan product/service line diversification and new market entry strategies

Unlike its ideal never-ending characteristics, you must know where to begin and when to stop an iteration of the audit. Seven key nonlinear steps involved in the audit process illustrated in Figure 5-1 are described below. These steps can be categorized in three broad phases: (1) initiation, (2) reference measure and method selection, and (3) execution of the audit.

1. *Define audit goals.* The KCRM team agrees on the key expectations of the audit, its key objectives, and constraints. Specifically, marketing and sales representatives on the team must help identify what the projected benefits of both the audit and the KCRM project are. Goals must be defined unambiguously, and must be measurable if achieved.

2. *Assemble the audit team.* Key members for the audit team, which is also the project implementation team, are selected. This step is described in detail as Step 3 in Chapter 6.

3. *Identify constraints.* Financial, technological, resource, time, and strategic constraints are identified.

4. *Define customer clusters.* Following one-to-one marketing ideas, determine criteria on which your customers are identified as most valuable, most growable, and below zero in terms of their long-term value to your business.

5. *Establish a reference measure.* Determine the state of customer relations and retention that your business would like to achieve in an ideal situation. This measure will be used as a benchmark for measuring KCRM performance. Make sure that a select few variables are accounted for in this measure, and that you do not make it immeasurable or meaningless in your attempts to make it all-encompassing. Progression from the stage when the audit is performed for the very first time to later stages allows for easy comparison with the initial benchmark state.

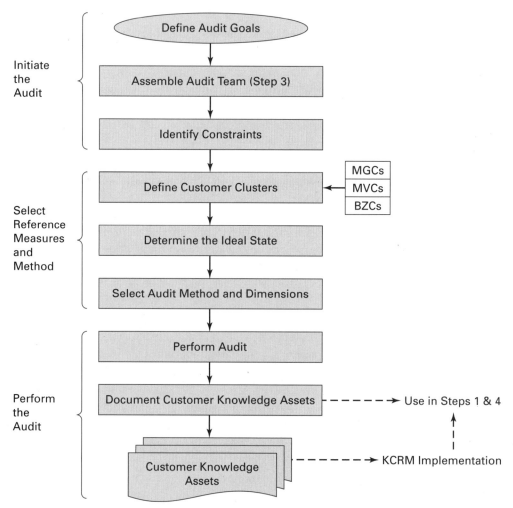

Figure 5-1
Key activities involved in a customer knowledge audit.

6. *Select an audit method.* The audit method flows along the lines of Figure 5-1, except that specific instantiations and requirements vary according to your specific business.

7. *Perform the audit.* The actual customer knowledge audit is carried out, and knowledge assets of your business are identified and documented. The outcome of this audit is used in Steps 1 and 4 illustrated on the roadmap. This provides an internal benchmark to evaluate the effects of knowledge management and KCRM initiatives after they have been put in place.

··

BRITISH RUGBY: THE ROUGH WAY

> The 120-year-old British Saracens Rugby Club based in North London moved to the Web (www.saracens.net) to help build its fan following and loyalty of ticket buyers. The club uses the Website more for strengthening its relationships with fans—most of which are U.K. based—by building a community. A forum allows fans to discuss games and players. Chat rooms allow fans to talk to players, management, and other fans. Members can buy merchandise, find the latest news, gossip, and injury reports (remember, British rugby is a rough game). The club is increasingly slicing and dicing customer data to find new and interesting patterns that can help redirect marketing dollars (well, pounds!) more effectively.

INITIATING THE AUDIT ····················

The three phases of the audit process—namely, initiation, reference benchmarking and method selection—and execution are described in the following sections. The process begins by defining key goals that you hope to achieve through the audit, and the limitations placed on them by existing constraints. Goals must be defined very narrowly and specifically because they provide the basis for many decisions that follow, as illustrated in Figure 5-2.

Aiming too much or too broadly can result in a futile exercise and wasted investments, so identify specific goals such as the following:

- How can we identify the lowest rank of *below-zero customers* (BCGs) by looking at their 2000 spending patterns? Examples might be customers who only responded to your free offers, or only bought goods with price matches that might have invoked your price guarantees at substantial loss. If I were BigOfficeSupplyStore.com, I might want to look at customers who purchased significant amounts of goods but only when my businesses took losses in each sale. What knowledge of most valued customers (MVCs) located outside the 50 United States do we have? How can we improve that knowledge to grow their purchase volume? What do competing firms offer to the same customers? Is that a viable option for us?

- How can we increase sales volumes involving our top strata of *most growable customers?* How can we increase this figure by 30% by November this year?

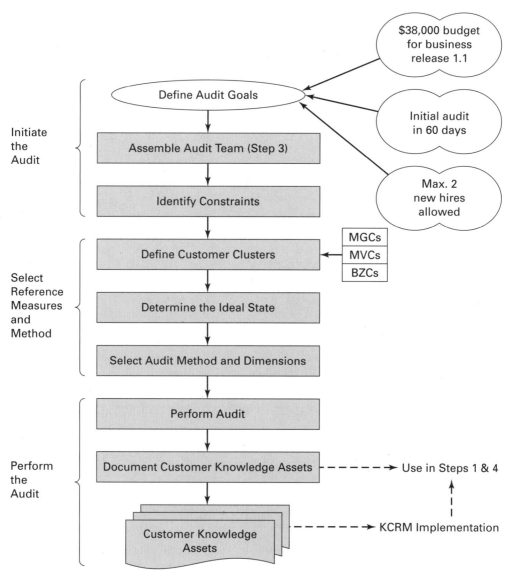

Figure 5-2
Defining audit goals.

Assembling the Audit Team

A multidisciplinary team with membership that accurately represents the various needs of your business' divisions must perform the knowledge audit. Due to the diverse membership structure of the team, a certain degree of discord and disagreement should be expected, but as the team members learn to resolve these differences in an amicable manner, this diversity becomes its key strength. This team must have representative from the functional areas listed in Table 5-1, at the bare minimum.

Table 5-1 KCRM Team Membership

Member Representation	Role
Business strategy	Sets goals, determines optimal performance benchmarks, brings the bigger knowledge management perspective into the analysis
KCRM evangelist	Brings a short- and long-term knowledge management and CRM vision, integrates viewpoints and needs of functional representatives, and helps aligns corporate strategy and technology implementation aided by a good understanding of both the business and business implications of your business' customer knowledge assets
Marketing and sales	Identifies needs and requirements to enable one-to-one relationships with customers, provides base criteria for segmenting customer bases, and identifies MCVs, MGCs, and BZCs
Finance	Allocates and manages project funding
Information technology	Brings expertise for implementing KCRM technology and integrating it with existing infrastructural pieces

The actual team formation process is described in detail in Chapter 6.

Tech Talk

Most Valued Customers (MVCs): Customers who currently influence most of your revenues and of whose business you have the largest share.

Most Growable Customers (MGCs): Customers who are the most promising candidates for growing your business with in the near future. It is this segment whose "share of the customer" you want to maximize.

Below Zero Customers (BZCs): Customers whose lifetime value falls far below the time, money, and resources that you must invest to retain. These are customers whom you can either "lose" or derive additional streams of revenue from by differentiating the level of service provided. These are discussed in further detail in the next section.

Identifying Constraints

Constraints—both for the audit and for the overall KCRM initiative—must be identified next. A comprehensive customer knowledge audit can often be an overambitious, long-term, and expensive undertaking that is best done if divided into smaller segments. Budget, time, and resource constraints can provide initial bases for such segmentation (see Figure 5-3). These constraints might be difficult to comprehensively identify upfront, and must be incorporated into the audit and implementation plan as they emerge—for example, knowing that the KCRM project must demonstrate some tangible payoff within three months, or knowing budgeting limitations or hiring caps provide natural boundaries for narrowing down the audit process.

REFERENCE MEASURES
AND METHODOLOGICAL CHOICES . . . .

The second phase of the audit involves clustering and definition of customer categories, determination of the ideal reference benchmark, and selection of the audit method and associated specifics.

Clustering and Defining Customers

Before a full-blown customer knowledge audit can be done, you must differentiate your customers according to the lifetime value that they have for your business. The concept of not treating all customers equally comes from the realm of one-to-one marketing. Brick-and-mortar stores have done this for a long time; treat your most important customers very well, and ignore customers who only cause you losses! While that might be exaggerating a bit, customer relationship management centrally relies on differential treatment of various customers depending on which group they belong to:

- Most valuable—those who give most of your business at present, those you want to retain, reward, and provide the highest level of service
- Most growable in the near future
- Customers with zero or negative value to your business

The many functional areas and departments that your team represents might not be in agreement as to who constitutes a valuable customer. Besides, a customer of little value to one division of your business might be a key account of another. Without effective knowledge sharing among these departments, customer value can be misjudged, often at your business' peril.

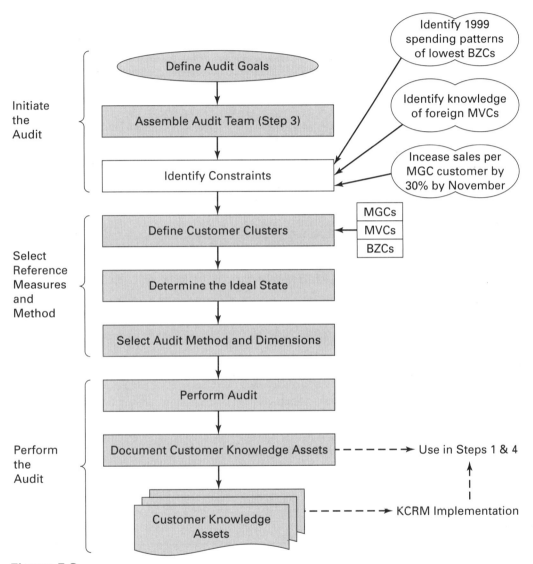

Figure 5-3
Identifying constraints during the audit process.

Two primary customer types that must be identified to focus on are what Martha Rogers and Don Peppers define as *most valued customers* and *most growable customers*. Besides these two, another group must be identified to take focus *away* from, your business' *Below Zero Customers* (BZCs). The audit team must collectively establish criteria for classifying customers under each of these three key categories. Classification criteria for MVCs are relatively straightforward to determine from

··

JENNY CRAIG'S NEW BAG OF TRICKS

The controversial La Jolla, California-based diet program maker, Jenny Craig Inc. went online with its Website (www.jennycraig.com) in an attempt to focus its directed marketing effort. However, the company realizes the importance of each of its 65,000 active customers and the role of personal relationships that drive the business. The information systems mostly assist at the back end rather than on its Website because knowledge about specific customers is largely tacit. A customer database is used to analyze, identify, and segment customers based on their behavioral patterns, but most data is collected informally at over 500 weight loss centers nationwide. The typical customer receives an average of six mailings every year, each of which contains promotional discounts, incentives, and advice based on personally collected and aggregated data. Automation through the Web that works well for many businesses would have had a negative effect on Jenny Craig's high-value customers. A loyalty-enhancing relationship management approach targeted at a relatively wealthy customer base resulted in double-digit increases in customer retention during 1999–2000.

existing transaction records and purchases. The second cluster is trickier to define. Again, principles of knowledge management can assist in making accurate similarity-based judgments for past and future MGCs. No hard-and-fast rules exist; criteria for defining MGCs should therefore be a collective judgment of your KCRM team with above-ordinary inputs from marketing and sales.

A national car rental company defines an MGC using the following set of criteria:

- Rents 25 cars per year
- Rents at least 8 cars from us
- Did not use any discount coupons over 40 percent of the time
- Owns a "frequent-renter" card with a competitor
- Never refills gas before dropping off cars at the airport parking lot

A major U.S. specialty stationery and pen Web store defines an MGC as a customer who:

- Buys more than $7,000 worth of goods every year
- Buys refills for high-end imported fountain pens, typically not purchased in the same store

- Has 70 percent of her purchases gift wrapped before shipment
- Holds a senior management position in the financial services industry

You must also identify below zero customers—those who do not turn a profit, and neither do you have a hope that they will. Identifying who exactly these customers are is again based on criteria that are best determined by your KCRM team working collaboratively. Once identified, you must divert resources and expenses *away* from these customers and redirect them toward serving your MGCs and MVCs.

Similarly, an office supply store may have different criteria for defining BZCs. For example, a customer who:

- Returns 35 percent or more of his purchases
- Price matches most purchases to take excessive advantage of the store's "155% price guarantee"
- Regularly places unreasonable demands on store staff
- Accounts for under $700 in annual purchases

Resources funneled unproductively toward below-zero customers can be redirected in four possible ways, as described in Table 5-2. Again, exact implementation must take into account your own business, and inputs from your own team members.

CUSTOMER SEGMENTATION AT *MCI*

Telephone companies have long practiced the art of differential treatment for customers through multiple long-distance calling plans; the Web had made their customers even more differentiable. MCI, a long-distance telephony provider, uses the Web to differentiate among customers. MCI offers highly discounted rates to customers who are willing to manage their account through the Web. Whether it's changing mailing addresses, reviewing bills, adding new credit card numbers, or asking billing or service questions, customers who sign up under this plan have no support number to call—everything is self-serve and every interaction is Web-based. This lets MCI offer lower rates to self-serving customers instead of splitting support fees incurred due to a few customers across the entire customer base. In effect, what MCI did was charge a premium to subscribers who needed human assistance (and valued it) in the form of higher rates. Although MCI was one of the first companies to have adopted this model, many others in the telecommunications industry soon followed suit.

Table 5-2 Tactics for Redirecting Resources Away from Below-Zero Customers

Tactic	Implementation
Reduced service	Provide fewer options
	Reduce available choice
	Offer slower shipping methods
	Limit quantities
Alternative service methods	Offer limited technical support
	Provide customer service only through the Web
	Force customers to use automated voice response and fax back services
	Charge for live support
Charge for additional services	Charge for services that are otherwise free to more valued customers
Reduced communication	Infrequent paper and electronic mailings
	Reduce frequency of discounts
	Provide automated, electronic-only service and support channels

Based on an extension of D. Peppers, M. Rogers, and B. Dorf, *The One to One Fieldbook*, Currency Doubleday, New York 1999, 356-357.

Determining the Ideal State Reference

Once customer classification criteria are established, the team must identify the optimal high level at which each component of their customer knowledge assets must operate. This provides a benchmark reference to measure impact of KCRM initiatives. As Figure 5-4 illustrates, point B provides the *ideal state* value that the team must target, and point A marks the starting point. As the project progresses through various stages and time frames (such as financial quarters) of implementation, changes are tracked in relation to these benchmark values.

Let us assume that the parameter being tracked is the average number of purchases per MVC per year. Point B indicates the ideal value that might have been calculated as a 15 percent increment over your competitor's average figure, and point A indicates the point at which you began. Several such trackers must be used to measure various aspects of CRM, and can be aggregated into a single composite measure in the end.

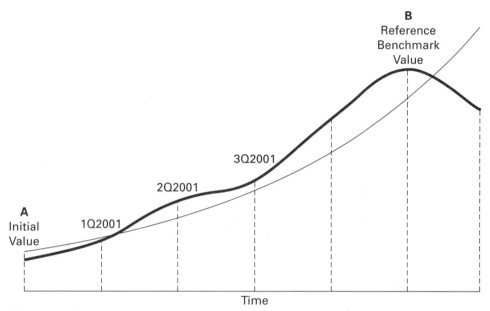

Figure 5-4
The ideal state reference point.

Process performance need not be based on an arbitrary figure; it could be based on a function such as 118 percent of the industry average derived from publicly known industry averages, competitor fiscal figures, or future market predictions.

THE AUDIT METHOD . . . .

The choice of method primarily involves selection of key dimensions that you will measure. Take a quick look at *Bohn's Knowledge Growth Framework* in Chapter 10 to determine these dimensions. The pre-KCRM state of your business' customer knowledge and channel relationship assets must be accurately reflected in the results of your audit, and these must provide a stable foundation for guiding your implementation plans and reinforcing investments in KCRM technology (see Figure 5-5).

For example, if you determine that customers cancel existing orders, and never order again because of their irritation with poorly coordinated billing issues (a very common problem in Web stores), you must document this in your audit. Several sources can provide you various measures that might be needed: Customer surveys, interviews with clients, analysis of sales data, cost of sales, market reputation measures, analysis of competitor data, analysis of cash flows, analysis of knowledge flow bottlenecks and focus groups can provide more insights into the actual state of your company's knowledge assets than pure guesswork can. Market pull for your products and services, return on investments in IT and knowledge/discussion databases, employee skills, sharing of best practices across the enterprise, and development of core competencies are other feasible indicators. The choice of technologies implemented and integrated to address each issue will be heavily influenced by the accuracy and depth of this documentation. With each problem dimension identified in the audit, make sure that you also record the following associated parameters: employee expertise and skills/knowledge, reputation-related perceptions created or negated, organizational culture as it relates to the issue. It helps to think in terms of the issues of protection, maintenance, enhancement, and advantage of these intangible customer-influencing assets. Customer knowledge that is already available as information in electronic format as well as what is "on file" in nonelectronic format including sources such as your company's invoicing system, warranty service records, and complaint handling system must be taken into account.

SAMPLE DIAGNOSTIC QUESTIONS

A comprehensive set of diagnostics questions relating to the four processes of CRM (i.e., identification, differentiation, interaction, and customization) along with customer knowledge management are listed below. These can be used as the basis for selecting the minimally sufficient dimensions of the customer knowledge audit that you conduct.

Identification

- Do you have mechanisms for identifying each customer individually?
- Do you have data on customer transactions, and in a form amenable to analysis?
- Is that data accurate? Will it stay accurate through maintenance?
- How much information about each customer do you collect?
- Does each business unit in your business have its own customer records?
- Are these records shared across units?
- Do you use any other sources of customer-identifying mechanisms?

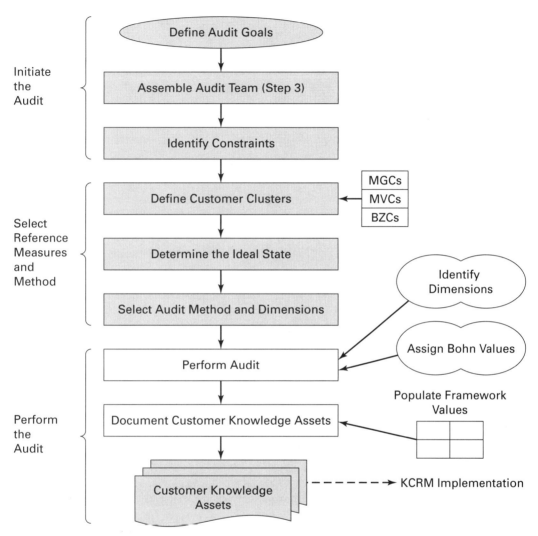

Figure 5-5
Auditing dimensions and assigning Bohn's scores.

- Do you aggregate analyses of customer data and match individual customers against those profiles?
- Do you mine your customer data for knowledge about their preferences, viability, and behavior?
- Do your customer acquisitions costs vary significantly across product lines?

Differentiation

- Do you currently have criteria for identifying MVCs, MGCs, and BZCs, even if you do not actually use those terms to describe those categorizations?
- How do you calculate customer acquisition costs?
- How do you calculate the cost of servicing in terms of both allocated fixed costs and variable per-customer costs?
- Do you currently use any measures or predictors of customer loyalty?
- Do you identify key influencers besides key customers?
- How are these influencers differentiated?
- How do you currently measure returns on investment for "servicing" these influencers?
- How do you manage relationships with influencers?
- What steps can be taken to differentiate both customers and influencers into subcategories according to their long-term value to your business?
- Do you track and aggregate purchase frequency according to multiple units of analysis such as person, division, and customer business?
- Do you track and aggregate service delivery frequency according to multiple angles of analysis such as by product, product line, and incident type?
- Do you track breakdowns of costs involved in the above?
- Do you track the number of business units, divisions, and related concerns of your customer organizations?
- Do you track the number of purchasers at each customer unit as described above?
- Is seasonality of purchase patterns of significance in your line of business?
- Do you track and correlate ancillary purchases associated with each key purchase?
- Do you track effectiveness of cross-selling and up-selling attempts?
- Do you measure or evaluate expectations about future loyalty and attrition rates from newly acquired customers?

- Do you measure correlations between promotional discounts and "specials" and future loyalty from newly acquired customers?
- Evaluate what percentage of your total customer base and what percentage of your total business can be attributed to your MVCs, MGCs, and BZCs.
- For each segment, what objective defines your relationship management tasks:

  Retain

  Grow

  Lose

  Migrate

Interaction

- What interaction channels do your customers use?
- What type of information is gathered in these interactions?
- What type of information is transparently collected in Web-based interactions?
- Are interactions captured at all customer interaction points?
- Does your business track the value of customer interactions to the customer?
- Is current customer knowledge leveraged in an unobtrusive yet useful manner?
- Is knowledge of past interactions and individual differences applied in future interactions?
- Does interaction enable gathering of customer knowledge that is only obtainable directly from the customer?
- Does each interaction pick up where the previous one left off, i.e., is there continuous dialogue over spaces of time?
- If the customer interacts with one division of your business, is this knowledge accessible across the enterprise, and in other unrelated interactions?
- Can the customer interact with other customers who share similar profiles or interests (e.g., Amazon.com)?

Customization

- How does your business match customer needs and customization through:

  Configuration management of services or products

  Bundling of related or complementary products or services

  Delivery and logistics

  Bundling of ancillary services

  Integration with customer's existing product or services infrastructure

- How are assumptions about the customer managed and reevaluated?

- What objectives apply to the following customization and how is this knowledge managed on a customer-to-customer basis?

  Relationship development

  Creation of additional sales leads

  Customer retention and loyalty enhancement

  Increasing lifetime value of individual customers

  Maximizing cost-efficiency

  Increasing share of the customer

  Boosting customer satisfaction

  Increasing customer dialogue

- Generating feedback and learning to build your own products further

- How does customization delivery add value to your product or service's design modularity?

Customer Knowledge Management

- Are customer knowledge management processes adequately rewarded?

- Does your business' culture support collection and application of customer knowledge? Is it an open, trusting, and sharing culture?

- Does your company's culture reflect internal competitiveness?

- Is customer-centric behavior enabled by existing customer-interaction management technology at an enterprise level?

- Are most of your company's software applications built to automate existing customer interaction processes?
- Are any of these applications capable of identifying and targeting your best and most profitable customers?
- Do these systems integrate customer information across contact channels such as your Website and toll-free number?
- Do these applications consider the customer's past buying behavior?
- Do they offer real-time personalization for services for each customer?
- Are customer-centric knowledge, skills, competencies, and best practices in your company shared across the enterprise, across locations, across business units, and within departments?
- Are customer knowledge management technologies unobtrusive by design?
- Where do you think your business falls on the Bohn knowledge scale (Chapter 10)?
- How would you characterize your company's structure and organization?
- What other types of customer- and product-centric knowledge do you think are critical to your business competitiveness?
- Would you agree that most business units in your company have a great deal of freedom to act and have a bottom-line responsibility for their own actions?
- How do these systems compare with those in use by competitors?
- Do your employees have sufficient training to use them?
- Can knowledge of multiple team members or stakeholders be added to create synergy?
- What does your company reward—team performance or individual performance?
- Does your senior management focus on financial performance alone or both financial performance and future growth planning?
- Are your employees responsible for creating additional value in customer-interaction processes? Does it count in their compensation arrangements?

DOCUMENTING CUSTOMER
KNOWLEDGE ASSETS ·

Customer knowledge assets audited in the preceding steps must be recorded in the capability framework in Table 5-3 so that they can be compared over time both before and after your KCRM strategy has been implemented. This framework also simultaneously facilitates uniform comparison with your key competitors. Add categories specific to your own business within this framework.

Table 5-3 The Capability Framework for Positioning Customer Knowledge Assets

Regulatory Capability Level	Positional Capability Level
Patents	Path-dependent capabilities
Trademarks	Reputation
Registered designs	Value chain configuration
Trade secrets	Distribution networks
Licenses	Installed and repeat customer base
Proprietary technology	Market share
Methodologies	Liquidity
Databases	Product and service reputation
Average value (= total/number)	Average value (= total/number)

Functional Capability Level	Cultural Capablility Level
Lead times	Supportive corporate culture
Accessibility of past knowledge	Knowledge sharing without fear
Innovative capabilities	Tradition of risk sharing
Individual and team skills	Perception of quality standards
Distributor know-how	Capability to respond to market challenges
Employee skills	Innovation
Applicability of knowledge to customer interactions	Entrepreneurial drive in employees, employee initiative, and motivation
Aggregation of customer knowledge across all channels of interaction and contact	Team-focused reward structures
Average value (= total/number)	Average value (= total/number)

Measure each entry recorded in Table 5-3 on a scale of 0 to 8 as described in Table 5-4. This allows you to measure both the level of each entry as well as the degree to which it is tacit, and must be deliberately supported and enhanced by knowledge management processes. The lower the value on this scale, the more important it might be to account for it in the KCRM design initiative in order to make it readily applicable and actionable.

Table 5-4 *The Tacit-Explicit Scale for Measuring Entries in Table 5-3*

Stage	Description/ Diagnostic
0	We do not know good from bad outcomes.
1	We have no knowledge; each time we have to make a decision, it is by trial and error.
2	We have only tacit knowledge that is in the form of personal knowledge held by the following persons: _____.
3	We have tacit knowledge; we have converted it into heuristics and rules of thumb; it usually works well.
4	Some knowledge exists in explicated form, but no one really uses it.
5	We use explicitly codified knowledge but need tacit knowledge possessed by person _____ to be able to apply it well.
6	We use explicitly codified knowledge but need tacit knowledge possessed by person _____ to be able to apply it in some circumstances; but unless things are significantly different from normal, we can manage without the tacit component. Whenever we use this explicit knowledge, we revalidate it.
7	Tried and tested models now exist and we have effective mechanisms to unlearn irrelevant practices. We can simulate conditions; do what-if analysis in complex circumstances; modify behavior accordingly; it always works. Explicit knowledge is continually revalidated on every occasion of its use, and tacitness of key knowledge is low. Corporate culture is supportive of knowledge sharing, and loss of employees does not hurt our stock of knowledge.
8	Difficult to characterize.

USING THE AUDIT RESULTS TO DRIVE KCRM   . . . .

At the end of the audit process, you will have populated Table 5-3 with values and additional dimensions. These values represent ratings assigned collectively to each key aspect of customer knowledge and strategic capabilities as posed by your diagnostic questions (you might either arrive on consensus or calculate average values for each cell across multiple participants).

Analyzing Cells

Some cells will have low values such as 1, 2, or 3 assigned to them. These indicate that (1) those customer knowledge and strategic assets are highly tacit in nature as they exist at present and (2) they cannot be directly applied or shared across your entire business enterprise because of their inexplicability. It is these cells that must either be made more explicitly sharable, or suitable technology must be put into place to facilitate sharing of this tacit knowledge that is impossible to feasibly codify or explicate. Some other cells will have higher values such as 5 or 6 and indicate high levels of capability maturity and suitability for sharing. Indication of such suitability should not be taken to mean that these are in fact being shared and applied across your business.

Analyzing Quadrants

Add entries in each quadrant and divide by the number of entries to calculate the average value for each of the four quadrants. Quadrants with the lowest scores are the ones that most likely need KCRM support. Do not use these scores alone as the basis for further decisions; instead, use them only for getting a feel for the relative levels at which your company operates along the four dimensions. Since the number of diagnostics in each quadrant is not standardized and the significance of each question (as perceived by a number of stakeholders) will vary from one company to another, these *Bohn's scores* will help your audit team decide and weight each of these quadrants on a composite basis. The populated cells of the framework therefore help determine the quadrants representing four types of capabilities that need the most strengthening and those that are already healthy.

···

CUSTOMER DIFFERENTIATION AT E-MACHINES

E-machines is a leading manufacturer of entry-level Windows personal computers. After its unexpected founding in late 1998, the company shot up to one of the top PC brands in the United States within a matter of months. The secret is well known: good-quality systems assembled in Korea from brand-name parts, bundled with Windows and basic productivity software at half the price of the average American PC brand. The company fueled a price war within the industry. In the end it was folks like you and me—the consumer—who benefited. However, to keep the razor-thin $10 per machine profit margin, the company began to differentiate among customers based on their support needs. Each machine came with 15 days of technical support; those 15 days began counting down only when the customer called the company for the first time. The customer could buy an extended warranty plan for $59; this would give her unlimited technical support and an added year of warranty. By setting the base level of service, the company watched its costs by differentiating among customers who needed more support and those who preferred a good price bundle instead.

Analyzing Progression Over Time

Beginning with the base values derived from the pre-implementation audit, you can recalculate scores over different points of implementation progression. Declining values will indicate a failure to improve processes, and improving values indicate success. Specifically ask the following questions for each resource as you use this framework to track progress over time:

1. Is the stock of this asset/capability increasing?
2. Is it being shared more, if not being explicated more?
3. Is it being applied and used more?
4. How does it compare with both past and present equivalents for our key competitors?
5. Do our employees recognize the value of this specific asset?
6. Have we made it more easily imitable by extensive sharing or explication?
7. Do we still need to retain the current level of focus on this parameter?

The initial audit values therefore serve as a common point of reference against which payoffs from your own KCRM initiatives can be compared over time, and those of your competitors can be evaluated directly, and over time. The key pitfall that you must avoid through thorough initial analysis is that of missing out a key company-specific parameter on Table 5-3.

SUMMARY . . . .

You cannot know where you want your KCRM investments to take your business unless you know where your business stands now. This is where the audit and analysis step helps. Specifically:

- *The audit provides a snapshot of the present state.* A customer knowledge audit provides the basis for planning, aligning, and implementing KCRM by taking both explicit and tacit knowledge about customers and business partners, and business processes into account. The first audit can then be used as a reference point for evaluating future investments in building networked knowledge and relationship capital.

- *An audit involves three phases.* The three phases are (1) initiation, (2) reference measure and method selection, and (3) execution of the audit. These consist of seven steps: defining audit goals, assembling an audit team, identifying all relevant constraints, defining customer clusters or segments, determining the ideal state, selecting audit dimensions and method, and finally executing the method to document customer knowledge assets.

- *Customers can be classified in three broad categories.* Customers that are most valuable (MVCs—those who give most of your business at present, those you want to retain, reward, and provide the highest level of service), those who are most growable (MGCs), and those with zero or negative long-term value to your business (BZCs—ones whom a business is better off without).

- *Different customer clusters are treated differently.* MVCs, MGCs, and BZCs must be identified, differentiated, addressed, and interacted with differently to maximize their value to your business. We discussed how additional value can be divered to MVCs and additional value be extracted from BZCs.

- *The Capability Classification Framework can help document knowledge assets in a trackable format.* Functional, regulatory, positional, and cultural capabilities can be documented using this framework to facilitate future comparisons and for tracking progression over time.

In the next chapter, we examine the third step on the roadmap and see what issues are of significance in putting together a team for building a KCRM strategy and deploying supportive technology.

TEST YOUR UNDERSTANDING . . . .

1. How does audit and analysis of existing knowledge and relationship assets contribute to strategy formulation?

2. What is a reference measure and how is one selected?

3. How are constraints identified during the audit and analysis stage? What do these constraints mean?

4. What is the meaning of an ideal state? Can it be achieved?

5. What tactics can be used to *dump* below-zero customers or increase their value to your business?

6. What are the four key phases of customer relationship management and how do they relate to knowledge-enabled relationship management?

7. How are audit results documented in a consistent manner? Why is future comparability of interest to businesses?

8. What are the four quadrants of the capability framework and what do they mean?

9. Audits generally provide a snapshot of the current state of a business. What is the problem with such snapshots?

10. What determines the choice of an audit method?

6

Building an Implementation Team

In this chapter...

- Understand the implementation team design.

- Balance conflicting requirements for project design.

- Understand the tasks and expertise involved in implementing KCRM.

- Understand the differences between pre- and postchasm team members.

- Avoid common team formation pitfalls.

The third step in implementing a knowledge-enabled customer relationship management initiative involves building an implementation team. Customer knowledge management initiatives operate in the customer dimension, while most businesses operate in the product or service dimension. A KCRM initiative must necessarily cross a large number of functional, departmental, divisional, and even organizational boundaries. A knowledge-enabled CRM system is built on expertise, knowledge, understanding, skills, experience, and insights aggregated across a variety of stakeholders who represent a multitude of functional specializations. IT staff and end users who collectively form deployment teams in traditional IT implementation projects fall short of capturing the complexity and cross-functional nature of work involved in implementing KCRM. Successful implementation critically hinges on the quality of collaborative relationships that characterize such multifunctional teams, and the extent to which this is achieved determines CRM success. The inherent complexity embodied by such relationships necessitates selecting just the right blend of team members to lead the project.

In this chapter, we will begin by understanding the core structure of the team that implements both the KCRM strategy and the technology. By examining key tasks, we will be able to better comprehend the balancing-act nature of implementation. We will also see how external consultants can be carefully chosen to supplement in-house skills. We will examine the concept of laterality, and see how a well-structured team can deliver that. Finally, using a risk assessment framework, we will analyze how problems can be predicted before they occur. An effective team will facilitate execution of the project in a manner that is both efficient and effective.

TASKS AND EXPERTISE . . . .

A knowledge-enabled CRM project requires expertise from several domains, all brought together in the context of *your* business.

Figure 6-1 highlights six key task areas within which expertise is needed at the lowest common denominator of analysis.

1. Leadership for the project at management and operational levels
2. Technology design and development
3. Training and educating both end-users of the system and senior management
4. Implementing cultural enhancements, rewards tied to performance, and incentives for employees, partners, and customers to use KCRM-supporting systems

....

How Allianz France Strengthened Its Alliances

Allianz has over 5,000 offices in France. The company receives hundreds of calls each day. Customer focused, as it was, a series of mergers and alliances such as those with German Allianz Group AG, Assurances Générales des France (AGF), and Credit Lyonnais complicated matters. In France, customers can buy insurance from traditional brokers and agents, as well as through third-party branded contracts from banks such as Assurances Fédérales. Fortunately, one of the largest French banks used Allianz as the generic insurer whose contracts the bank sold. As the business grew, disparate pieces of information prevented claims agents from operating in a cost-efficient way, or expeditiously meeting customer needs. Until 1996, a mainframe-based claims department in Paris managed customer calls.

To address these challenges, Allianz moved away from its mainframe operations, opened up a TeleClaims office for Assurances Fédérales customers in Strasbourg, and built an integrated, enterprise-wide, customer interaction platform to help increase sales, improve customer loyalty, and reduce costs. A unified view of each customer is now possible through the seamless integration of customer-facing functions that ensure that everyone has rapid access to accurate information no matter what the activity they pursue on behalf of the client.

5. Sales and marketing processes, procedures, and mechanisms

6. Measurement of performance, results, and returns on investments

KCRM teams, especially in an e-business context, involve people from inside and outside your own business. External and internal coordination is needed to bring these stakeholders together in a synergistic fashion. Since participants who bring such expertise might be internal or external to your business, effective project management calls for good coordination among all stakeholders involved.

Tech Talk

Stakeholders: Groups of people or businesses that have some stake in the outcome of a project. In a typical KCRM project, stakeholders might include the customer service department, business development department, the shipping business partner, and the corporate strategist.

Figure 6-1
Key tasks and processes involving KCRM team members.

Your business can potentially draw upon the following sources of requisite expertise:

- Internal information technology department
- Internal departmental experts and specialists
- External strategic partners and supply chain allies
- Technology vendors and deployment contractors who supply various technological pieces
- Front-office marketing, sales, and customer relations staff
- Consultants

Remember that your KCRM project is not merely a technology implementation project. It is therefore essential to involve technology enthusiasts within various functional areas such as marketing and sales during the technology design stages as well. Various participants in the KCRM team must simultaneously balance several counteracting requirements of the project, as illustrated in Figure 6-2. Balancing these conflicting needs necessitates a delicate balance, the loss of which can throw the entire project off course.

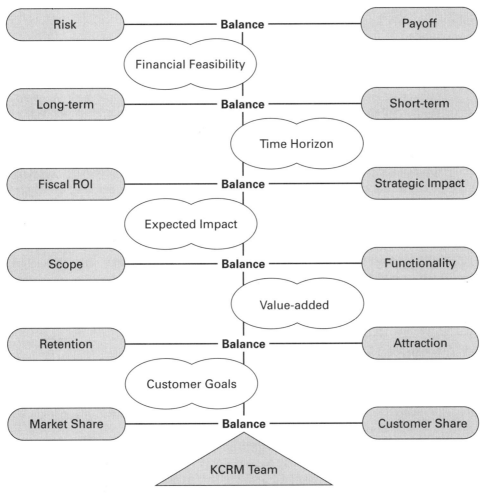

Figure 6-2
Contradicting needs of a KCRM system that must be balanced.

1. Risk versus payoff

2. Long-term versus short-term impact of CRM

3. Financial returns on investment versus strategic, nonfinancial returns

4. Scope versus functionality of the system

5. Potential for retaining existing customers versus acquiring new ones

6. Focal balance between increased share of the customer versus market share

If done right, a well-balanced deployment team will become the key strength of your customer relationship management strategy, and a potential contributor to success.

Tech Talk

> **Chasm: A figurative separation between adopters and skeptics of a new technology or paradigm. People who adopt that new technology or paradigm are said to have crossed the chasm. For example, when the Internet became available to the public, people who actively created it come first on the curve and were called innovators; people who adopted it immediately ("crossed the chasm") can be described as early adopters or visionaries, those who followed; masses that soon followed are described as the early majority; people who might eventually adopt it are the late majority; those who have sworn to never adopt it until they are forced to, are the laggards or skeptics. So, with any given innovation, people can be classified into these four groups depending on when they "cross the chasm."**

As Figure 6-3 illustrates, there will be knowledge-enabled CRM proponents and visionaries on one extreme and skeptics on the other, and early and late majority adopters in the middle. Though every effort should be made to maximize inclusion of prechasm participants, a healthy dose of skepticism from postchasm participants or observers within your company will keep the project grounded in reality.

TEAM COMPOSITION . . . .

Due to the enterprise-spanning nature of knowledge-enabled CRM, functional diversity in the deployment team is almost a given. The team's design has much to do with the nature and scope of the project. A well-structured team will result in the possibility of creative innovation, and renewed customer retention and revenue maximization focus, while a poorly structured one will lead only to conflict, tension, and loss of tangibly beneficial business outcomes. For the former to happen, highly lateral teams that accommodate members' different backgrounds, values, skills, perspectives, and assumptions, as summarized in Table 6-1, are needed.

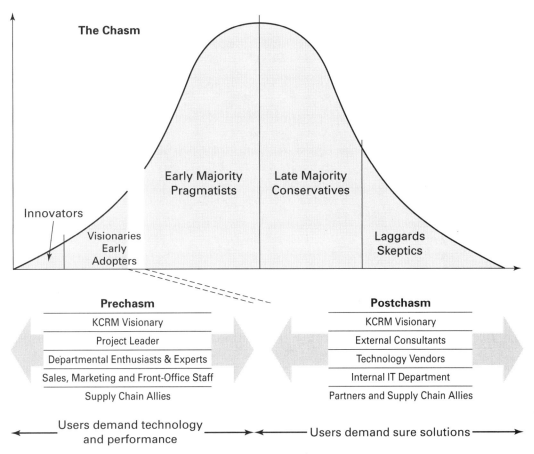

The Chasm

Early Majority
Pragmatists

Late Majority
Conservatives

Innovators

Visionaries
Early
Adopters

Laggards
Skeptics

Prechasm	**Postchasm**
KCRM Visionary	KCRM Visionary
Project Leader	External Consultants
Departmental Enthusiasts & Experts	Technology Vendors
Sales, Marketing and Front-Office Staff	Internal IT Department
Supply Chain Allies	Partners and Supply Chain Allies

◄——— Users demand technology ———► ◄——— Users demand sure solutions ———►
and performance

Figure 6-3
Pre- and post-chasm groups surrounding technology-enabled KCRM.

Tech Talk

Laterality: The ability of team members to accommodate other members' different backgrounds, values, skills, perspectives, and assumptions to effectively collaborate across functional and organizational boundaries.

Functional specialists are the early adopters of technologies that emerge from within various departments within your business. These people often tend to have specializations other than IT, and have a well-articulated vision and opinion of how they think technology can be used to improve the operation of their own specialization. For CRM systems, look for such functional specialists and enthusiasts in your marketing, sales, customer relations, and middle management rungs. Even though these people

Table 6-1 The Two Basic Elements of Lateral Team Design

Team Design Element	Characteristics of the Knowledge Management Team Members Selected
Defining the knowledge management project leader's role	The leader of the team must be credible, stable, have sufficient authority and access to resources, be callable of facilitating conflict resolutions among participating divisions, lead project management operations, facilitate collaborative teamwork, schedule and coordinate, be actively involved in team formulation, have experience in a multitude of management roles within your company, and must be selected from upper of upper middle management.
Defining the team composition and selection criteria for team members	Members must be drawn from the various functional areas within your business and possess specialized expertise, sufficient experience with your business, and required competencies that truly represent respective functional areas. These members may either be dedicated to work full time on the KCRM initiative or participate on a part-time basis. Most importantly, they must have a clear opinion or vision of potential outcomes of knowledge enablement that they are participating in. They must exhibit laterality and strong teamwork.

often tend to be nontechnologists, they are the best people to gauge potential usefulness of each bit of functionality that your CRM system might provide. And, on the other hand, these also are among the first to realize limitations of technology that might have been proposed and its possible misfits with the emerging needs of their colleagues and functional domain users. Including such participants on the team will give every decision healthy reality checks along the way, and reduce potential frontline user buy-in resistance in the future.

Internal Information Technology Staff

Internal IT participants bring in knowledge of interdependencies between complex systems such as Websites, supply chain management and electronic commerce platform management, and the networks that they operate and integrate through. This expertise supplements technological vision and possible application ideas that emerge from functional specialists and KCRM/KM/CRM proponents. Specifically, IT staff members bring in knowledge of:

- Electronic commerce and enabling infrastructure
- Customer contact channel integration methods

- Viability of solutions proposed by specialized domain experts
- Limitations of existing infrastructure
- Connectivity and compatibility issues involved in proving enterprise-wide support for customer-centric knowledge management
- Issues related to standardization across different software platforms and mobile devices for in-field use
- Standardization across multiple applications and tools
- Integration of new technology with both active and pure legacy systems

Make sure that IT participants whom you select have credibility among customer relations and marketing participants. If internal IT cannot work cohesively with the aforementioned groups, they might lean toward considering outsourcing an external developer. Technical skills and the ability to work in team environments are the two key factors that should influence their selection.

Laterality Providers

Laterality refers to the ability to cut across functional boundaries and relate to people from different areas. People who exhibit this characteristic are best suited to be on a KCRM team. They have often worked in many roles, in many divisions of your company, so they know what it is like to be in other participants' shoes because they have "been there." Such participant team members bring five strengths to the team as described in Table 6-2.

Table 6-2 Lateral Members Bind KCRM Deployment Teams Together

Dimension	Laterality is promoted by their ability to...
Bridge and interpret	Act as a bridge and as interpreters between people from different backgrounds, skill areas, and specializations
Promote despecialization	Learn faster than the average person in your company
	Not be defensive about their lack of understanding or knowledge in areas other than their own area
Create synergy	Bring value to the overall team synergies, as they tend not to be egoistically constrained
Promote team learning	Learn to understand the collaborators' frames of reference
Encourage collaboration	Have the ability to deal creatively and rationally with the problems stemming from the above differences

External Consultants

Shortcomings in in-house functional, technical, and managerial skills can often be overcome using external consultants. A word of warning is in order: External consultants might lack the common frame of reference, your organization's culture, and values that bind internal participants together. However, by potentially bringing in a balanced—possibly biased—outsider perspective into the process, this liability of external consultants can be turned into an asset. However, four issues must be considered before deciding on an outside consultant or consulting firm:

1. Level of trust and confidence that your internal team members can place in the consulting partner
2. Consulting firm's reputation for integrity and confidentiality, especially when backed by nondisclosure agreements (which are highly recommended)
3. Track record of the firm
4. Contractual agreements with your business' competitors and possible conflicts of interest

Senior Management and Buy-In

No matter how team oriented and collaborative your company is, politics and interdepartmental rivalry can keep your KCRM project from making progress. Power, politics, and functional rivalry are so critical to project success that information systems research has a whole stream dedicated to researching these aspects. Buy-in and support from a senior management executive or CEO are essential to secure *before* you begin. Senior or middle managers must constitute at the very least a minority of your team, and must be kept in the loop throughout the implementation process. This ensures strong commitment to implementing the project and provides a venue for resolving disputes, conflict, and making budget allocations among other equally deserving projects. Recent research has shown that senior management support is one of the foremost contributors to knowledge management and CRM success.

Team Lifecycle

Although the need for specialized expertise will vary along the stage of KCRM deployment, a small part of the team—the *core team*—must be retained on a permanent basis. Unlike typical enterprise resource planning (ERP) and business process reengineering (BPR) technology implementations, knowledge-enabled CRM does not have a definite stopping point. It cannot have a stopping point if it must maintain its effectiveness over time. The team's size should be kept to the minimum possible needed to actually do the implementation. The core team should consist of only the following participants, and the rest temporarily brought in along various stages of development on an as-needed basis:

1. Knowledge and customer-relations visionary or champion, often a senior manager who also serves as the project leader
2. Corporate strategist, often a senior manager or market development middle manager
3. Marketing, sales, and customer service manager; could be also the project visionary
4. User delegate from finance or human resources to build and deploy metrics
5. Information technology staff members to design and develop IT infrastructure for CRM and knowledge management

Figure 6-4 illustrates the structure of the typical KCRM team. The project leader in the middle coordinates various participants, and leads the project. She also forms the link in the chain between various functional departments and senior management. Project sponsors and senior management must actively support the project. Various activities and business processes that the team is jointly responsible for are shown in the shared space under the hub and spoke.

Stakeholders on the team should typify and accurately represent the interests of the group that they represent, and should be familiar with your existing business model, practices, and work culture. Project-related roles and desirable characteristics of these stakeholders are detailed in Table 6-3.

LEADERSHIP . . . .

The KCRM project leader's role is not to direct or control, but to facilitate a supportive, unobtrusive, and focused environment within which team members can concentrate on their tasks with minimal distraction and requisite collaboration. In addition, traditional project-related tasks such as progress tracking, scheduling, workload distribution, effort-goal alignment, and budgeting also fall on the shoulders of the project leader. The project leader may be the customer relationship visionary (CRV)—a continued leadership role that melds the responsibilities of the so-called *one-to-one manager* and the *chief knowledge officer*. That role is discussed in detail in Chapter 9. Table 6-4 describes four key activities that the project leader must effectively manage.

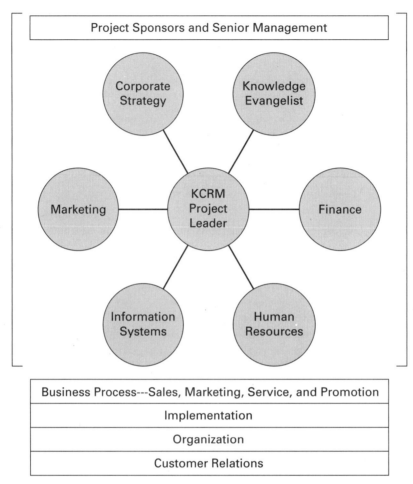

Figure 6-4
Structure of the KCRM team and key responsibilities.

The KCRM team must begin by collectively understanding the project's strategic intent, your business' immediate and long-term customer valuation, and a well agreed upon comprehension of financial, technological, and organizational constraints that apply to their projected work.

Figure 6-5 provides the initial set of questions that the team must begin by addressing. Each step in the flowchart identifies questions that must be addressed while assembling the KCRM team. One of the first tasks that the management team needs to undertake is that of understanding the project's strategic intent, organizational context, technological constraints, monetary limitations, and short-term as well as

Table 6-3 *Structuring the Knowledge Management Team*

Stakeholder Group	Project Role	Desirable Characteristics
Teams User teams Finance Marketing Customer relations	Provide functional expertise Provide business expertise in their specific area Participate in the process design stage Help in the implementation stages of the system	Able to understand work processes in their area Good interpersonal and team skills Possess a certain degree of credibility within other participating groups. Willing to see from other functional viewpoints
Technology Internal IT staff External consultants Functional technologists.	Provide technology expertise Participate in the actual implementation and design Represent the internal and internally proficient technologists Write the code Bring in a perspective on functional capabilities and limitations of existing systems	Able to understand technology in depth Good interpersonal skills Strong team skills Willing to consider the perspectives brought in by other team members and actually incorporate them into the design Willing to learn. Credibility Possess a customer orientation.
Leadership and Vision Senior management/ CRV/ project sponsor	Support the legitimacy of the project Bring in vision that correlates with the overall company wide vision Serve on steering committees (if needed) Commit the resources needed.	Understand the management and strategic processes Possess credibility and a strong leadership position that almost everyone on the team accepts. Possess a clear idea of the bigger picture. Must "eat their own dog food," that is, believe what they say.

Table 6-4 Leadership Responsibilities and Activities

Responsibilities	Activities
Managing internal dynamics	Help members objectively resolve differences, using structured decision-making techniques
	Encourage creative conflict in moderation
	Contain excessive departmental conflict
	Balance stakeholder needs and concerns
	Clarify differences and their underlying assumptions; facilitate resolution
Translating needs Delegating tasks	Act as a translator in the startup stages of the project when the user teams and the IT participants fail to understand each other's viewpoints because of vocabulary differences
	Help build shared understanding.
	Facilitate effective and well-moderated brainstorming
	Keep strategic goals and functional needs aligned
	Brief senior management on progress and project milestones
	Facilitate cross-functional interaction through employee meetings, surveys, interviews, and focus groups
	Protect project direction from ill-representative stakeholders
Ensuring user participation	Ensure participation of frontline sales and marketing staff
	Ensure that technology blueprints meet their actual needs for CRM
	Design and implement incentives for such participation
	Obtain feedback from frontline staff throughout the KCRM strategy and technology development process
	Field test prototypes versions of tools and obtain feedback on features, interface, functionality, and design
Arriving at customer classifications	Facilitate classification of customers into most valuable, most growable, and below zero on co-evolved bases that team members representing various divisions of your business unanimously agree upon

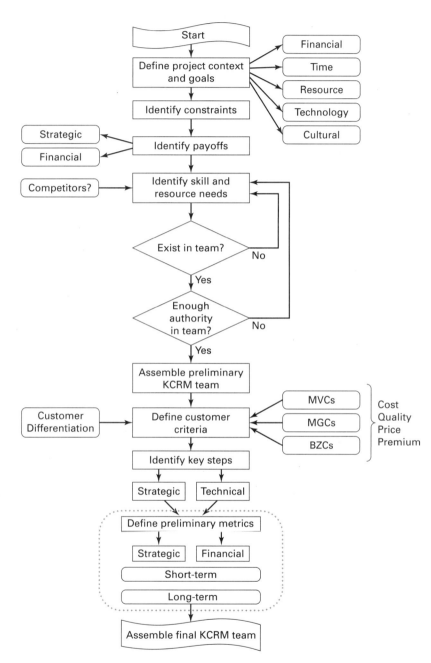

Figure 6-5
Assessing the KCRM team's task-structure fit.

long-term goals. When your team begins to consider customer differentiation, its cost and customer perceptivity as well as its impact on perceived price premium should be considered. Members of your team should be able to provide adequate answers to these questions collectively. A well-designed team should be able to identify customer knowledge management processes and relationship-enhancing activities across the entire value chain—that includes business partners, suppliers, and e-business service providers.

RISK ASSESSMENT AND COMMON PITFALLS . . . . .

A study of a group of 2,600 CEOs, CIOs, and technology managers by the *Cambridge Information Network* in 1999 revealed that approximately 90 percent of IT projects exceeded their budgets—20 percent by more than 100 percent. Since knowledge management, CRM, and knowledge-enabled CRM are technology-intensive projects, several key lessons can be learned from IT project failures and applied to minimize KCRM project risk. Figure 6-6 illustrates four key risk types involved in such projects, a derivative of Mark Keil et al.'s seminal Framework for Identifying Software Project Risks (*Communications of the ACM*, 1998).

Key concepts and accompanying project risks underlying this framework are described as follows:

- Project risks can be classified according to both the level of control (high or low) that a project manager has over it, and according to its relative importance to the team (moderate through high).

- Lack of an active role of the top management has been identified as the primary reason why many projects fail; and the second reason is the failure of users to see the need for, or be convinced about, the value of the project.

- The risks that must be taken most seriously are those that you have little or no control over, and those that are also significant at the same time. Customer mandate—representing the level of buy-in of various "customers" of the project—is one such risk. You can mitigate customer buy-in problems by (1) selling the project harder, (2) including representatives from the actual user community and partner firms, and (3) gauging frontline user needs accurately. This further necessitates both senior management and sales/marketing staff commitment—one without the other will rarely suffice.

- Certain risks such as changes in business environment are both beyond control and relatively less damaging to the project (or as damaging to competitors' projects). These are represented by the lower-left quadrant in

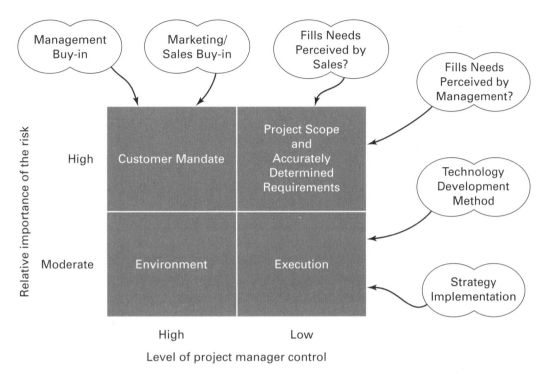

Figure 6-6
Identifying, assessing, and prioritizing project risks.

Figure 6-6, and must take a secondary place *in comparison* to other risk factors.

- Senior management involvement not only mitigates risks in the upper left quadrant; it also ensures that (1) senior management's "bigger picture" vision is accounted for in the project and (2) a steady stream of developmental funding is received. Knowledge-enabled customer relationship management projects can get politically charged because of the multitudes of functional areas and businesses or business units involved; senior management involvement can help defuse such political controversy.

- While all these risks must be thought of together rather than independently, the focus must be on the risks over which you have little control. Formally presenting an initial set of objectives and methods identified by the KCRM team can help compare the project's objective with stakeholder expectations and perceptions, and resolve emergent differences before they turn into problems.

The risk assessment framework can be used to identify, map, prioritize, and better manage risks involved in the KCRM project.

SUMMARY . . . .

- *KCRM initiatives are necessarily collaborative.* Implementation teams must be representative of the actual needs for strengthening customer relationships through customer knowledge management. They must include mid- and high-level managerial participants, and external business partners who represent a variety of functional specialties.

- *Teams must be boundary spanning.* Implementation teams extend beyond your own business' boundaries; internal and external coordination must be facilitated by high team-level laterality. Pre- and postchasm membership ensures that there is a healthy dose of optimism and a healthy dose of skepticism and realism in team-level decisions.

- *Balancing conflicting requirements is an art.* Various requirements of designing a KCRM strategy and system will contradict others. Managerial and technological skills must be well balanced. Senior management involvement helps diffuse political tensions and conflict among team members.

- *Leadership must be unanimously accepted by all participants.* Many team members may not be from your own organization. Rather than spinning wheels over who is in control, the team leader must act as a facilitator for collaboration, not as an issuer of directives. Managing internal dynamics, translation of needs, task delegation, user and customer involvement, and co-assignment of customer classifications are some of the responsibilities that fall on the leader's shoulders.

- *Risks must be prioritized jointly.* Use the *Risk Assessment framework* to determine threats and risks that are within the team's control and those that are not. Once the controllable risks are being well managed, address the less-controllable ones by "selling" the project to front-line staff and being attuned to external business changes.

TEST YOUR UNDERSTANDING . . . .

1. What are the key tasks involved in implementing a customer knowledge management strategy and expertise needed for putting the technology in place and making it deliver results?

2. What is a chasm and what does it have to do with KCRM implementation?

3. What does *laterality* mean? Who needs it, why, and how can it be acquired?

4. What issues should your consider before hiring an external consultant to work on your internal knowledge management, KCRM, or e-Business project?

5. Who are the key stakeholders in an implementation team?

6. Why do you think leadership even matters? What should be the role of the leader: giving marching orders or facilitating collaboration?

7. How is the Keilean *Risk Assessment framework* helpful in implementing knowledge-enabled customer relationship management? What insights should it lead to?

8. If team members are brought from your own business and from other businesses, who should lead the team?

9. What is the role of senior management in the project team? Why bother them?

10. Some team members might think that an interactive chat window must be built into your Website, others might want Personal Digital Assistants (PDAs) for themselves, and the geek on the team might ask for a new database schema. Unfortunately, there is often a limit of how much money can be spent. How are conflicting requirements balanced by the team?

7 Blueprinting the Technology Infrastructure

In this chapter...

- Understand the design challenges in creating a KCRM technology blueprint.

- Compare the requirements against customer relationship management objectives.

- Understand various pieces of the customer knowledge management technology framework.

- Identify the collaborative platform for use in a Web-based environment.

- See examples of customer knowledge systems used in B2C and B2B e-businesses.

- Analyze the relative fit of 10-key business intelligence methods in e-business settings.

- Understand various pieces of the KCRM technology architecture.

- Examine various long-term design considerations, including the build-or-buy choice.

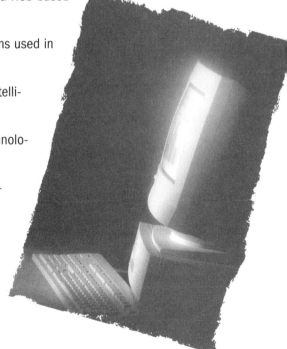

Knowledge-enabled customer relationship management (KCRM) both drives and is driven by technology. The ideal KCRM technology infrastructure guarantees real-time, seamless integration of e-business processes and activities including online selling, marketing, knowledge management, and customer service, irrespective of which *channel*—voice, Web, e-mail, wireless, or proprietary—a transaction originates. Channel strategy must be integrated both across channels and across functional units of your business. Real-time operational information flow and communication across the entire enterprise are an operational necessity for e-businesses. KCRM therefore spans all portions of the value chain including marketing, sales, product development, distribution, customer service, support, finance, and e-business technology development. When such real-time information value chains exist in the business, foolishness is the best word to describe the act of not interpreting and acting on them.

The strategic intent of blueprinting the technology infrastructure needed for facilitating KCRM is to recognize (1) how existing infrastructure can be leveraged to provide an infrastructural foundation without being tied down by its limitations in the context of supporting e-business, and (2) additional functionality that must be added to support your business' relationship building goals.

In this chapter, we examine the fourth step on the KCRM roadmap and see how technology is blueprinted. We examine the objectives of creating a technology blueprint; analyze the requirements of such as system; understand why informal communications are so germane to customer knowledge; understand various business intelligence tools and platform choices that are relevant to KCRM; compare search and retrieval methods; and see the factors that help decide whether it is worth building it from scratch or buying an off-the-shelf system. Finally, we take an up close look at design factors that help future proof the system to save it from the tragedy akin to that of three-year plans with two-month lives.

DESIGN CHALLENGES . . . .

The strategic intent of a knowledge-enabled customer relationship management system is not one of throughput and efficiency, but that of enhancing the customer experience that leads to increased customer retention and loyalty. Competition is increasingly shaped by pre- and postsales support, and by relationships in addition to the traditional formatives such as price, quality, and speed. This necessitates an integrated interaction strategy that enhances overall customer experience; seeing KCRM purely as an initiative to cut costs can have catastrophic effects. Six key challenges described below must be addressed in the KCRM technology-blueprinting phase, especially in e-business settings:

1. *Interaction consistency*: e-businesses are often geographically dispersed. Many electronic commerce retailers such as Staples, Office Depot, and Walmart also have brick-and-mortar stores. Imperfect integration of systems across such business—whether born on the Web or initially brick and mortar—often results in inconsistent customer interaction. Many companies give the customary lip service to customer relationship management and apply the results of their knowledge management efforts separately at different customer touchpoints rather than in an integrated fashion. This leads to inaccuracy, a sense of lack of urgency, and inconsistency in dealing with current and prospective customers. Systems must be integrated to deliver consistent interaction facilitated by a total view of each customer.

2. *Customer expectations:* If you are an e-business or transforming into one, your customers might not be certain what to expect when you offer them Web-based services. Mismanaged expectations can disappoint your customers enough to make them turn elsewhere with just one click. Just the right balance between operational cost-efficiency and the provision of customer service must be struck. KCRM technology plans must also account for the hard-to-predict future usage of interaction channels, not just the known current usage levels.

3. *Balance*: Although self-service has long served businesses as a cost-cutting mechanism (predating even McDonald's), Web-based interaction must balance self-service and (human) agent-assisted service. More importantly, the e-business system must be smart enough to recognize when a potential customer needs more help than the system can offer, and transfer her over to a live human agent.

4. *Customer driven:* Knowledge-enabled customer relationship management must align your business to deliver what the *customer* perceives to be of high value, not what your business thinks the customer perceives. Such customer-driven (not merely customer-focused) value maximization is possible only through intimate knowledge of the customer—a challenge that well-designed knowledge management technology addresses.

5. *Adaptability*: As business changes occur, your business' information systems—the KCRM system, the e-business architecture, and the e-transaction processing system (e-TPS) — must not inhibit rapid adaptation (a phenomenon called *systems drag*). Instead, they must facilitate adaptation. A good KCRM system must be growable—flexibility and scalability are therefore essential ingredients. This necessitates blueprinting e-business supporting systems in a modular, adaptable,

plug-and-play-like fashion as described in detail in Chapter 8, but initiated right at the blueprinting stage.

6. *A single face*: The lack of integration at an enterprise level shows up in customer interactions in the form of inconsistent information, lack of coordination, and the presentation of multiple faces of the same business. Office supply stores that went on the Web are exemplars of such lack of integration—the brick-and-mortar store, the toll-free catalog store, and the Web store of the same business can rarely answer customer queries for transactions initiated at channels other than their own. The idea is to integrate enterprise information systems, silo CRM systems, e-commerce front ends, e-business back ends, eTPS, business systems, business intelligence initiatives, workflow tools, and enterprise application integration (EAI) approaches with the unifying thread of knowledge-enabled customer relationship management. Data flowing through e-business systems can further be captured and integrated with decision support systems for analysis. Applying the principles of knowledge management to e-business systems necessitates inclusion of internal business users, trading partners, suppliers, and customers in the development of e-business KCRM applications and services with one goal: *competitively* delighting the customer. Presenting a single face to an individual customer or a client business requires information integration in real time. More importantly, knowledge must be available across multiple customer touchpoints. This is a challenge that the ideal KCRM system must address.

Tech Talk

Systems Drag: Occurs when a business' information systems cannot be changed at the same pace as the business itself is willing to change in response to new market and customer needs. This occurs primarily because of inflexible systems that have not been well thought out from the start.

These challenges apply whether you sell tangible physical goods such as books, CDs, clothing, or groceries, or you sell intangible goods such as services, information, music, digital products directly through or facilitated by the Web. Although they are discussed here in the context of business-to-consumer (B2C) electronic commerce, they also apply to varying degrees in the business-to-business (B2B) context.

THE CUSTOMER LIFECYCLE . . . .

The objective of any business is to acquire, retain, enhance, and maximize its relationships with customers. The key processes underlying customer relationship management are described in Figure 7-1.

As these processes occur in a business, they are facilitated by tools and technologies that help align the business' products and services with its customers' existing and emergent needs. Although traditional CRM adopts a simplistic view of this process by integrating sales, service, and marketing. However, in a customer-driven business, other areas and functions are also influenced by basic CRM activities. Knowledge gained from customer, supplier, and partner interactions can drive business strategy and consequently, profitability. KCRM is not constrained to individual customers—it encompasses suppliers, partners, and even competitors.

Technology's role in building KCRM systems is that of broadening reach, enhancing the speed of knowledge transfer and real-time knowledge sharing, enabling informed decision making, and facilitating collaborative success. (Customer relationship software alone is expected to be a $5.6 billion industry by 2002 according to Aberdeen Group estimates.) Such systems must facilitate mapping of the *sources* of know-how, not just know-how *per se*. This necessitates the introduction of

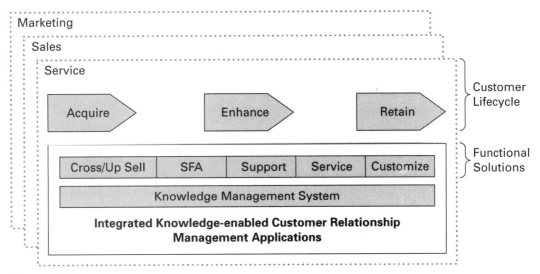

Figure 7-1
Technologies supporting the customer lifecycle.

integrated knowledge-enabled customer relationship management applications as described in Figure 7-1. At the very least, a KCRM system must support three functionalities: customization, personalization, and predictive anticipation, as explained in Table 7-1.

Table 7-1 The Barebones Capabilities of a KCRM System

Functionality	Description
Customization	If I explicitly or behaviorally tell the system my preferences, it changes accordingly.
Personalization	The system is gleaning information from my usage pattern and it changes its behavior accordingly.
Predictive anticipation	The system monitors every contact that I make with the business, learns my behavioral patterns and preferences, and then anticipates my future needs, sometimes even before I can.

The Levers of KCRM Technology

The good news about knowledge-enabled customer relationship management technology is that most components used to build the necessary infrastructure have been around for years, and your business probably already has several of these in place. The key to successful KCRM technology implementation lies in leveraging the *existing* infrastructure, primarily operational data warehouses and communications capabilities already in place. In a highly distributed and diverse technological environment, interoperability between systems that would not normally "talk" is imperative. Thanks to the Internet, the glue to bind these islands of systems now exists. Implementing KCRM technology then becomes a matter of integrating these systems in a certain way and adding the missing components. Therefore, customer knowledge management systems can—and must—build on existing technological investments to mitigate risks, sustain management support, and integrate with the extant infrastructure.

While there is no perfect formula for building a KCRM system, prescribing one will only be fraught with the risk of not taking contextual differences between similar businesses into account. Because such systems must be built on "Internet time," incremental pragmatism—not perfection—is key. KCRM technology implementation is described at a blueprint level rather than a hands-on level to stay clear of prescribing formulas and to keep in line with the explanatory focus of this book. Readers interested in the technical details of developing such systems should examine my *Knowledge Management Toolkit: Practical Techniques for Building a Knowledge Management System* (Prentice Hall 2000).

For God, Country, and ERP

Although enterprise resource planning (ERP) overpromised and underdelivered, it has had a positive side effect on many businesses that fell for it: better data and operational integration at all levels of the organization, and beyond traditional business boundaries to include suppliers and customers. That is good news for a potential KCRM implementer because the grunt work has probably already been done!

> **Tech Talk**
>
> **Enterprise Resource Planning: Modular, enterprise-spanning system that was supposed to be perfectly integrated and customized to a business' needs. Major ERP software makers such as Baan, Peoplesoft, and SAP abandoned ship when ERP's failures became obvious. ERP systems typically cost several million dollars and took anywhere from two to five years to install.**

CUSTOMER KNOWLEDGE MANAGEMENT: TECHNOLOGY FRAMEWORK . . . .

In this section, we examine the knowledge-enabled customer relationship management technology framework that is used to make judgments about what existing infrastructural components in your business can be taken as is, and what else needs to be added. By being able to look before you take the leap, you can better evaluate your business' needs and identify existing infrastructure that can (or cannot) meet those needs.

The basic customer knowledge management technology framework is illustrated in Figure 7-2. We will examine how this framework forms the basis for the KCRM architecture in a later section in this chapter. The concepts indicated on the arrows are the business processes (or activities) that the system must support, and the circles represent the technology components that facilitate these activities.

Various components of the framework support one or more of the five key objectives of creating, packaging and assembling, retrieving, validating, and applying knowledge, as described in Table 7-2.

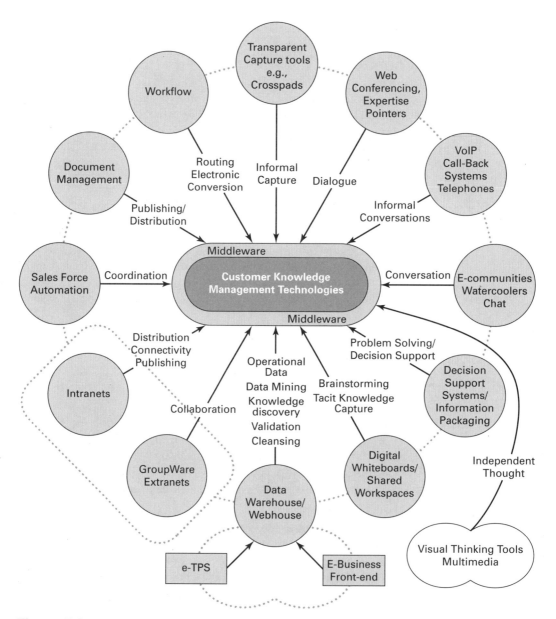

Figure 7-2
The customer knowledge management technology framework.

Table 7-2 Five Key Knowledge Objectives and Associated Enabling Technology

Knowledge Objective	Customer-focused Technology Enablers
Retrieve/find	Knowledge-bases, intelligent agents, meta-search engines, data mining tools
Create	Distributed decision support systems (DSS), clickstreams, discussion repositories, multimedia
Package/assemble	Information refineries, Web publishing, push delivery, WAP, pattern matching
Communicate/apply	Networked, multichannel, structured-unstructured customer KMS
Reuse/revalidate	Support knowledge bases, discussion databases, rating mechanisms, and nonintrusive history capture devices

Let us examine each of the technology components in this framework and understand how they fit into the big picture.

The Collaborative Platform

The collaborative platform is the core foundation of the KCRM system. Along with the communications network services and hardware, it provides a pipeline to enable the flow of explicated knowledge, its context, and a medium for conversations. The collaborative platform provides a channel for converting your business' intellectual capital and customer knowledge into what Don Tapscott calls *digital capital*. By incorporating informal communications channels, pointers to expertise (e.g., skills databases, expert locators) in addition to traditional information resources, they facilitate distributed work and collaboration within and across individual businesses. Informal content becomes especially important to support with the collaborative platform when loose social bonding exists between potential users of the system. Rich communications support in the form of video conferencing, voice, multimedia, and conversations must therefore be a feature of effective KCRM platforms, and not an afterthought.

Tech Talk

Collaborative Platform: Technology infrastructure—the network, software, and hardware—that allows knowledge workers to perform tasks and work on projects together. Such platforms can often allow workers sitting several thousand miles apart to collaborate, often through the Internet.

Out-of-the-box collaborative platforms such as Lotus Notes are often quicker to implement, replicate, secure, and deploy, but there are tradeoffs that shift the balance toward more open, nonproprietary systems. Because e-business is facilitated by the Internet—an open standard—and both intranets and extranets use the same set of protocols as the e-business platform, the Web is certainly the collaborative platform of choice. In addition, portability, scalability, consistency, flexibility and adaptability, security, efficiency, channel-spanning integration, maturity, training costs, and deployment time must be taken into consideration. These features define the ideal collaborative platform as described in Table 7-3. Although there are tradeoffs involved, it is highly recommended that the Web be used as the collaborative platform.

Platform independence, tool independence, performance, and scalability merit further elicitation.

- *Platform and Tool Independence*: Data that flows through a firm's information systems and e-business systems often exists in a multitude of platform-specific formats. The collaborative platform must be capable of manipulating highly distributed data regardless of its platform—Windows, Linux, MacOS, PalmOS, WAP-specific, or Unix. The Web provides the ideal channel through its hypertext markup language (HTML), extended markup language (XML), and hypertext transfer protocols (HTTP).

- *Performance and Scalability*: Scalability defines how well the system can handle increasing numbers of users and transaction loads. A system that works well with 50 users but grinds to a halt when 400 users adopt it is poor on scalability. Scalability problems might not show up right from the start, but when they do, they are usually the hardest and most expensive of problems to fix. In addition to selecting software and hardware components that have proven scalability, three other factors must be kept in mind: (1) plan for additional system response delays as usage grows, (2) plan for delays in automated real-time updates to back-end repositories and databases as usage grows, and (3) plan for response delays when a system is accessed through multiple channels (e.g., a Web-based order tracking system accessed through a wireless application cellular phone).

GroupWare Systems

The process of creating, sharing, and applying knowledge inherently involves collaboration—a key determinant of innovation and responsiveness. Complaint resolution, problem solving, brainstorming, idea generation, and strategy planning meetings are usually highly interactive, involving multiple people, often from different locations, functional areas, operational divisions, and even different companies. The basic technological element to support such collaboration is GroupWare (a trademarked term

Table 7-3: Features of the Ideal Collaborative Platform

Requirement	Description
Portability	It must allow different computing platforms such as Macs, Windows PCs, Unix workstations, WAP devices, and PalmOS systems to seamlessly interoperate. The HTTP protocol and Java used with the Web browser as the primary client are usually strong candidates.
Consistent and easy-to-use client interface	Using Web browsers as the front end facilitates building a simple, easy-to-use interface with a consistent look and feel.
Scalability	The number of users may increase exponentially without any significant degradation in the platform's performance. This is a function of both hardware and software platform choices.
Integration	The platform must be able to integrate with existing applications and legacy systems and data. Legacy systems are integrated especially well using Web protocol-based software translators called wrappers.
Customizability	The platform must be capable of being customized by the end user and must be sufficiently flexible for accommodating yet-unknown integration needs. Proprietary solutions usually provide higher degrees of customizability but at the cost of portability, scalability, and cost.
Security	Sufficiently high levels of security must be implemented. Using the Web as a base platform does not usually allow for out-of-the-box security solutions, but very high levels of security are possible in most Web browsers.
Structural flexibility	Both structured data (such as database records) and highly unstructured data (such as video clippings) must be supported.
Protocol efficiency across all channels	Data transmission protocols used within the platform must be capable of adjusting themselves to the richness/bandwidth of the channels that they might be using at any given time. Furthermore, multiple customer contact and access channels must be usable.
Technological maturity	The platform must be relatively mature. The Web does not fit the bill well, but the tradeoffs between cost and maturity still make it a good choice.
Training costs	The costs incurred in training users and customers should be reasonable. The Web browser is a tool that many corporate users are familiar with, so training costs can be expected to be lower with web-based systems front ends.
Project decomposability	The platform must not require an all-or-nothing approach to system building. The project itself must be possible to implement in small results-driven increments (see Chapter 8)—each stage of which can "go live."
Implementation cost	The Web-services market is characterized by a significantly high level of competition, therefore Web-based tools, services, software, and server hardware/software/space can be acquired price-competitively. However, the actual cost of development might be higher if a system is built from ground up.
Deployment time	Deployment time is influenced by technology complexity and familiarity. This is usually lower with Web-based projects because of the availability of numerous development tools that facilitate rapid prototyping.
Open architecture	The platform must have an open architecture and not a proprietary one.

GAINING INTEREST AT INDEPENDENCE COMMUNITY BANK

Independence Community Bank (ICB) (www.nycbny.com) is a Brooklyn, NY-based small bank with 65 branches and $7 billion in assets. ICB's target markets are working-class immigrant neighborhoods in metropolitan New York. The company embraced relationship management technologies, initially to begin developing customized communication with new customers. The bank initially answered inbound calls in different departments for all its branches, transferring callers on an as-needed basis, and referring them to other branch locations.

A new integrated channel system adds several capabilities that not only allow ICB to make its operations more efficient, but also allow it to add value to its specific group of customers. Speech recognition systems that recognize 26 different languages using an automatic phone-tree technology are now integrated with telephone, Web, and branch-specific data. For a regional bank that added services focused on its customer group—like multilingual capability on its incoming call systems—these moves indicate a strong potential for continual differentiation and future lock-in. ICB could do this because it approached the problem beginning with the customer, not fancy technology.

that is now loosely used to refer to collaborative systems). GroupWare tools provide a document repository, remote integration, collaboration support, and shared workspaces. However, most GroupWare tools tend to be used solely as e-mail clients and document management systems. Examples include Lotus Notes, Netscape Collabra, Microsoft's freebie NetMeeting, Novell GroupWise, and Webflow. Existing tools are being increasingly integrated with the Internet and often being replaced by it. The shift toward intranets and extranets is clearly visible in most businesses as GroupWare systems fall out of favor. For understanding KCRM systems, we will not consider specific proprietary GroupWare systems any further.

Intranets and Extranets

In the pre-Internet days, businesses normally needed to lease or own telecommunications lines in order to connect to other geographically distributed internal systems. The Internet has changed everything: Instead of relying on expensive networks, businesses have begun using the Internet to simulate secure, cost-effective, and unrestricted private networks. Intranets and extranets are hybrid information systems built on open

Internet protocols such as HTTP and TCP/IP and related Web technologies. They enable business partners to efficiently share resources to accomplish common goals such as information exchange, collaboration, invoicing, electronic funds transfer, and supply chain management, document exchange, conversations, deliberations, and discussions. The technology that enables this is commonly known as a virtual private network (VPN) (illustrated in Figure 7-3).

Tech Talk

Virtual Private Network (VPN): Technique that allows one to create a secure, private network using the Internet, without having to build a network. Using a special (tunneling) protocol, computers of both ends simulate a private pipeline for exchanging data.

Rapid Application Development (RAD) Tools: Software tools that help speed up the process of developing new software applications by automating many complex development and programming tasks.

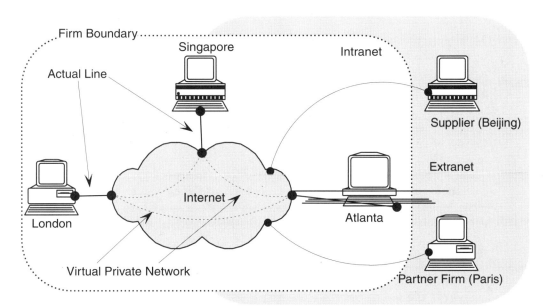

Figure 7-3
Intranets and extranets use public networks to create cost-effective, robust, and secure channels.

When such simulated networks are created, a business needs to pay primarily for Internet access (the actual line in Figure 7-3). When the simulated network is used to connect systems within the business, it is called an intranet, and when it is used to connect to outer-organizational systems such as those of suppliers, vendors, and partner businesses, it is called an extranet. Figure 7-3 shows how an intranet is used to connect a business' offices across London, Singapore, and Atlanta without incurring otherwise prohibitive network building costs. The same level of connectivity is extended to its supplier in Beijing and a partner firm in Paris—all through the Internet. Intranets and extranets are platform-independent and not bound by proprietary protocols or technologies. Tools and services that use open protocols can be introduced with relative ease as business environments and functionality evolution necessitate change. The system itself is accessed through a Web browser, which eliminates the need for being at a certain location to be able to access it (though such restrictions *can* be enforced). This unprecedented global business-to-business connectivity has led critics to hail the Internet as the biggest happening after the invention of the wheel. Data that moves across Intranets and extranets goes over the exposed, public information superhighway where security becomes a concern. Rapid application development tools that are available for building intranets and extranets usually address security design features; however, readers who are interested in examining security issues in further depth are pointed to my book *Web Security* (Butterworth Heinemann/Digital Press, 1999).

Networks

Although the Internet provides a powerful channel for building intra- and inter-organizational systems, it does not eliminate the need for each computer in your business to be actually connected to the Internet. In other words, the path to the Internet (the *actual line* in Figure 7-3) must be present, and have sufficient bandwidth to support rich communications and interactions. If you are implementing a KCRM project, it is assumed that you already have internal networks connected to the Internet in place. Table 7-4 contrasts three different categories of systems that are often confused with customer knowledge management systems. The differences are highlighted specifically in the context of their relationship with customer knowledge, the nature of their content, their scope, and knowledge generated from activities within a business.

Tech Talk

Data Warehouse: Large repository of data that aggregates data from over the entire organization and makes it all accessible from a single source. A well-developed data warehouse allows employees to find all relevant data—cleaned and tidied up—there, instead of having to scramble for inconsistent pieces all over their company.

Table 7-4 *Systems Commonly Confused with Customer Knowledge Management Systems*

	Intranet/Extranet	Data Warehouse	Groupware
Type of content	Structured and semi-structured	Highly structured, raw data	Semistructured, archival
Context	Fast, low-cost, mass-customized delivery throughout the enterprise	Source of aggregated, cleansed, structured, and context-devoid data	Collaborative work, largely internal
Size	Might grow over time	Always large	Might grow over time
Focus	Information delivery and publishing	Scrubbed, raw, clean, and organized data	Enabling collaborative work through electronic channels
Performance	Varies	Computing resource intensive	Not resource intensive
Network dependency	Very high	Varies; high in data Web houses	High
Scope	Limited to extensive, intraorganizational (intranet) or interorganizational (extranet)	Internal	Largely intraorganizational, limitedly interorganizational

Document Management Systems and Workflow

Document management (DM) systems marked the attempt of businesses to create a paperless office by converting volumes of hard-copy information from paper to an easier-to-transfer and searchable electronic format. Unfortunately, converting every paper document into electronic form creates two problems: (1) It strips the document of its context—i.e., it sanitizes it, and (2) the cost of such conversions is rarely worth the expense if conversion is blindly done. Simply cataloging information is often sufficient and more efficient. Commercial-grade document management systems play a small part in customer knowledge management systems, especially when they are supported by tools such as versioning and automated tagging and time stamping (described later in this chapter). Some document management also includes the ability to develop a database of documents and automatically classify them. Newer standards such as Document Management Association (DMA) and WebDAV facilitates tighter, Web-enabled integration of document management systems with the KCRM infrastructure (PC Docs, FileNet, Documentum, and Hyland are popular vendors; see www.aiim.org for details on the standards). Workflow management systems that automate the procedures by which documents, information, and tasks are routed among participants based on predefined rules and process sequences, are increasingly integrated with document management systems.

Informal Knowledge Networks

Several informal technology solutions support knowledge sharing with customers and partners. Examples of some along with details of activities that they facilitate are shown in Table 7-5.

Table 7-5 Technology Applications and Informal Customer Interaction Facilitated

Technology	Activities Facilitated
Web collaboration tools	Web-initiated inquiries can be integrated with voice calls assigned to a representative with the most *relevant* skill set
	Web pages can be pushed to customers in real time
	Escalated agent-unassisted calls can be routed to a company representative for real-time resolution
Interactive chat	Direct interaction with human agents
	History of customer interactions can be captured by Web-housing clickstream data
Intelligent agents	Intelligent software agents can monitor customer clickstreams and look for clickstream data patterns that initiate agent-initiated suggestions
E-communities	Customers can query discussion archives to resolve previously encountered issues
	Customers can interact with e-business hosted communities to resolve questions (such as on Amazon.com)
Intelligent routing	Computer telephony integration (CTI) provides intelligent routing of incoming queries based on (1) customer requirements, (2) customer history, (3) agent skills, and (4) representative availability.

Expertise pointers and multimedia are two mechanisms that facilitate sharing tacit knowledge that cannot be formally expressed or codified but can be explicated.

Expertise Pointers

Besides their basic roles in publishing and information distribution, collaborative knowledge platforms can provide pointers to expertise when they reach a level beyond which it is impossible to codify knowledge in systems. Tacit knowledge develops naturally as a byproduct of action; it is more easily exchanged, combined, distributed, and managed if it is converted to explicit knowledge. However, good technology does not necessarily translate to good information or knowledge. Beyond this fatigue point, pointers (yellow pages, skills directories, and automated knowledge-based routing) to the person who actually holds relevant knowledge are needed to facilitate knowledge flow. The scope of such pointers can be both internal (such as employees in your own location or in foreign offices) and external to the organization (such as consultants and researchers). There are three approaches to implementing such pointers:

1. Web-searchable database with contextual comments added by referrers
2. Collection of links at the end of relevant knowledge objects such as documents
3. Automated intelligent routing systems that look for keywords in employee or customer queries and match them with expert profiles to automatically redirect them

Multimedia

The value of multimedia in customer knowledge management comes from its ability to capture what cannot be figuratively expressed in a thousand words. Informal content that is too cumbersome to describe in words can be captured in audio files (often in Real Audio or MP3 format), pictures, and video clips (such as product descriptions, shapes, color, etc.) that can be attached and manipulated with other knowledge objects, records, transactions, and discussions. Multimedia also helps overcome language barriers in internationally distributed teams where all members do not necessarily speak the same language. Customer software development teams, for example, often upload screen shots of error messages to share and troubleshoot with client participants. Web-based, real-time, distributed collaboration lets team members work together with many other participants on documents or information in real time, or share an application running on one single computer with other people in a meeting.

Everyone can view the information shared by the application, and any participant can take control of the shared application to edit information in real time. In addition, many tools such as electronic whiteboards and digital pens allow informal content to be captured in a transparent manner without demanding additional work from the participants in a meeting. Mind maps and visual thinking tools (such as Inspiration, www.inspiration.com, and Mind Manager, www.mindmanager.com) make extensive use of multimedia to capture and organize independent or collaborative thought processes that can later be shared, distributed, posted, printed, exchanged, or e-mailed. Several tools such as ConceptDraw (www.conceptdraw.com) for Mac and Windows also provide a rich set of features that can be mobilized to express concepts and process understanding in a graphical, electronically sharable form.

P&G's Marketing Net: High-Speed Internet Marketing

When it comes to the Web, Procter and Gamble is not just counting on Web-based retailing; e-business is transforming internal processes even in its traditional departments. To deploy collaborative knowledge sharing for improved decision making, P&G created Marketing Net, a Web-based digital library that lets marketing managers, sales groups, and executives view their proposed advertising copy, videos, and competitors' advertisements over the Internet, without having to resort to physically shipping videotapes from office to office. Web-enabled knowledge sharing-networks and brainstorming software tools allow teams distributed around the world to deliberate, debate, and refine their marketing material. The results: more widely shared tacit knowledge, 50 percent reduction in new concept development time, quicker business decisions, and reduced travel expenses.

Web Conferencing, E-Communities, Water Coolers, and Chat

Informal conversations contain vast amounts of untapped *tacit* knowledge. Such knowledge can be shared and widely deployed through mechanisms that allow informal discussions and conversations. Web conferencing enables virtual meetings where users from different locations connect, conduct meetings, and share information as if everyone were in the same room. Electronic communities such as those at Amazon.com allow groups of customers to share their opinions and experiences with specific product offerings (see Figure 7-4).

Figure 7-4
Communities at Amazon.com allow customers' interest to share knowledge.

Similarly, Dell capitalizes on such discussion forums (support.dell.com, Figure 7-5). Both Dell customers and support personnel participate on these forums. Very often, other customers help resolve issues that a customer might be facing. This builds a strong community, possibly increases Dell's goodwill, and reduces support overheads.

Mechanisms that allow community members who benefit from these discussions to allow leaving feedback and add comments encourage social exchange of information and knowledge (this concept is called *social exchange theory*). As interaction complexity rises, the KCRM system's focus must become more social, cognitive, behavioral, and less technical. For example, Amazon.com provides reviewers' details on how many other customers found their reviews useful, what their relative level of contribution (shown as a rank in Figure 7-6) is, and what purchase circles they fall

Figure 7-5
Dell uses an asynchronous Web self-service and support strategy through its support forums.

under. Such helpful feedback encourages continuing contributions in groups where ties are solely sociodigital.

Tech Talk

Social Exchange Theory: Members of a community stay loyal as long as they feel that their efforts are being reciprocated by other members and that they are gaining respect among their peers through their contributions. Amazon.com, for example, assigns "Top 500 Reviewer" to the top 500 contributors.

Electronic communities (e-communities) can be among any combination of internal employees, partner firm employees, and customers. As increasing amounts of information is put into the hands of customers by the e-business, it tends to create what is described as lock-in—a powerful reason for the customer to keep coming back to

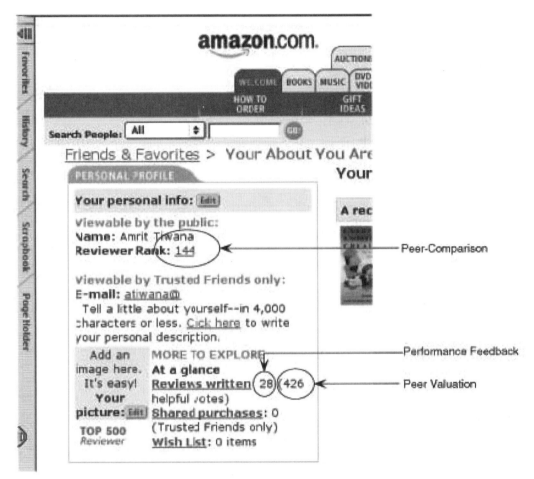

Figure 7-6
Amazon's version of a peer feedback system that ties contributions to recognition-based rewards.

the same site. Lock-in increases the intangible and tangible switching costs for the customers and therefore makes it increasingly hard for the customer to take his business elsewhere. Mobshop, a reverse auction B2C site, offers e-communities that allow customers to collude and drive prices down through information sharing and joint strategy planning. B2B hubs operate much like trading *bazaars* and flea markets, deriving much of their attraction from the communities that constitute them. Figure 7-7 shows one such B2B trading hub that specializes in steel trading (www.eSteel.com). Other industry specific B2B hubs like eSteel.com include VerticalNet.com, equipp.com (Figure 7-8), and Chemdex.com.

Figure 7-7
eSteel.com is an online business-to-business steel trading community.

Tech Talk

> **Reverse Auction: Auction mechanism where sellers bid on buyers' needs and change their terms and prices because of collective bargaining. Elements of reverse auctions can be seen at Priceline.com and Mercata.com.**

Technologies that enable such e-communities have been around for years. Now they need to be implemented as an integral part of e-business hubs to deliver results.

Such integration also allows businesses to put data in the hands of customers to add additional value without compromising privacy. Amazon.com, for example, lets customers uniquely analyze aggregated data. For example, if you work at MIT and want to know which books are uniquely purchased by people there and not by the

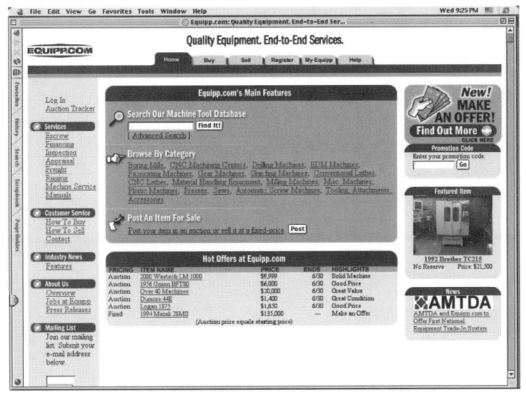

Figure 7-8
Equipp.com is a B2B industrial equipment-trading hub.

average Amazon customer, you can search for unique best-selling titles (see Figure 7-9) within that specific community.

What makes e-communities so different from traditional communities is their ability to facilitate real-time, bidirectional conversations that can also be continued asynchronously. Microsoft's NetMeeting, Caucus, Web Crossing, Notes discussion databases, REMAP, Optimus, Microsoft Messenger, and AOL Messenger are examples of tools that allow such collaboration.

Voiceover IP

Amid a sea of abandoned digital shopping carts, several Web-based interaction technologies have emerged to enable human interaction in an environment that otherwise lacks human touch. Much of this is made possible by Voiceover IP (VoIP), an Internet protocol that facilitates real-time voice communications over the Internet. Voice is con-

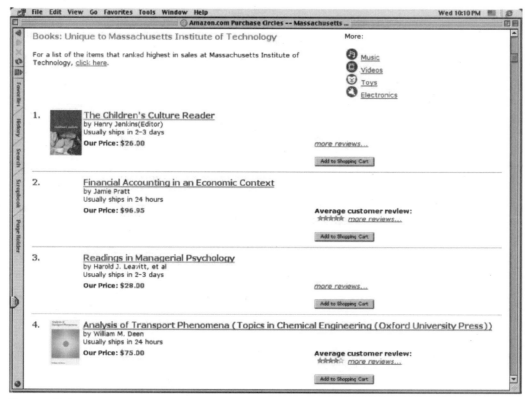

Figure 7-9
Letting customers slice and dice aggregated data add value to the total customer experience, as Amazon.com's community-specific filtering allows.

verted into information packets that are sent as streamed data and reconverted into voice on the receiving end. Voiceover IP is a growing market, as Figure 7-10 illustrates.

When integrated with collaboration technology (such as systems developed by Silknet, eGain, and netDialog), a customer support representative can take shared control of the customer's browser and interactively push relevant information through. A variant of VoIP is call back mechanisms where the customer can schedule a call-back from the host business, or even talk through the browser itself. In addition, businesses can reduce their long-distance calling expenses (especially when the customer is located in a different country) and enable customers to talk without having to tie up a telephone line. More importantly, the integration of the browser and voice allows support staff to pick up from where a customer left rather than have the customer describe the problem all over.

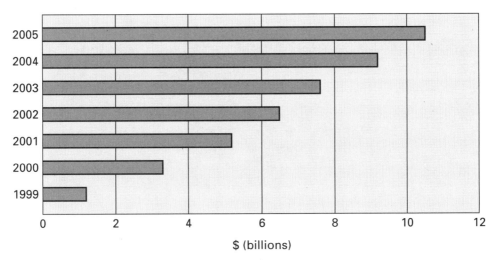

Figure 7-10
The Voiceover IP market's growth represents the need for human interaction even in purely digital customer relationships.

Several B2C e-businesses have also capitalized on the potential for real-time text chat—a resource-stingy alternative to VoIP. Planetoutdoors.com, a sporting goods retailer, for example, allows customers to ask questions about specific products in real time through its Web browsers. Figure 7-11 shows an example of such an interaction where a customer decides to ask a customer support representative a question about a specific pullover that he is interested in purchasing. From within the page displaying the pullover, the customer can click on a chat button to activate a chat window that immediately connects him to a live representative who can answer his questions.

Opportunities for knowledge capture abound in such scenarios. For example:

- The entire chat transcript can be automatically recorded and referenced to a customer, maybe even added to her profile. The next time the same item goes on sale, that customer can be specifically targeted with the promotion.
- The customer does not need to explain from scratch what she is looking for. When the company-side representative responds, she is looking at the same Web page that the customer is looking at. That provides the context for a focused discussion that does not waste the customer's or the representative's time.
- It eliminates the need for the customer to move away from her computer and pick up the telephone to ask the same question.
- Analyzing the clickstream data from that session can also reveal what else the customer might have looked at, and is possibly interested in.

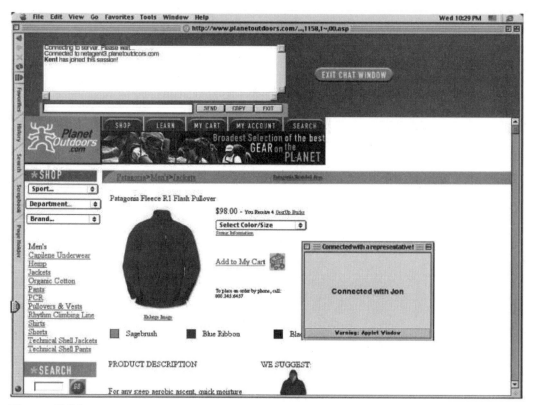

Figure 7-11
At Planetoutdoors.com, real-time chat is a bandwidth-efficient alternative to VoIP.
Based on data from Frost and Sullivan, 2000.

Such systems increasingly encourage Web self-service and reduce operational costs for e-businesses. Apple Computer, like Dell and Gateway, allows customers to self-configure their personal computers before purchase (see Figure 7-12).

Using a powerful repertoire of configuration rules sorted in a knowledge base, customers can assemble and purchase a computer with one of several thousand possible configurations. No wonder most customers of such businesses tend to be repeat buyers. Other examples of Web-based self-service include Microsoft's and Apple's troubleshooting knowledge bases and frequently asked question (FAQ) lists on many Websites. Many of these concepts are seen in a B2C e-commerce context but are highly applicable in a B2B context as well.

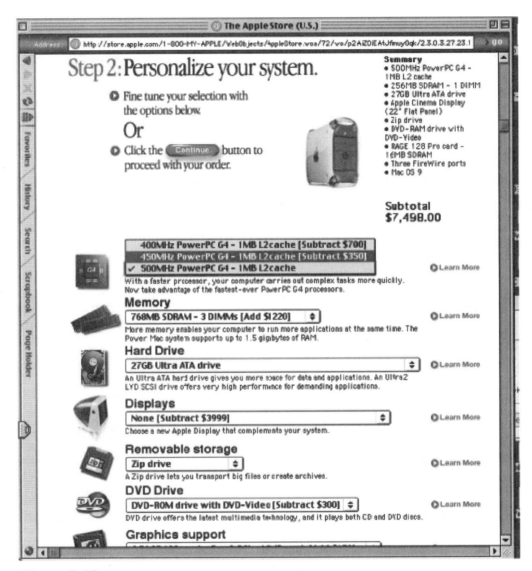

Figure 7-12
Online configurators such as this one used by Apple encourage Web self-service.

Business Intelligence Systems

Transactional, Web, historical, and third-party data is extracted, transformed, cleansed, loaded, and deployed in a data warehouse (or one that goes under a pseudonym such as a customer data store), semistructured information is stored in a combination discussion databases, clickstream Web houses, and ill-structured information is stored in conversational repositories and multimedia systems. These repositories collectively hold explicated formal and informal knowledge and the rules associated with them for accumulation, refining, managing, validating, maintaining, annotating (adding context), and distributing the contents. These repositories collectively hold declarative, procedural, causal, and contextual knowledge as described in Table 7-6. In addition, integrated communication channels provide pathways for transferring and sharing (but not always capturing) tacit knowledge that flows among customer, business employees, and partner firms.

Table 7-6 Four Different Types of Knowledge Are in KCRM Systems

Knowledge	Type Description
Declarative	Significant, meaningful concepts, categories, definitions, and assumptions
Procedural	Processes, sequences of events and activities, and actions
Causal	Rationale for choices, alternatives, and rejected decisions and associated informal knowledge
Context	Decision circumstances, assumptions, results of those assumptions, and informal knowledge such as video clips, annotations, notes, and conversations

Business intelligence systems are defined by the collection of decision support systems, case-based reasoning (CBR) systems, and contextual information retrieval systems, which provide the needed historical base from past experience that help make decisions rapidly and accurately. In addition, these systems provide pointers when the limits of codification of knowledge are reached. For example, if an employee helping a customer troubleshoot a piece of equipment using a customer problem resolution system encounters a problem that is not recorded in the system, he would know whom to call for help while the customer waits; the business intelligence system would tell him that.

Several technological tools such as artificial intelligence subsystems, intelligent data warehouses, genetic algorithm tools, neural networks, expert systems, CBR applications, rule bases, and intelligent agents can be combined to endow the customer knowledge management system with business intelligence capabilities. A summary of these tools and their role in customer knowledge management appears in Table 7-7.

QUICK DIAGNOSTICS FOR EXISTING INTERACTION CHANNELS

1. Are most of your company's software applications built to automate existing processes?
2. Are any of these applications capable of identifying and targeting your best and most profitable customers?
3. Do these systems integrate customer information across contact channels such as your Website and phone ordering system?
4. Do these applications consider the customer's past buying behavior?
5. Do they offer real-time personalization for services for each customer?

Table 7-7 Business Intelligence Tools and their Applications in Customer Knowledge Management

Tool	Description
Case-based reasoning	Searches a collection of previous cases known as its case base for past cases with attributes that match the current case. The user defines the problem to be solved based on some attributes (each with varying degrees of importance as indicated by their user-assigned weights). A search engine then searches through all the cases in the case base and retrieves those that match closely. As new cases are added, the case-based reasoning becomes increasingly powerful and accurate. Concepts are stored as real images and the context of past decisions is satisfactorily retained. However, CBR requires the user to define all expected attributes in the initial stages of its development.
Data mining-based inference modeling	Data mining tools analyze customer information embedded in vast amounts of operational data and facilitate knowledge-based market segmentation and customer profiling. These techniques have limited applicability for new customers.

Table 7-7 *Business Intelligence Tools and their Applications in Customer Knowledge Management (cont.)*

Tool	Description
Data Web houses and warehouses	A data warehouse acts as a unifier of a multitude of isolated, distributed databases and aggregates, cleans, scrubs, and consolidate disparate data. Although data warehouses do not possess the ability to deliver real-time data, Web-enabled warehouses known as data Web houses are moving in that direction. By aggregating data across multiple sources, they give decision makers the ability to run complex queries, slice-and-dice data, and most importantly, improve information quality and accuracy. Document management systems
Document management systems	Make vast amounts of documents such as product literature, electronic forms, specifications, and correspondence easily accessible and adaptable through electronic media (often a Web front end). These systems often include workflow functionality that allows documents to be intelligently routed to select relevant employees.
Fuzzy logic systems	Need to be trained by domain specialists or experts—often too expensive or unfeasible. There might be experts available and accessible but their opinions might differ, or none of them might have comprehensive understanding of the problem. Even if you do get experts, they might have problems explicating their decision-making process in sufficient detail. Several companies have invested millions of dollars in expert systems but to little avail—simply because the experts were unable to exactly state what they knew and how they knew it.
Genetic algorithms	Apply Darwin's *survival of the fittest* theory to computer programs and data. A genetic algorithm experiments with several new and novel problem solutions simultaneously. The programs and data sets that solve a problem survive (ranked high and retained for genetic refinement) and others are assigned a low rank and discarded. They are very effective in making decisions where the amount of data to be taken into account is very large; there are discontinuities in available data, and near-optimal solutions are acceptable.

Table 7-7 Business Intelligence Tools and their Applications in Customer Knowledge Management (cont.)

Tool	Description
Collaborative filtering	Automatically compares attributes of one set of customer data with other customers and provides ideas for personalization. This approach relies on an extensive base of similar customers. Collaborative filtering requires scalable personalization capabilities that can handle effective personalization as customer data volume grows. A good example of collaborative filtering that actually works can be found on Amazon.com's site wherein the site recommends books based on past purchases by other customers with similar interests.
Neural networks	Networked computing architecture in which a number of processors are interconnected in a manner suggestive of the connections between neurons in a human brain and which can learn by a process of trial and error. They are especially useful when very limited inputs from domain experts exist or when you have the data but lack experts to make judgments about it.
Rule-based systems	Embed existing rule of thumb and heuristics in systems to facilitate fast and accurate decision making. However, five conditions must be met for them to work well: (1) You must know the variable in your problem/question, (2) you must be able to express them in hard, numerical terms (e.g., dollars), (3) the rule specified must cover all these variables, (4) there is no overlap between rules, and (5) the rules must have been validated. These systems require continuous manual change and conflict resolution between rules requires additional rule making.
Sales force automation	Designed to increase the effectiveness of sales representatives by integrating customer knowledge bases, marketing literature, product configuration knowledge, and analysis tools that connect multiple distribution channels and functional areas within a business. Though these tools are not intelligent in themselves, they interact with other intelligent tools to deliver results at the physical point of need.

Data Mining

Data mining tools help extract trends and patterns from data warehouses. External information retrieval systems provide the key financial and nonfinancial indicators of the company's health. E-businesses use operational metrics in addition to ROI metrics. Data mining tools can assimilate these operational metrics and help deduce patterns that are latently embedded in them. In a typical B2C e-commerce site, metrics such as those described in Table 7-8 are often used. Data to calculate these metrics can be collected through clickstream tracking that is well supported in most data Web houses (the Web-centric data warehouse). However, as they are collected over time, data mining can help determine unobvious correlations and patterns in these numbers.

Table 7-8 *Some Clickstream-based Metrics in B2C Transactions*

Metric	Description
Click-through rate	Percentage of users who click on a link, banner, or picture
Impression count	A measure of click-through rate obtained from an external source (such as a partner site)
Look-to-click rate	Percentage of product impressions that are converted to click-throughs
Click-to-basket rate	Percentage of click-throughs that are converted to placement in the shopping cart
Basket-to-buy rate	Percentages of shopping cart placements that are converted to purchases

The provisional construction of a messy array of rules, tools, heuristics, and guidelines that produce results according to the expertise and sensitivity of the *craftsman*, not the empirical accuracy of the rules, tools, and guidelines is needed. Patterns deduced by data mining tools provide a more defensible basis for changing or adding new rules.

Flexibility, expert dependence, processing overhead, ability to deal with complex problems, accuracy, speed, tolerance for dirty data, and response time must be considered when making a choice about a business intelligence tool. Response time is critically important when a KCRM system is used to answer customer questions on the phone; however, accuracy is more important when a technical bug needs to be

INTELLIGENT AGENTS

> Emerging intelligent agent-based search mechanisms allow synchronous and asynchronous searches to be performed in an intelligent manner while simultaneously reducing the bandwidth requirements typically demanded by conventional search mechanisms. Mobile agents—which depart from a "home" location, hop across networked servers scouring for information, and return home when they find it—are the most promising development to watch out for commercialization.

resolved. Similarly, when customer or businesses credit-worthiness-related decisions are made, the ability to interpret incomplete and fuzzy information (i.e., dirty data) is important. These characteristics always involve tradeoffs and there is no *one best* business intelligence tool to pick. Table 7-9 maps these characteristics to facilitate comparison across categories and across tools.

Table 7-9 A Comparison of Performance and Accuracy Tradeoffs Among Intelligence Tools.

Intelligence Tool	Response Time	Scalability	Flexibility	Ease of Use	Embeddability	Processing Overhead	Expert Dependence	Tolerance for Dirty Data	Implementation Speed	Tolerance for Complexity	Accuracy
Genetic algoritym	▲	▼	▼	▼	▲	▲	▼		▲	▲	▲
Neural networks	▲	◆	▼	▼	◆	▼	▼	▲	◆	▲	▲
Fuzzy logic systems	▲	▼	◆	▲	◆	▲	▲	▲	▲	◆	◆
Rule-based systems	∎	▼	◆	▲	▲	◆	▲	▼	▲	◆	▲
Case-based reasoning	▼	▲	▼	◆	◆	▲	▼	▲	◆	▲	▲

Legend: ▲ = High   ▼ = Low   ◆ = Medium   ∎ = Deteriorates as the number of active rules grow

Search and Retrieval

Without powerful search and retrieval tools, valuable, actionable codified customer knowledge cannot be retrieved, nor can codified pointers to tacit knowledge distributed throughout the business be traced. Creative retrieval schemes can potentially enrich acquisition, management, aggregation, conversion, and dissemination functions. Conventional keyword-based search mechanisms are of limited value to knowledge-enabled customer relationship management because of their (1) inability to narrow down searches from a range of excessive hits, (2) breadth tradeoffs in those that use relevancy rankings, and (3) insensitivity to the *user-intended* meaning and context of the search.

PERSONALIZED CONTENT FILTERING

Personalized content filtering refers to the process of categorizing items by their content: images, video, sound, text, etc. A user profile—automatically updated through automatic refinement and derivation by statistical learning algorithms—defines the relevant content *types*. These tools may collect such preferences passively from a simple registration process or actively by profiling, clustering bookmarks, and learning from browsing patterns. Marimba, Netscape, BackWeb, and Pointcast all provide personalized content filtering tools.

Information Packaging and Meta-Information

Information packaging refers to the collective activity of filtering, editing, searching, and organizing pieces of knowledge. Packaging ensures that what is aggregated is useful, provides value, and encourages application in guiding business decision making. High-level knowledge about possessed information is needed to be able to package information. Such information about information—*meta-information*—assists in defining, categorizing, and locating knowledge resources and provides insight into information users, types of information being accessed, where and which information repositories are being most frequently accessed. In e-business settings this poses additional challenges: Information must be aggregated in real time, and in a manner useful at the point of need. For example, intelligent meta search tool-based customer service systems can automatically route incoming complaints to qualified specialists. Table 7-10 describes how automated clustering, categorization, taxonomy generation, synonymies, and translation tools can enhance search and retrieval processes.

Tech Talk

Meta-Information: Information about information that assists in defining, categorizing, and locating knowledge resources and provides insight into information users, types of information being accessed, where and which information is being accessed most frequently .

Table 7-10 Automated Mechanisms that Enhance Explicit Knowledge Search and Retrieval.

Tool Function	Description
Clustering	Automatically finds groups of related documents and knowledge elements such as technical reports, news feeds, patents, manuals, and press releases by analyzing key concepts in textual and non-textual information (using tags).
Categorization	Assigns new knowledge elements to one or more categories from a user-defined taxonomy.
Taxonomy generation	Generates categorization taxonomies of relevant concepts and keywords from a base knowledge artifact/document set.
Translation	Recognizes and translates key concepts from one language to another. Machine translation—an inexpensive solution for transnational businesses—results in only about 60 percent accuracy. CISCO, for example, uses Uniscape's translator (www.uniscape.com). Many translation systems use a Web front-end. Figure 7-13 shows the Go Translator (translator.go.com) converting a site (www.kmtoolkit.com) from English to German.
Thesaurus	A thesaurus integrated with the system can be an indispensable too for automatically cross-referencing related but inconsistently defined concepts in search queries.

Off-the-shelf tools such as Excalibur (www.excalibur.com) provide search solutions based on semantic networks (that use built-in thesauri, dictionaries, and lexical databases) that help distinguish between multiple meanings and contexts of a single word or phrase. Altavista, CompassWare, InText, Lycos, Microsoft Index Server, Oracle, Thunderstone, and Verity sell meta-attribute searching tools, and Netperceptions, Alexa, Firefly, GrapeVine, and NetPerceptions are visible collaborative filtering tool vendors. Tools based on Adaptive Pattern Recognition Processing (APRP) can further enhance the system's ability to recognize fuzzy queries.

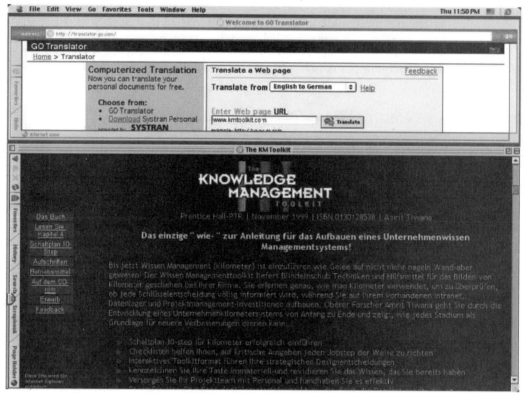

Figure 7-13
A Web-based multilingual translator in action.

Five types of search strategies can be deployed in varying combinations:

1. Metasearching
2. Hierarchical searching
3. Tagged attribute searching
4. Content searching
5. Combinatorial

These search strategies are described in Table 7-11. Implementing any given combination of these strategies is usually a snap with commercially available pluggable software components.

Table 7-11 Five Search Strategies for Search and Retrieval of Codified Content

Search Strategy	Description
Meta	Based on metacategories and dependent on keywords and attribute tags
	Minimizes time spent in locating the right, general high-level category
	Clarifies the context intended by the user through refinement and rejection
Hierarchical	Organizes knowledge items in a fixed hierarchy
	User can traverse links to efficiently locate the right knowledge element
	Often uses hyperlinks that facilitate "digging deeper"
Tagged attribute	Matches user input attributes against attributes/tags associated with documents and pointers
	Results are ranked according to their relevance (which can be improved through feedback)
Content	Matches search term, keyword, or text string to return results with relevance scores based on the frequency of matches
	Inefficient, slow search strategy
Combinatorial	Combination of two or more of the above executed in parallel
	Improves retrieval quality across information of various types (textual, informal, etc.)

Tagging Attributes

Although the aforementioned search and retrieval strategies are directly applicable to explicit knowledge, they can be useful in retrieving tacit knowledge as well. If pointers, skills directories, and employee yellow pages are maintained well, they provide pointers to people (internal or external) with the most relevant expertise. Though they cannot search through tacit expertise per *se*, they can search through pointers and references to its sources.

While most of these methods are based on some mutant of text string searches, one that stands out is attribute tag searching. Attribute tag searching works by searching through tags that define concepts not inherently captured in the content of a knowledge object. For example, a report can have several searchable attributes attached to it. Even common software tools such as word processors automatically tag documents with details of the author; a creation and last modification timestamp; people who might have read it, approved it, or modified it, its size, etc. When used in combination with automated indexing, tagging can provide powerful, automated retrieval capabilities. For a KCRM system, tags can define activities, work domains, formats, products and services, time indicators, and locations associated with a knowledge object, as described in Table 7-12.

In addition to search and retrieval effectiveness and efficiency, a good user interface will determine how easy it is to actually use the system. Table 7-13 provides a set of guidelines for its design.

Table 7-12 *Seven Attributes for Tagging Knowledge Objects*

Tagging Attribute	Description
Activities	Relates organizational activities to the given knowledge element. This attribute is defined in nonexclusive groupings based on an explicit model of business processes and customer-related activities that occur in your business, and can be incrementally improved.
Domain	Tags the knowledge item to its subject matter, broad domains of expertise, and skill areas.
Form	Specifies the physical representation (paper, electronic, multimedia, formal, informal, tacit, heuristic) of the knowledge element. Each knowledge element can have multiple, overlapping form attributes associated with it.
Type	Specifies what type of document a given knowledge element exists in. For example, explicit type attributes include procedures, manuals, guidelines, time lines, best practices, memo, press releases, annual report, and competitive intelligence feeds.
Products/services	Specifies the specific, ideally nonoverlapping product or service to which the knowledge element relates.
Time	Marks the creation of that object, which might have a value different from the actual creation of that knowledge. This attribute is useful for narrowing down the retrieval process when an approximate time block associated with it is known. Not every knowledge element can have a time attribute assigned to it.
Location	Specifies the approximate physical or logical location of the knowledge element.

Expiration Dates for Knowledge

Some KCRM implementations actually allow the creators or authors of a knowledge content unit to tag an expiration date to the content. This ensures that invalid, inapplicable, or outdated content is automatically relegated to an expired status and is not accidentally used to make a current decision

Table 7-13 User Interface Design Considerations

Considerations	Implications for Interface Design
Functionality	Allow users to accomplish their tasks quickly, effectively, and without frustration by implementing an exceptionally intuitive interface.
Consistency	Use a consistent set of menus and buttons that have the same meaning across the entire enterprise-spanning system. Maintain consistency in presentation, access, retrieval, and use of information throughout the system.
Relevancy	Present all information that relates to the user's task on one screen if possible and hide unrelated options. Make generous use of white space, use jargon-free, lowest common denominator interface terms, and use hyperlinks to facilitate "digging down" for details.
Navigation	Use a site map, provide visual cues to indicate which of many applications a user is using at a given moment, and use a consistent navigation scheme for collaborative messaging, document repository navigation, retrieval, and discussion.
Customizability	Allow users to customize the client-side system to their specific interests.
Stickiness	Interactive intelligent agents can learn from user-initiated changes and remember them in the future. Use them to make the system remember any such preferences.

THE KCRM ARCHITECTURE . . . .

Having examined various pieces of technology that collectively provide the technological framework for building a knowledge-enabled CRM system, we will now see how the pieces fit into the KCRM architecture. The basic architecture of a knowledge-enabled customer relationship management system is shown in Figure 7-14. Remember, although KCRM is customer-driven, it also includes business partners (logistics, distribution, shipping, etc.) and suppliers. The system-level description here is specifically in the context of e-business.

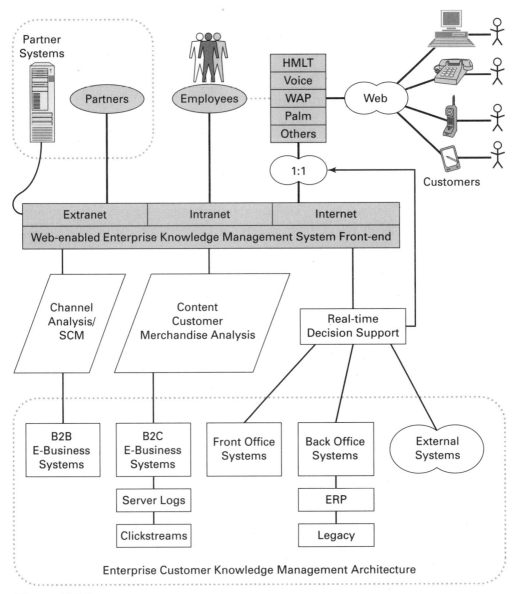

Figure 7-14
The KCRM system architecture.

At the bottom layer are e-business systems. These include business-to-consumer (B2C) and business-to-business (B2B) systems. These systems are supported by several data sources such as data warehouses and Web houses that aggregate real-time (e.g., clickstream data) and historical data that result from transactions between businesses and customers. Next, we have front office systems such as those used to input pricing information and back office systems that are more transactional in nature. In addition, there are external data sources and systems such as those used for obtaining dynamic pricing, shipping information, etc.

The top layer represents the actual system-level front end (not to be confused with front office applications) through which customers, employees, and business partners interact. The front end can be divided into three clusters, all of which are Web-enabled.

The primary cluster is the Internet segment. This portion of the logical architecture connects customers to the business through the Web. Customers can interact through a multitude of interaction channels such as Web browsers (HTML, ASP, etc.), voice (telephones, VoIP interfaces), wireless handheld devices (such as WAP protocol enabled cellular phones), hand-held computing platforms such as PalmPilots, and WebTV interfaces. By being able to manage and integrate customer knowledge into the interactions that occur through this cluster, one-to-one marketing is perfectly possible. Each customer can be identified individually, and pricing and other offers can be specifically designed and individualized based on prior knowledge of each customer.

The second cluster is the Intranet. This provides a medium for collaboration among the firm's own employees, however distributed they might be.

The third cluster is the extranet. As described earlier in this chapter, the extranet connects both external systems and individuals to the internal ones. Typically these entities represent partner firms and business collaborators. Access privileges and rights are controlled at the lowest layer.

The middle layer is where the action is: Knowledge management activities occur between the front-end and back-end systems. For example, between the transactional events (financial and informational) that occur through the extranet, there are opportunities for applying customer knowledge management techniques for creating, sharing, and applying knowledge relevant to supply chain management and channel analysis. Similarly, in the business-to-consumer context, real-time decision support can be provided to assist with sales. The previously mentioned examples of real-time interaction and automated decision/selection support like Planetoutdoors.com (and others like 1800flowers.com, Buy.com, and Gofly.com) fall in this category. Similarly, content, merchandise, and customer analysis can be done using data mining techniques and calculating placement performance metrics from clickstream data. If your e-business is B2B focused, then the same set of customers is replaced with individual businesses.

WANG GLOBAL SERVICES' KNOWLEDGE LOSS ANTIDOTE

Wang Global Services, a $4 billion network technology services provider based in Billerica, Massachusetts, was faced with a worsening knowledge loss problem driven by high turnover at the help desk. Maintaining service quality delivered to the employees of its strategic enterprise customers (which include Dell Computer and Microsoft) needed effective mechanisms to capture that relatively mobile knowledge.

To address this problem, Wang built a Web-based advisor that was built on a continually replenished repository of support issues and troubleshooting cases. As 150 service center analysts access and add to this repository, a team of "knowledge builders" create and maintain formal explicit knowledge bases that increase the scope of knowledge captured and allow the company to also apply this customer support knowledge to actually create new contracts and new business bids. The Web-based system has facilitated consistent responses, faster time to resolution, and a unified means to access resources.

The architecture described here is a high-level explanation; for implementation level details, I recommend reading my *Knowledge Management Toolkit* (Prentice Hall, 2000) and Ralph Kimball's *The Data Webhouse Toolkit* (John Wiley, 2000).

INTEGRATION

Businesses that have no legacy applications—outmoded pre-e-business applications tying up valuable data—to deal with can often get a head start by customizing off-the-shelf knowledge management and customer relationship management suites. Born-on-the-Web companies precisely fit that bill. However, most businesses that have been around for a little longer and have diverged into electronic commerce and e-business are tied down with valuable data in their legacy systems. Legacy systems, computer telephony and voice, data warehouses and Web houses, decision support systems, and e-TPSs need to be seamlessly integrated. As Figure 7-2 shows, middleware binds the system together; it connects systems that would normally not communicate. Although we discussed that Internet protocols can connect a multitude of systems such as mainframes, they need to be able to "talk" to the Net in order to take advantage of the Internet's inherent platform independence.

· ·

YAPI KREDI BANK: THE TURKISH EXPERIENCE

Yapi Kredi Bank (YKB) is the largest private commercial bank in Turkey. As part of its long-term strategy, the bank undertook drastic measures to revamp its structure and organization to maximize operational efficiency, commercial effectiveness, and asset realization. In 1998, Yapi Kredi saw an opportunity to use technology to penetrate profitable segments and increase its presence in Turkish banking. It soon recognized the need for sophisticated marketing strategies to build competitive barriers.

Even though the bank operates in a country with one of the lowest percentage of Internet users in the world, a customer-facing Interactive Voice Response (IVR) system, and employee-facing integrated, enterprise-wide, customer interaction platform has helped YKB increase sales, improve customer loyalty, and reduce costs to the lowest levels in Turkey.

Middleware: Data and Information Integration

Middleware is a glorified extension of legacy integration; any Web-centric system's binding glue. The term *legacy system*s is often used in the context of mainframes; legacy integration provides connections between legacy data and existing and new systems such as those supporting e-business processes. A number of companies have used wrapper technologies similar to TCL/TK and Knowledge Query Modeling Language (KQML) to integrate data sources such as those on mainframes that were otherwise hard to integrate. Middleware is much like legacy integration except that it also integrates systems that are not-so-legacy (made incompatible by the introduction of new e-business systems, i.e., e-legacy systems).

Tech Talk

Wrapper technologies: Software tools that allow legacy systems to exchange data with more popular computing platforms such as Windows PCs. Many of these technologies use the Internet protocol as an intermediary.

Middleware can range from simple (interface integration that transports information from one system to another in order to complete a business transaction) to integral. Business requirements for information integration should drive the choice of middleware. The alternative of handcrafting middleware (in the form of a point-to-point interface) is unappealing because of high levels of instability that accompany changes in business needs, system technologies, and software upgrades. Well-designed middleware can connect islands of data in situations where the intranet is not expansive and new information is being generated at a high rate. Several other benefits accrue from the use of middleware for enterprise-level integration.

- *Information utilization:* Existing legacy and not-so-legacy data and information are integrated with operational KCRM systems.
- *Adaptability:* Plug-in modules provide support for new data formats and delivery mechanisms as they emerge to provide unprecedented extensibility and adaptability.
- *Automated tracking:* Intelligent agents and Web crawlers navigate through integrated internal repositories and external sources to inform users of new content (pull- or push-based delivery), as it becomes available.
- *Chaotic structuration of information:* Automated content aggregation and electronically cataloging of new information in real time help patterns and structure emerge from chaos of information flows.

Rapid technological change has brought and will continue to bring new information sources, as well as unpredictable communication, information transfer, and knowledge sharing services and requirements that go with them. An open architecture allows for the integration of new transmission methods, data sources, and technologies as they emerge. To ensure compatibility with existing systems as well as newer ones, make sure that you rely on industry-wide open standards. In order to be open and flexible, the architecture should adhere to Internet protocols, have broad database and repository support, and open, well-documented application programming interfaces (APIs), as described in Table 7-14. This will allow you to take advantage of multiple market vendors who might have open-standard offerings. More importantly, should an open standard go out of favor it is more likely that a migration path will become available. In essence, an open standards-based knowledge-enabled customer relationship management system can prevent systems drag by keeping pace with e-business as it evolves.

To delve deeper than the explanatory intent of this section, I highly recommend reading David Linthicum's *Enterprise Application Integration* (Addison-Wesley, 1999), which offers an excellent treatment of hands-on data-, application-, and enterprise-level middleware-based integration.

Channel Integration

In traditional businesses as well as e-businesses, several channels of communication connect a company to its customers and partners. In customer relationship management, these channels—Web browsers (HTML, ASP, etc.), voice (telephones, call cen-

Table 7-14 Open Standards and Protocols that Improve the System's Adaptability.

Protocol	Description
LDAP	Lightweight Directory Access Protocol is a format to store contact and network resource information, register Web clients and application servers, and store certificates in a directory.
PPTP	Point-to-Point Tunneling Protocol permits network protocols to be encrypted inside the Internet TCP/IP protocol so that proprietary protocol networks can communicate over the Internet. This is what allows businesses to have Internet-based global networks without having to pay for them.
S/MIME	Secure MIME is a standard that lets users send secure e-mail messages by using certificate-based encryption and authentication.
vCARD	Virtual Card is a format for storing and presenting contact or registration information.
SMTP POP	Electronic mail protocols. Simple Mail Transfer Protocol and Post office Protocol
MP3	Audio streaming support for digitized audio content.
RealAudio H.323 H.324	Video conferencing protocols.
Signed Objects	Format for automating trusted software and document distribution.

ters, interactive voice response systems, and VoIP interfaces), wireless hand-held devices (such as WAP protocol enabled cellular phones), hand-held computing platforms such as PalmPilots, direct contact (brick-and-mortar stores and mail), and WebTV interfaces—are described as customer *touchpoints*. As illustrated in Figure 7-15, customers can often choose which channel to use and when to use it.

The relatively minor technological issue is to seamlessly integrate various computing platforms such as Macs, Windows PCs, Unix workstations, WAP devices, and PalmOS handheld computers. The more significant issue is the logical integration across all channels at all touchpoints and across functional units. Responses like "But I don't have access to your information," and "The system will not let me do that for you" are commonly encountered in stores, banks, and other businesses. Such responses are often indicative of poor channel integration and organizational management, and rarely acceptable in e-business environments. A specific customer's history, information, and interpreted knowledge must be integratively accessible across all business processes including pre- and postsale contacts, ordering, delivery, support, problem solving and

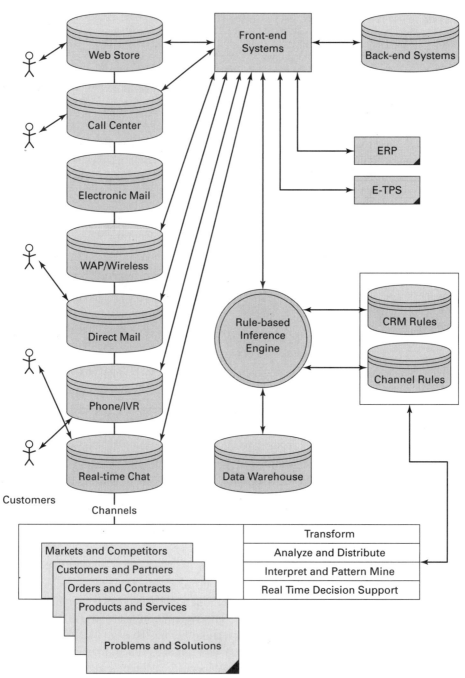

Figure 7-15
Multi-channel information and knowledge integration is a necessity in all businesses.

complaint resolution, and any other interactions. This knowledge must be updated and made available in real time—a challenge that is best addressed by enabling technology. Furthermore, based on this knowledge of the customer, the system must help the business decide on the most appropriate channel for contacting the customer in a given context at any time. An e-mail from an online broker advising a customer to immediately sell his stock following a 70 percent drop is worthless if the customer is not online. That information is perhaps best delivered through a WAP-enabled telephone or beeper.

AMERICAN AIRLINES' DOT-COM APPROACH TO FLYER LOYALTY

American Airlines' approach to customer knowledge management focuses on integrating information about its 11 million loyal customers (and 24 million infrequent flyers) across all touchpoints—Web, phone, in person—and across all functions—reservations, customer service, marketing, baggage check-in counters through flight gates. The system's objective is to be more than just informative. If a customer meets American's profile for its Admiral's Club membership and is not a member, the relationship management system intuitively identifies that customer and suggests viable incentives that can be offered to the customer to join the club. When a customer goes online (www.aa.com), American's Web systems recognize the customer and offer added bonuses such as extra frequent flyer miles, discounts, and upgrades based on the customer's history. If the customer is not recognized, different incentives are offered automatically to persuade the customer to join.

American introduced its customer e-mail program several years back, offering discounts, last-minute bargains, and packaged tours to subscribers. Wireless alerts about changes in flight schedules and delays are delivered over cell phones and PDAs. American is not alone, with Delta (www.delta-air.com), Airtran (www.airtran.com), Alaska Airlines (www.alaskaair.com) doing exactly the same thing. Technology can add value for a temporary time frame, but is soon copied. Differentiation must therefore rely on building in-depth customer knowledge and forging loyal relationships.

KCRM must extend beyond the Web, and it must address the customer's needs—in ways that create lock-in, increase levels of dependence, and raise switching costs. In addition, the channels must include business partners and ally firms. The need for integrating all channels and making channel-specific decisions regarding each customer based on her historical-contact knowledge must therefore be kept in view while designing the KCRM infrastructure.

LONG-TERM CONSIDERATIONS . . . .

Two decisions have long-term impacts on KCRM strategy: (1) the decision to build or buy the technology and (2) the level of future-proofing and adaptability that are incorporated, beginning with the initial implementation stages.

To Build or to Buy

Implementing a new system of the scope of a KCRM system is often constrained by time, money, and resources. Often, a choice needs to be made whether to build or buy the system. The choice between buying and building the system is rarely black and white. If built, it is rarely done from scratch, as many components of the system are bought prebuilt and integrated to assemble the system. If purchased off the shelf, some degree of customization and adaptation are always required. So deploying a system can be considered along the build-buy continuum and characterized as the one it is closer to. When you begin development, your choices are usually limited to one of the following:

- Build the system in-house, often involving internal IT staff and end-users, and maybe bring a consultant with specialized expertise on-board.
- Buy an off-the-shelf solution and customize it internally or with the help of a systems integration consultant.
- Buy in part and build in part.

Each choice comes with its own set of problems and strengths as described in Table 7-15. Often, the best choice is to take the middle ground, build in part and buy in part.

The final choice will be influenced by four factors:

1. Time, money, and resources that are available.
2. System's potential to create an immediately inimitable advantage for your business.
3. Dynamicity of your market and the breadth of your window of opportunity.
4. Scope and level of complexity that the system's deployment entails.

These choices are mapped in the matrix in Figure 7-16. Time constraints are represented on one side of the matrix. *No time* indicates that the system must be deployed in a short time frame and *more time* indicates that time is not a decisive issue. In most

Table 7-15 A Comparison of Build versus Buy Approaches to System Implementation

Option	Build	Build and Buy	Buy
Up-front costs	High	Medium to low	Low
Time	High	Medium	Low
Flexibility	High	High	None
Customizability	High	Medium	Low to medium
Integration ease	High	Medium	Varies
Comments	Quality may vary with available skills	Usually the best compromise for fast-paced yet highly customized projects	Installation and configuration time

e-business projects, time *is* an issue. Implementing a perfect system on a closed window of opportunity will produce no results; so a far-from-perfect solution that is implemented rapidly is of essence. Correspondingly, choices in e-business-focused KCRM projects tend to lie within the upper two quadrants. Map your business' situation to one of the quadrants to determine whether a building- or buying-side bias fits better with your own company's case.

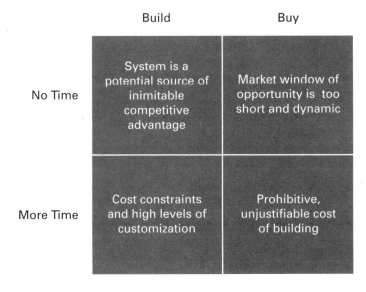

Build   Buy

	Build	Buy
No Time	System is a potential source of inimitable competitive advantage	Market window of opportunity is too short and dynamic
More Time	Cost constraints and high levels of customization	Prohibitive, unjustifiable cost of building

Figure 7-16
The build-buy selection matrix.

Should you decide to buy the system rather than build it, consider the following set of questions while short-listing prospective solutions:

1. Does the system offer a comprehensive set of features to support Internet commerce and e-business?

2. Are customers, partners, and resellers well integrated?

3. Is customer information from multiple channels consolidated?

4. Is the system interoperable with existing systems? If not, what additional costs will be incurred in ensuring interoperability?

5. Is the system scalable?

Future-Proofing

Future-proofing the design of a knowledge-enabled customer relationship management or customer knowledge management system refers to its flexibility for future adaptation. Eight strategic choices (see Table 7-16) can make the KCRM system more robust, adaptable, and flexible for unpredictable and unanticipated market changes.

SUMMARY . . . .

At any given moment, you cannot bring to mind all that your organization knows about any given customer or partner. KCRM technology attempts to help overcome that limitation. The following points are germane to the blueprinting step of the KCRM system's design:

- *KCRM technology must be experience centric.* The objective is not one of boosting throughput and efficiency but that of enhancing the customer experience that leads to increased customer retention and loyalty. Interaction consistency, meeting and exceeding customer expectations, a balance between personal contact and automated efficiency, and future adaptability must therefore be considered.

- *KCRM is not limited to individual customers.* It encompasses suppliers, partners, and even competitors that the system must help acquire, retain, enhance, and maximize their relationships with.

- *Technology broadens reach.* Technology's role in building KCRM systems is that of broadening reach, enhancing the speed of knowledge transfer and real-time knowledge application, enabling informed decision making, mapping sources of tacit knowledge, communicating and integrating

Table 7-16 Considerations for Future-Proofing the KCRM System

Strategy	Approach
Open standards	What might be state of art today might be outdated long before you recoup your investment. Internet-based systems inherently have a high degree of modularity, extensibility, and compatibility (content might be distributed across multiple platforms, devices, servers, and locations); unlike proprietary standards, they will not leave you in a lurch if one vendor goes out of business.
Mission-focused design	Technology design must be driven by business objectives, problems, and opportunities.
Results-driven	Use a results-driven incremental deployment process to build the system in a modular fashion. This will permit future expandability and component swapping, and reduce project risk.
User involvement	Users do not exist in vacuum but in relatively stable communities. Make sure to involve them in the initial design and prototyping stages so that a sense of ownership is nurtured.
Intuitive	Make the system intuitive to use. Tips in Patrick Lynch and Sarah Horton's excellent book, *Web Style Guide: Basic Design Principles for Creating Web Sites* (Yale University Press, 1999) perhaps defeat your $600-an-hour consultant.
Integration	Integrate old legacy systems if they contain valuable customer data.
Optimization	Balance performance, scalability, and flexibility. Remember that transaction-processing delays will amplify by orders of magnitude as you begin to scale the system upward.
Pragmatism	Avoid the philosopher's trap of building an all-encompassing knowledge management infrastructure. Instead, use clear models of limited scope to focus on enabling specific objectives, customer processes, actions, and results. The initial focus should be on building or implementing solutions that facilitate finding, summarizing, interpreting, and analyzing large volumes of customer information efficiently and effectively.

diverse channels and touchpoints, and facilitating collaborative success. Interoperability and leverage of existing systems are a crucial necessity. The system itself must not be confused with intranets, extranets, data stores, or groupware.

- *Informal communications must be facilitated.* Web collaboration tools, multimedia, pointers, e-communities, Voice-over-IP, and intelligent routing exemplify some mechanisms that facilitate informal associations in Web-centric environments.

- *Business intelligence tools must be applied selectively.* Flexibility, expert dependence, processing overhead, ability to deal with complex problems, accuracy, speed, tolerance for dirty data, and response time must be considered when making a choice about a business intelligence tool. Several tools such as artificial intelligence subsystems, intelligent data warehouses, genetic algorithm tools, neural networks, expert systems, case-based reasoning applications, rule bases, and intelligent agents can be combined to endow the customer knowledge management system with business intelligence capabilities.

- *You cannot use what you cannot find.* Powerful search and retrieval mechanisms facilitate tracing and retrieval of valuable, actionable codified customer knowledge as well as codified "people pointers" to tacit knowledge. Various combinations of metasearching, hierarchical, tagged-attribute, combinatorial, and content searching may be used. Attribute tag searching allows searching through tags that define concepts not inherently captured in the content of a knowledge object.

- *User interfaces should meet actual user needs.* Functionality, consistency, relevancy of context, navigability, customizability, and stickiness are key considerations.

- *The system must be future-proofed.* Rapid technological change has brought and will continue to bring new information sources, as well as unpredictable communication, information transfer, and knowledge-sharing services and requirements that accompany them. Open standards, mission-focused design, results-driven design, modular integration, and a pragmatic outlook help build a system that can adapt to unpredictable future needs.

In the next chapter, we examine the process of actually developing and deploying the system in a results-driven manner—the fifth step on the roadmap.

TEST YOUR UNDERSTANDING . . . .

1. What is a technology blueprint?

2. What design challenges are involved in creating a KCRM technology blueprint?

3. How can the requirements of a system be compared with customer relationship management objectives during the blueprinting stage?

4. What are the various pieces of the customer knowledge management technology framework?

5. What does predictive anticipation mean? How can this capability be created in e-business settings?

6. What are various long-term design considerations that must be taken into account during the technology design stage? Why do they matter if the system might be obsolete in a few years?

7. Why should you choose to build a system instead of buying it? Under what circumstances would you do the opposite?

8. What characteristics should one expect in a robust collaborative platform that lays the foundation for a KCRM system? Do you think that the Web is suitable for this?

9. How do intranets and extranets differ from e-business customer knowledge management systems?

10. What is the role of informal knowledge networks? Do you think that these can often be more important than databases and traditional collaborative information systems?

8 Results-Driven Development and Deployment

In this chapter...

- Understand what it takes to deploy KCRM systems successfully.

- Understand the role of prototyping and pilot testing.

- Recognize the limitations of traditional big-bang deployment methods.

- Understand how results-driven incrementalism overcomes these problems.

- Create incremental, cumulative business releases.

- Recognize potential pitfalls and avoidance strategies in using RDI.

T he *ruthless execution test,* a rule of thumb attributed to Cisco, suggests that if five people cannot complete an e-business systems implementation project within 90 days, it's too ambitious and must be dropped. Alternatively, it must be broken down into smaller sub-projects until each of them passes the ruthless execution test. Indeed, this reflects the pace of Internet time—a concept of the rate of change that far exceeds the proverbial "dog years" measure that we knew before the emergence of e-business. Even the of best intentions and technological capabilities cannot ensure smooth development and deployment—step five on the roadmap—without a results-driven incremental approach. Traditional approaches that have fared well in stable systems development do not hold up in an e-business environment, because objectives and goals of the final system are a moving target—one that is moved by changing market needs, rapid technological innovation, and unstable outcome expectations. Businesses that assume that a creatively designed customer knowledge management system will be enthusiastically adopted by employees who will learn about its fallacy the hard way.

In this chapter, we identify the shortcomings of systems development methods that have served us well for many years. We see how the waterfall method and traditional old age big-bang methodologies no longer allow building adaptive systems at a ruthless pace and with unfailing accuracy, as today's e-business environment unforgivingly demands . Finally we examine results-driven deployment methods that overcome various shortcomings of traditional methodologies, and see how these are used for deploying knowledge-enabled customer relationship management systems.

HIDDEN COSTS AND OTHER SURPRISES . . . .

Systems development for complex projects such as KCRM systems often begin to resemble an ad hoc undertaking more than something with a clearly defined and followed plan. Technology costs are only a small part of the equation, and nontechnology costs—training, reward systems, integration of business processes—often take up a larger chunk of the development and deployment costs of such complex systems.

Deploying a new system is a learning experience in which the knowledge management team can learn much from users' perceptions about the system, its usability, suitability to task in the users' opinion, level of functionality, etc. Identifying oft-unanticipated changes at this stage can save your company from much grievance, financial loss incurred in pulling the plug on a new system, and lost market potential that might otherwise become visible only once that system is delivered in its final form. It is always safer to field-test a scaled-down version of the system early on in the process and letting a few users find holes in its design and implementation rather than discovering the same after your company has come to critically depend on it. Two good ways of doing this, early-stage prototyping and pilot testing, are described next.

Prototyping

Prototyping is one of the most inexpensive yet underutilized forms of rejection insurance that your development team can buy. Prototyping requires that a team in the middle of developing a system put a working version of their unfinished product or its functional subparts in the hands of future users. For example, if you have a working model of how the interface of your company's CRM system might look, you could run it by field workers in your customer support and sales offices. This allows them to touch, feel, and see the system well before it is actually ready for use to generate comments, suggestions, and feedback that will prove invaluable in the long run. At the same time, by involving these select, key users in the development and deployment process, the likelihood of user buy-in problems or rejection is reduced. Being able to prototype portions of a system requires that your development team be able to concretize rather abstract details from the system's specifications to produce a working model. Choosing the right portions of the system to show to end users is a tricky process that is addressed in further detail later in this chapter.

The Value of Pilot Projects

Pilot testing refers to the idea of implementing a system with almost full functionality, but only in a small portion of the actual organizational units and offices that it is planned for. You might pilot-test a new system in a single small office of your company. This must be done before a full-blown version is implemented across the enterprise. For example, in an electronic commerce retail business, customer service representatives could provide you feedback on the usability or comprehensiveness of customer detail presented on one screen that is activated once a customer calls your company's 800 support line. They might feel that requiring managerial authorization for an online price-match request creates a bottleneck in the process and causes many customers to lose patience and hang up—a relatively simple problem to fix that can otherwise cause increased levels of customer dissatisfaction. Knowing such problems ahead of time can provide your development team a sufficient time buffer to fix the problem *before* the system is rolled out across the enterprise. Feedback such as this is impossible to get without actually putting the system in its final users' hands.

Chunking and Prototyping for Pilot Projects

Chunks refer to a set of technology modules that fit together and can be implemented together as a single whole. Chunks are a good way of conceptualizing how and when feedback from pilot-stage users can be incorporated. It is impossible to logistically or financially justify making individual changes based on each user's comments. These suggestions, gripes, and modification suggestions collected from users must be aggregated and implemented in chunks such that change implemented within such a chunk is large enough to enable potential users to accomplish a task in a *measurably* improved way.

Pilot testing and prototyping are not mutually exclusive approaches to predeployment testing. On the contrary, they often follow a sequential order wherein each project chunk is implemented in the form of a prototype and then deployed in a pilot setting as described in Figure 8-1.

Pilot testing helps reveal significant—and often fundamental—design flaws early in the deployment process. When problems are identified at that early stage, it is still possible to rework the system's design to meet users' actual needs without any significant investment of time and resources.

Choosing a Pilot Project

As a first step toward choosing the right pilot, find a tightly scheduled project that the team agrees (user mandate coupled with managerial mandate) will have a significant potential impact. Nevertheless, be careful not to force the technology on a stream of work that constitutes the lifeblood of your business. Follow these tips for evaluating the viability of potential pilot projects:

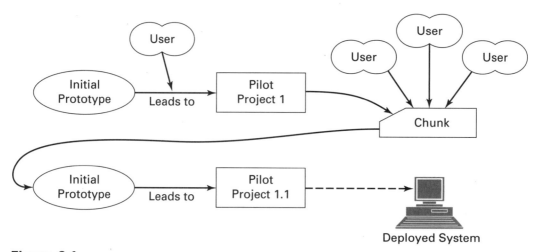

Figure 8-1
Prototyping and pilot projects must be combined in a repetitive sequence to generate pre-deployment feedback from future users.

1. Avoid trivial projects.

2. Favor projects with widespread visibility and noticeable effects (such as customer retention).

3. Select a process-intensive project that can be highly impacted by the use of a knowledge management system.

4. Select a project that will last long enough to build necessary synergy within the team and the user community.

5. Set tangible deadlines and metrics for determining success.

6. Stay away from your company's lifeblood.

The hazard of implementing and experimenting with such a pilot is that its success can lead to rapid proliferation of independent, disconnected "mini-KCRM" systems. This can rapidly lead to the proliferation of small, independent, and specialized knowledge management systems that can rapidly create disconnected silos of knowledge—which bring us back to square one.

AN OVERVIEW OF BIG-BANG SYSTEMS DEVELOPMENT METHODS . . . .

The waterfall method, named so for the semblance of its shape—and the direction that it will take your KCRM project—is one of the earliest and perennially popular approaches to systems development. This method depicts the natural order of events that occur in the process, and is a useful tool for gaining a conceptual understanding of systems development. All big-bang application deployment methods are variants of the waterfall method; they assume that requirements between analysis and deployment phases remain relatively stable and that the system can be delivered in one large chunk at the end of the process. This method consists of a series of sequential steps as illustrated in Figure 8-2.

Tech Talk

Waterfall Method: Structured approach to systems development that consists of sequential phases beginning with requirements analysis and ending with implementation and evaluation. This approach was popularized by Ed Yourdon in the 1980s and has been the most widely followed method for several decades since.

The horizontal spacing between the steps implies that any stage can be begun only after the preceding stage has been completed. This model involves verification; that is, checking that the product of any stage is a faithful translation of its specifica-

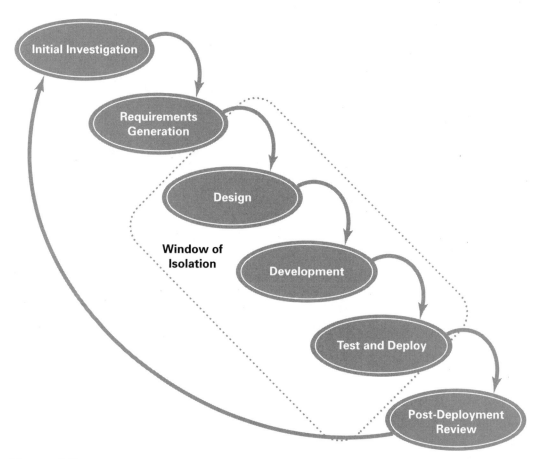

Figure 8-2
The waterfall method consists of a series of sequential steps.

tion—the product of the previous stage. If an error occurs in this translation of require-ments into features of the system, it is carried over to the next stage. In this manner, if such errors are not caught at any given stage, they propagate until the last stage. Therefore, there is a window of isolation between users and developers of the systems as shown in Figure 8-2. This is an extended time frame between which users tell sys-tem developers what they want from their system, and then do not see them again until the review stage is reached. Aha! There lies the catch: Requirements of electronic commerce systems, customer relationship management tools, and knowledge man-agement infrastructure change so fast that by the time developers managed to make their way through the first couple of stages, the requirements, expectations, and needs from their system might be very different from what they are working on delivering.

The requirements determination phase is the point within the waterfall methodology where many projects start out on the wrong foot. The waterfall method allows little scope for the last phase, the postdeployment review, which was later added to the original model. In addition, as end users often express opinions or preferences much later in the process, not all requirements are captured in the initial phases. Without stable requirements, sequential development activities deliver unsatisfactory results. The waterfall method does not let intended users try or see the target system well until it's ready; by then, it is often too dated, mismatched with their actual needs, and too well defined to be altered inexpensively.

For this reason, despite having remained the mainstay development model for many years, this method has started to fall out of favor. For critical projects like developing a knowledge management system and CRM support infrastructure, this method should not be the first choice.

The V Method

An alternative model that emerged from the waterfall method was the V model. This model allows for verification of each step in the development process. As illustrated in Figure 8-3, these steps are represented on the left-hand side of the V, beginning at the top. To the right are various stages corresponding to these systems development steps. For most purposes, the V model is principally the same as the waterfall model but reveals more levels of detail. Further, the steps described in this model need not apply to the entire project; they might be applied to any single part of the project.

Tech Talk

V Method: More detail-oriented variant of the Waterfall method.

For reasons very similar to the near demise of the waterfall method, the V method is also unsuited for developing knowledge management-oriented systems, including KCRM systems and e-business technology architectures.

Incremental Development

Derivatives of the waterfall method such as the V model not only allow but also encourage implementers to focus on technology itself rather than on the changes needed at the level of your company to actually derive *business value* from the new functionality that the system provides. If the feedback and learning loop is incorporated into this model and the project is broken down into discrete phases that build upon each other, it gives us the incremental approach model as shown in Figure 8-4.

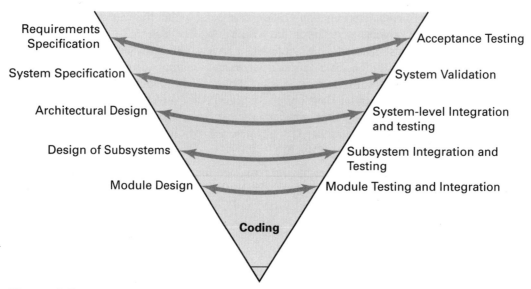

Figure 8-3
The V model represents the waterfall method in more detail.

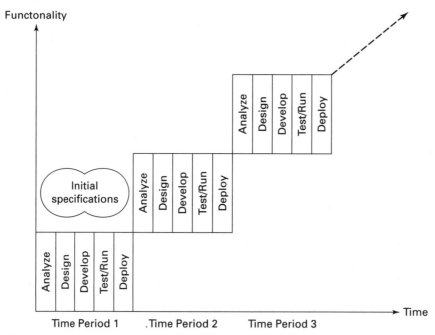

Figure 8-4
The incremental systems development method.

The incremental approach to systems development and deployment assumes that functions required of a system, such as a knowledge management system, cannot be known completely in the initial stages. This approach suggests that developers implement a part of the system and then increment it rapidly as new requirements surface. This way, the entire system can be implemented in increments, and changes can be incorporated over the course of development.

However, for their lack of flexibility and their relative inability to track complex relationships, this method provides little support for managing a relatively complex project like a knowledge management system. Alternatives that go beyond the limitations of the waterfall method are described next.

LOOKING BEYOND THE WATERFALL . . . .

Several methods for systems development gained prominence after the waterfall method. In this section, we take a closer look at their viability for KCRM development and deployment.

The Matrix Model

The matrix model is one of the earliest variants of the waterfall model that attempted to overcome some of its limitations. A matrix is used to diagrammatically represent various stages of the system lifecycle that are of interest at the time of using the model for the development project. The rows of this matrix (as shown in Figure 8-5) may or may not correspond to those of the waterfall model depending on whether the project is a development project (versus a maintenance or integration project).

Tech Talk

Matrix Model: Diagrammatic representation of various stages of the system lifecycle that are of interest *at the time* of using the model for the development project.

The columns of the matrix represent activities. When more detail is required, these activities can be defined in a more granular manner. The cell bodies of the matrix can be used for recording data related to these activities such as time spent on them, time periods during which they are carried out, and their relationships with other projects. The matrix therefore creates a simple repository for storing project data that can be used to guide further projects. Each such matrix could be used for smaller modules or "releases" within the larger project.

	Initial Investigation	Requirements	Design	Development	Testing and Deployment	Review
Initial Investigation						
Requirements						
Design						
Development						
Testing and Deployment						
Review						

Figure 8-5
The matrix method.

Information Packaging Methodology

Another alternative approach for developing the system is the learning loop (also known as the spiral model) approach to systems deployment. The key idea underlying this approach is that complex systems development can be broken down into four key phases as illustrated in Figure 8-6:

1. Business process design (BPD)
2. Functional design (FuD)
3. Interface prototype design (IPD)
4. Application prototype design (APD)

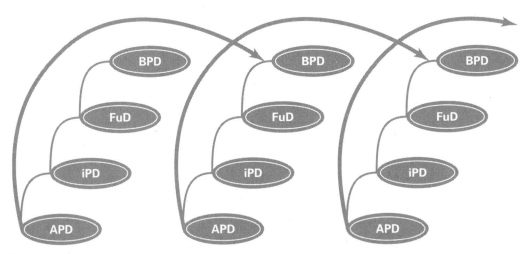

Figure 8-6
The spiral model-based approach for complex systems development.

Tech Talk

Information Packaging Methodology: Systems development approach that breaks down the process into four phases: (1) business process, (2) functional, (3) interface prototype, and (4) application prototype design.

These phases are repeated in a spiral-like manner to go through various stages of the system's development. As the process progresses through various iterations of these stage sets, knowledge of the project gained from each stage can be applied to the next one and so forth, hence the phrase *learning loop*.

The most common variant based on the spiral learning loop approach is the information packaging methodology (IPM). The basic processes involved in this approach are described in Figure 8-7. There are four key stages in this approach:

1. *Architecture-level system planning architecture and system planning*: Key knowledge and CRM problems that the system must address are listed, long- and short-term payoffs, stakeholders and user groups affected, strategic objectives of building the system are identified followed by a preliminary set of critical success factors and measures, financial, time, and resource constraints.

2. *Design and analysis*: Goals, alternatives, and associated risks are analyzed followed by a consensual definition of target users groups (e.g., customer service staff), an initial set of features that are needed, and a preliminary set of specifications to deliver those features.

3. *Technology implementation*: A detailed set of components is specified, built, and tested based on preceding conceptual design and analysis—both independently and together. A pilot project is selected, preliminary user feedback is incorporated, and the system is scaled up to an enterprise level.

4. *Deployment and metrics*: Users are trained to use the system, cultural issues are (rarely) addressed, and the system is formally deployed.

The distinguishing factor of this approach is the incorporation of softer issues such as change management, strategic alignment, cultural adjustments, and user training. Strategic alignment is the focal connection between the first and last stages of this method. Improvements that are made to the system itself follow the four-stage cycle, and are implemented in chunks rather than as discrete features, as described earlier. Unfortunately, this method cannot be easily scaled or feasibly deployed for developing systems of the level of complexity as are of interest to us in this context.

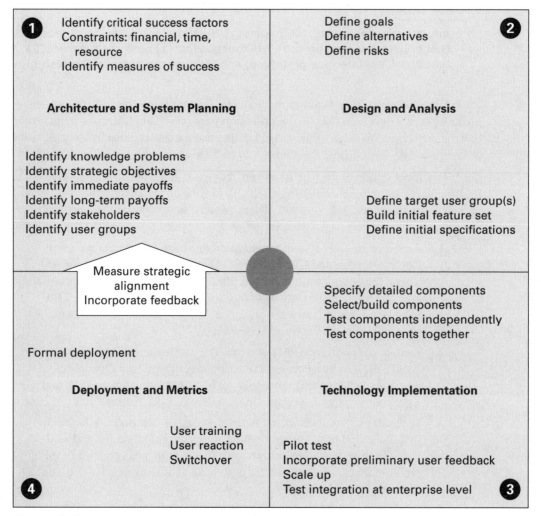

Figure 8-7
Four key stages of the information packaging methodology.

Beyond the Big Bang

Customer knowledge management strategy implementation is a complex process that is sometimes evolutionary, sometimes revolutionary. Changes in needs and requirements emerge as the system is being developed—changes that traditional development methods do not accomodate. In complex software systems, divisibility into independent modules is often the norm. As such projects tend to be rather expensive undertakings, knowing in advance whether it will deliver desired results is not only beneficial but also necessary for maintaining a stream of funding from your company's management. These are precisely the reasons why the big-bang methods—those that deliver the final system in a single, final step—of development and deployment do not live up to the needs of such projects.

The fatality of the big-bang methods comes from their implicit belief that delivery equals implementation. Contrary to the notion of developing the system in its entirety and implementing everything at once, KCRM deployment requires an incremental approach—one that incorporates feedback and learning from each development stage into the next one. Unlike software and ERP systems of the past, you cannot build a system with rigid assumptions about your company's structure, processes, and norms. Furthermore, if any of the preceding big-bang delivery methods is used, benefits of the system are not realized well until the system has been fully developed and implemented. Figure 8-8 illustrates this.

Various project milestones are indicated by successive stages. As development progresses through various stages, and as money is spent on the project, no benefits are realized until the development process is completed. The assumption behind the lengthy period of disconnected development effort is that it will end with the delivery of working product that will meet the needs of its users *at the time of delivery*. The system begins to give any projected benefits only after the big-bang delivery point is reached and the system goes live. Another problem inherent with this approach is that each stage builds on the preceding one, and if something goes wrong in, say, the second stage, work on the following stages will be built on a faulty foundation. By that

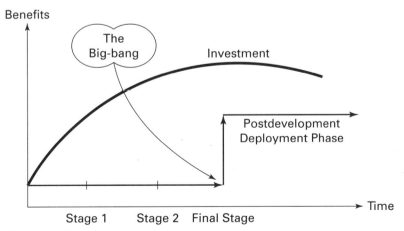

Figure 8-8
The big-bang approach delays benefits till the very end of the development process.

time, the system has aleady been developed and is often so rigid that changes can be very expensive, if even possible. If a new or changed need could have been incorporated in an early stage to keep the final system focused on users' *current* needs, the traditional model does not allow that.

RESULTS DRIVEN INCREMENTALISM . . . .

Results-driven incrementalism (RDI) is the single most promising method for development and deployment of a KCRM system, and one that overcomes the limitations posed by the deployment strategies discussed earlier. Using this method, the KCRM project is broken up into a series of short, fast-paced development cycles coupled with intensive implementation cycles, each of which delivers a *measurable* business benefit. There are several advantages of this approach:

- Expected business benefits of the KCRM system are realized much sooner than possible with the traditional big-bang approach—that is, as each discrete stage (also known as a *business release*) is completed (see the gray area under the curve in Figure 8-9) rather than cumulatively at the final delivery stage.
- Tangible benefits can be realized at a faster pace.
- Overall benefits gained over the lifetime of the project increase.
- The likelihood of completing the project on track and on time is increased.
- Points of failure are rectified right after each stage; it is therefore more likely that the project will *actually* be completed.
- Implementation time for the project can be drastically reduced.
- Investments are in smaller justifiable chunks rather than a singular larger amount.

Key Ideas Behind RDI

The RDI method links the KCRM system development team, CRM staff and end users throughout the project lifecycle. Five key ideas underlie results-driven incremental deployment:

1. *Incremental but independent results*. Deployment is segmented into a series of nonoverlapping increments, each of which delivers measurable business benefits and process improvements. Independence

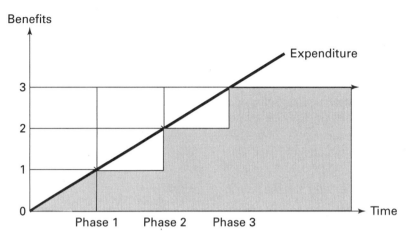

Figure 8-9
Benefits of each business release are visible immediately after it is completed.

implies that these benefits remain even if no further stages are implemented or if the project is killed at any given stage.

2. *Objective and results driven.* Targeted results and projected outcomes —that is, the "whys" and "whats"—are clearly defined before each stage of deployment. Results from each stage drive the following stages.

3. *Technical and organizational measures for each increment are clearly defined upfront.* Each increment of business release includes everything needed to product the target results. Both software functionality and necessary changes in policies, metrics, and work processes needed to derive business benefits from that functionality are included in the plan. Rewards that motivate end users to intcgratc that addcd functionality into their regular work processes are also included in each increment.

4. *Intensive, "bursty" implementation.* Implementation of the KCRM system is planned in short, intensive bursts rather than as a continuous, long-winded process. Typically, each incremental feature is allocated a deployment schedule ranging from two weeks to a maximum of three months. If a longer time frame is needed, the increment should be broken down further.

5. *Result-driven follow-ups.* Results of each increment form the basis for adjusting, modifying, and tuning subsequent increments.

Business Releases

Increments within an RDI deployment are called its business releases. Each release constitutes new software-based functionality and accompanying organizational measures to make that functionality deliver business benefits. The performance of each release is judged against selected *key performance indicators* (KPIs), which guide the next release. Business releases are short and do not overlap. The goal is to provide isolated, independent, and cumulative episodes of functionality and learning. Each business release should address at least the following questions:

- What is the targeted business result?
- What is the *exact* software functionality required to achieve these results?
- How will the results be measured?
- What complementary changes are needed in terms of:
  - Policies
  - Measures and metrics
  - Structure
  - Employee incentives
  - Procedures

Table 8-1 illustrates a sample business release for a portion of a KCRM implementation in a computer manufacturer's service and support department.

Metrics in such business releases can be subjective, especially when coming up with quantitative measures of success is difficult. In any case, whatever metrics are chosen, they should clearly articulate the basis for defining success and avoid creating a perfection of failure when a release has in fact successfully delivered expected business benefits.

Sequencing Business Releases

The ideal sequence of releases for deploying a KCRM system should maximize immediate business benefits. Three considerations guide their selection and ordering:

1. *Success expectations*: Because sustained management support and continued project funding partly depend on the "bang for the buck" that your project can demonstrate, select releases that have a high likelihood of success.

2. *Highest payoffs first:* Rank each release in terms of expected payoffs, and sequence those with the highest payoff expectations first and those with marginal payoffs toward the end.

Table 8-1 *A Sample Business Release*

Incremental Business Release #37	Details
Business release number	2001-37
Start date	10-22-2001
Due date	10-30-2001
Release manager	Smiley Norman
Target business result	Improve integration between in-warranty customer parts replacement requisition in Miami, Florida, and shipment center in Dublin, Ireland.
Software functionality	Integration of customer data between the customer case database in Florida and Dublin. An intranet front end should generate pages that combine data across the two distributed databases so that customer service representatives (CSRs) have access to all information related to a particular customer incident independent of where the problem was reported and recorded. The link must be secured and implemented using a VPN. Export restrictions for secure server link software from the United States no longer apply.
Preliminary metrics and success measures	Availability of all customer reports in both locations.
	Reduction in customer frustration because of having to explain background problems or "the sob story" with the defective unit every time he/she calls up the warranty support line.
Policy changes	Incorporate the following into partner appraisals:
	Use of the new system to access information
	Follow-up by corporate relations to assess customer satisfaction with CSR
	Reduction in coordination problems
	Reduction in long-distance expenses on the Miami-Dublin line
Accessibility	Not applicable
Other measures and notes	Increase in customer complaints due to CSR's inability to give them accurate responses to replacement order fulfillment noted between July and September.

3. *Cumulative results:* Begin with releases that have the most cumulative impact on the rest of the project. This way, learning and deployment can be divided into discrete, manageable, and meaningful chunks.

The above considerations need to be balanced because they have a tendency to pull the project sequence in opposing directions. Releases with highest payoffs might not be cumulative, and releases that are most cumulative might not have high chances of tangible success. Therefore, sequencing business releases necessitates striking a balance between these three criteria.

Process Divisibility and Release Decomposability

If KCRM business releases are used to break up the development and deployment process properly, accumulated business benefits will be retained even if subsequent releases are not implemented. Process divisibility can be approached from two perspectives, as illustrated in Figure 8-10.

1. *Narrow and deep*: The KCRM project is broken up into independently functional, incremental pieces. Each piece is implemented in the deepest level of detail within the same implementation round. This is illustrated by the vertical circled segments in Figure 8-10.
2. *Shallow and broad*: Successive increments involve the same software modules of the KCRM system, but in increasingly deeper levels of detail. This is illustrated by the horizontal circled segments in Figure 8-10.

The first approach is better suited for KCRM implementation because it does not leave the deployment team with the often-abused excuse that business benefits of the technology could not be realized because the implementation process was not completed. Note that the modules in Figure 8-10 not only represent the technology components but also the organizational components associated with that technology functionality.

Potential Pitfalls and Traps

Results-driven incrementalism is not immune to pitfalls in its execution stages. These traps can be avoided by keeping three points in consideration throughout the development and deployment process:

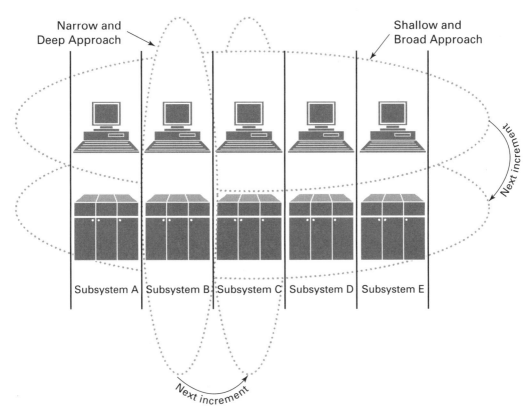

Figure 8-10
Two approaches to process divisibility using the RDI method.

1. *Avoid over engineering*: Do not attempt to implement system functionality that may never be used or is unnecessary for deriving desired business results. Maintain focus throughout the deployment process and maintain momentum by keeping only necessary functionality on the development schedule. This will also reduce risk and the potential for unexpected failure.

2. *Develop clear communication processes:* Explain your KCRM development team's expectations from end users who are involved, and involve them in decision making to ensure that there is buy-in from the user group. The same also holds true for management involvement.

3. *Address human issues:* A KCRM will be used only if your customer relationship management frontline workers and managers have any incentive for doing so. This necessitates addressing human issues, cultural change, reward systems, and clear-cut linkages between their compensation to the customer retention and management goals of your company.

SUMMARY . . . .

KCRM systems can be hefty investments. Seven key points discussed in this chapter should be kept in mind during the deployment phase:

- *Deployment must encompass technology and nontechnology issues.* Training, reward systems, and integration of business processes and systems must be explicitly considered during the deployment phase.

- *Decomposability facilitates modularity.* Complex systems must be decomposed into chunks—technology modules that fit together and can be implemented together as a single whole—to allow results-driven systems that solve current, not past problems.

- *Prototyping provides inexpensive rejection insurance.* Prototyping requires that a team developing a system put working version of their unfinished product or its functional subparts in the hands of future users. In the case of KCRM systems, this user population might include internal staff, external partners, and occasionally, customers.

- *The waterfall method family is a no-go.* These big-bang delivery methods worked well in more stable business environments but inhibit the stable translation of requirements into system features. They also encourage implementers to focus on technology itself rather than on the business-level changes required to actually derive business value from the new system. Variants such as the V method, the matrix model, and information packaging methodology also suffer from similar weaknesses.

- *Results-driven incrementalism overcomes these problems.* RDI helps build incremental but cumulative results through system-level chunking in the form of business releases, reduces risks of failure, and simultaneously addresses organizational and technical deployment issues that are measured by key performance indicators.

- *RDI is well suited to e-businesses.* Intensive, bursty, and rapid deployment of the system with built-in reality checks at each stage (release) reduce the logistical complexity in building such systems.

- *Avoid common pitfalls.* Overengineering, poor communications and coordination processes, lack of cumulative characteristics, relegated releases with the highest potential payoffs, and ignored human issues are commonly observed problems in the deployment phase.

Iterative perfection, not perfection from the start, should be the focus of deployment. Results-driven deployment reduces time-to-market and allows businesses to begin reaping limited benefits even before the entire system is deployed.

TEST YOUR UNDERSTANDING . . . .

1. What is the role of pilot testing in building complex systems?

2. What problems does prototyping solve?

3. What are some of the traditional big-bang methods for software deployment? What problems do they face when applied to e-business, knowledge management, and KCRM problems?

4. What is results-driven incrementalism and how does it differ from other popular alternatives?

5. What are business releases? How must they be structured?

6. Can you relate some of the pitfalls that we discussed to Web-focused projects that you might be aware of?

7. What is the *ruthless execution test*? Even though it's more of a rule of thumb than a test, what does it convey about the differences between traditional IT projects and e-business projects?

8. Why is the *Innovator's Dilemma* (Chapter 4) excellently evidenced by systems development approaches and their outcomes?

9. What hidden costs do businesses run the risk of discovering much later in the implementation process?

10. What is the role of clear interpersonal communications processes in KCRM systems deployment? Can you think of any nontechincal or technical project that you might have been involved in, and hated the experience because of politics and poor communications?

9

Leadership, Change Management, and Corporate Culture

In this chapter...

- Understand the role of corporate culture and leadership.

- Understand championing roles and goals.

- Understand what makes for a good customer relationship visionary.

- See how you can transform your organization's fear-based culture to a knowledge-sharing culture.

- Determine the process of cultural transition to support KCRM.

- Reconfigure reward structures to encourage knowledge sharing and relationship building.

- Understand the key elements of change management.

Technology is neither our enemy, friend, nor savior. The value of KCRM technology—like any other—is determined by the degree to which it can be profitably absorbed into your business and its culture, norms, and practices. Success of your KCRM system and associated strategy therefore depends as much on these softer issues as it does on harder technology issues, as illustrated in Figure 9-1. Akin to what I described in Chapter 3, a people, process, culture, and technology combination defines the initiative's fate.

Fear for their job security is a single dominant inhibitor that can keep employees from sharing their knowledge and expertise with other colleagues. Reward structures in most companies are set up to work in ways that reward employees for keeping their knowledge to themselves, not sharing it. Knowledge workers are not like mass-production-age troops, but are like volunteers who will share their knowledge and insights *if and only if* they are motivated to do so.

Successfully implementing KCRM solutions requires fundamental readjustment of corporate culture, strong leadership, and financial and nonfinancial reward structures that together gain the hearts and minds of employees and *motivate* them to share knowledge. Besides technology infrastructure, you need to minimize political divisions among your managers and employees, cultivate a corporate culture that encourages use and dependence on customer relationship management methods and enabling technology, and provide economic incentives for that to happen. Economic factors are indeed not limited to incentives that your business has for going the CRM route. In the following sections, we will see how these nontechnology factors can be taken into account and aligned with your KCRM strategy.

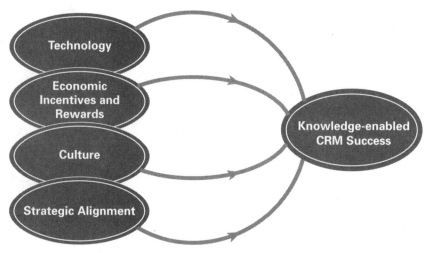

Figure 9-1
Drivers of KCRM success.

LEADERSHIP . . . .

Until this point, we have focused on KCRM strategies and supporting technology infrastructure. However, for people-intensive processes such as knowledge management and CRM to succeed, a champion, a zealot, and a capable leader is needed. Strong leadership and a complementary corporate culture are what it takes to succeed *after* a well-executed KCRM strategy and technology have been put in place. Therefore, we begin by examining leadership issues, development of knowledge activists, choice of the so-called *customer relationship visionary (CRV)*. To begin, let us look at how the average knowledge-focused manager compares with the typical manager on five personal traits. Table 9-1 describes differences typically encountered among managers who are successful in their respective roles.

Table 9-1 How a Typical Traditional Manager Compares with a Knowledge-Focused One

Manager	Emotionality	Extroversion	Openness	Agreeable	Committed
Traditional	3	3	3	3	3
Knowledge	2.3	3.6	4.2	2.9	3.3

Based on data from D. Duffy, "Knowledge Champions: What Does It Take to Be a Successful CKO?" *CIO Enterprise*, November 15, 1998, 66-71, and E. Scott, What Is a Chief Knowledge Officer? *Sloan Management Review*, Winter (1999), 29-38.

The table shows some interesting differences. Although knowledge-focused managers are more extroverted, open, and committed than your typical manager, they are also less agreeable and comparatively unemotional. Note that in many organizations the role of a customer relationship visionary is played by the CEO, in some by a CIO, and in some by the now infamous chief knowledge officer (CKO). Unlike the CIO who handles corporate leadership areas such as IT strategy, development of systems, connectivity, IT support, and general IT management—jobs that do not always demand entrepreneurial orientations—the CRV must be entreprenurially oriented to be successful.

Leadership Roles and Goals

A common weakness in knowledge-enabled customer relationship management programs is that the information technology component is often overemphasized at the expense of well-articulated knowledge management and relationship-building responsibilities. The CRV, whether officially or unofficially appointed, must have the following seven priorities on her agenda:

1. *Championing:* Actively promoting the KCRM, its adoption, and use.

2. *Educating users and management:* Management needs to be convinced that KCRM will have a financial payback and will not turn into a financial black hole; employees need to be convinced that it will not be yet another pain in the neck. Users must know not only how and why to use KCRM but also what is in it for them. Customer relationship and knowledge management objectives should be tied to personal monetary and promotional rewards. At the same time, the CRV must also demonstrate the value of the activity to senior management and ensure their buy-in and support.

3. *Mapping existing knowledge and devising metrics*: The CRV must help inventory critical explicit and tacit knowledge that already exists in your business, and devise metrics that objectively measure its value-creation impact on your business.

4. *Eliminating barriers*: The CRV must break down technical, cultural, and workflow barriers in communication and knowledge exchange processes.

5. *Creating the technology channels*: Technology channels are the socio-technical networks that help move knowledge around the organization—and these are best devised by a highly cross-functional team that the CRV must help bring together.

6. *Integrating business processes with the technology enablers*: KCRM systems must be built to support business processes and must deliver measurable business benefits. A high-level manager is usually in the best position to identify critical business processes that have the most latent potential. The CRV must also help watch the learning loop and ensure that your business is actually learning from its past mistakes.

7. *Cultural enhancement that embodies KCRM:* The CRV must initiate cultural enhancements and new reward systems that are not reminiscent of old-age thinking, but representative of customer centricity.

The CRV must serve the role of *organizational glue* that brings together many overlapping groups across your business: customer support representatives and marketing managers; corporate sponsors and senior management; knowledge and customer centricity proponents and cynics (who do not agree on the value of customer knowledge management); KCRM technology early adopters and zealots (that often include IT staff, intranet zealots, and human resources managers) versus laggards, each of which might pull your customer relationship management efforts in different directions.

· ·

KNOWLEDGE SHARING AT BUCKMAN LABS, AT&T, AND XEROX

Buckman Laboratories, a Memphis-based $300 million chemical company, uses a comprehensive intranet-based system, K'Netix, to share knowledge across 1,250 offices located across 80 countries. AT&T similarly uses a companywide system called its Information and Knowledge Exchange (IKE) to collaboratively share knowledge and build contract proposals. Xerox uses its Xerox Knowledge Network to share knowledge among 4,500 employees on a voluntary basis.

Success of these knowledge-sharing models is largely dependent on the active destruction of a knowledge-hoarding mentality that dominates businesses, often motivated by fear of job security. For this to happen, the interests of employees and the interests of the business must run in harmony. Reward systems and compensation must be driven by how much employees share, not just by what they know. The examples of Buckman, AT&T, and Xerox are successful by any measure; IKE, for example, receives about 200,000 hits per day and boasts the ability to cut the time needed to answer complex questions from 48 hours to 4. Buckman has seen a 49 percent rise in sales per employee, and a 67 percent increase in profit per employee.

Eventually, it is a strong knowledge-sharing culture that creates a win-win situation for both employees and employers. These cultural motivators become even more important when the span of these knowledge-sharing networks—formal or informal—extend across multiple collaborating firms as typical in e-business.

Table 9-2: Directions in Which Various Participants Can Pull KCRM Initiatives

Group	Oppose KCRM	Neutral	Support KCRM
Frontline staff	←	—	→
Senior management	←	—	→
Early adopters			→
Laggards	←		
Knowledge cynics	←		

Legend: ← = *oppose*   → = *support*   — = *neutral*

While having a few cynics is perhaps good, too many can be a hinderance. The CRV must bring together these stakeholders on common ground to begin putting knowledge-enabled customer relationship management to work. This does not mean that you will be able to convert the cynics into believers; however, it does mean that implementing the KCRM strategy should be kept from degenerating into an internal political war.

The Successful Leader

The successful leader and customer relationship visionary deals with both technology and managerial issues; a subtle balance of technical and managerial leadership ability is therefore expected. A reasonably high level of understanding of enabling technology can be fairly expected when the CRV is interacting with technology deployment staff. Equally, if not more importantly, the CRV also needs the skills and entrepreneurial spirit of an able manager. Most importantly, this leader must know your business very intimately (the reason why job history becomes a criteria, as described in the next section). Success of customer knowledge management in any business—big or small—depends on how this visionary-proponent brings together all stakeholders including managers, frontline workers and salespeople, business partners, and investors to share a common platform of beliefs, expectations, and commitment.

Not only must the CRV be able to see the big picture in your line of business and your particular business model, but also envision how it must look in the future and then set tasks, deadlines, and deliverables to create that vision.

First Steps for the Customer Relationship Visionary

The customer relationship visionary's actual initiatives can be classified into two broad categorical buckets: technical (shown in gray) and organizational as shown in Figure 9-2. These initiatives lie across the knowledge spectrum ranging from highly explicit and codifiable to invisibly tacit. Remember that the CRV's role on this matrix is to facilitate, not control.

Technological Imperatives

On the technological front, the CRV must facilitate the following initiatives:

  1. *Integrating channels*. Various customer touchpoints and sales and interaction channels must be seamlessly integrated. Many of these

Organizational   Technical

Level of Expression of Customer Knowledge

Scope of Work

Figure 9-2
The customer relationship visionary's task matrix.

touchpoints might extend outside your organization and may involve partner firms.

2. *Providing tools for collaborative problem solving.* Channels and tools for providing collaboration support and best practice diffusion must be built. Although the initial focus must be on explicit knowledge such as real-time sharing customer records—eventually, tacit knowledge-sharing mechanisms in the form of voice, video, and Web-enabled discussions must be introduced.

3. *Building skills directories.* When frontline staff are faced with a question that they do not have an answer to, systems should enable them to determine whom to ask. Skills and expertise directories provide such pointers to knowledge that may be tacit and highly specialized.

4. *Building repositories.* Build repositories to store "lessons learned." These can begin with simple discussion databases and later expand to relational databases tightly integrated with the intranet front end.

These collaborative tools and knowledge repositories must therefore integrate external knowledge.

Organizational Imperatives

Culture does not change on command. The CRV is therefore responsible for initiating and leading organizational processes that help embed customer-relationship building approaches into work routines of employees. On the organizational front, these tasks include the following:

1. *Identifying knowledge gaps:* Identify knowledge gaps that exist in critical work processes and assess ways and tools to bridge such gaps.

2. *Creating a culture of trust and knowledge sharing:* Change corporate culture from that of defensive knowledge-hoarding to a knowledge-sharing one by removing barriers to knowledge sharing, transfer, use, and distribution. The assumptions that retaining knowledge and keeping it to yourself works rather well for job security, respect among peers, and compensation rewards is counter productive. Breaking organizations out of this mold requires strong incentives and elimination of job risks and fears.

3. *Creating appropriate metrics:* Create metrics for knowledge work (see Chapter 10) and reward schemes for individuals who share their knowledge.

4. *Developing communities of practice:* Communities of practice must extend across the department(s), throughout the firm, and across collaborating firms, customer sites, allies, and partners.

5. *Training:* Educate knowledge workers about the value of knowledge management and then train them to use the KM system and related protocols. This includes showing knowledge workers how to ask better and smarter questions of their knowledge resources and repositories.

6. *Creating process triggers*: Improve the level of reuse of existing knowledge by creating *process triggers* and providing the context for reuse.

The CRV needs to have the breadth of understanding of a CEO and technological abilities of a CIO. Successful customer knowledge management leaders in the industry have come from diverse backgrounds: strategic management, human resources, internal consulting, finance, sales and marketing, new product development, and even academia. Leaders who are successful in this role are often not your typical job-switching managers but those who have stayed in a single company in many functional roles and departments. The key is to hire someone internally given that she has deep knowledge of your company from many perspectives and levels of observation in different roles, its culture, its politics, and the way things are done on the frontlines facing your customers. A strong record of accomplishment in a *variety* of roles is essential.

ENHANCING CORPORATE CULTURE . . . .

Corporate culture can be simply thought of as "the way we do things around here." Technology tools such as your KCRM system are mere artifacts, not your business' culture. In implementing KCRM, culture comes first, technology comes second; reverse them and you are in trouble. Corporate culture determines what your employees will do when no one is looking. Corporate culture is both invisible and formidable, and one that is difficult and expensive to change. Just because you now have a fancy knowledge-enabled CRM system that common sense says employees should use, does not make its use second nature. When management philosophy for being customer centric is at odds with the actual corporate culture, all that results is a stalemate. It does not matter whether the corporate culture in which you are implementing KCRM is characteristically "empowered" and participative, or is authoritative and exhibits power distance—knowledge management can thrive in either if the right motivators are in place. Contrary to popular belief, knowledge management can thrive even in an authoritative culture; in fact, that characterizes the Japanese businesses from which knowledge management practices first emerged. God bless your business if it spans the United States, Korea, Saudi Arabia, India, and South America! You must consider cultural motivators that work for *all* people—inside and outside your immediate company boundaries and among all people who will be using your KCRM systems and participating in customer relationship-building initiatives.

Fear and Knowledge Management

Businesses that fail to make knowledge management work have a pervasive atmosphere of fear and distrust. Driving out fear of knowledge management necessitates that an employee be confident that taking risks based on new information, customer insights, and knowledge will be rewarded, not penalized. A sharing culture in which problems, errors, omissions, successes, and disasters are shared and not penalized or hidden is mandatory. You must accept debate and conflict as ways of solving problems. On the other hand, a culture of fear will lead employees to repeat past mistakes, continue with old ways of doing things, and resolve past problems even when they know that there are better ways of doing things. More importantly, a culture of fear can characterize businesses if employees feel that sharing knowledge will lead them into a position where the company will not need them anymore. This fear is not without reason; part of the reason why total quality management (TQM) and business process reengineering (BPR) stalled was that employees, learning from widespread precedents and examples did not improve organizational processes so much, owing to fears that their jobs would be eliminated.

Cultures that do not drive out fear have two other side effects. First, they force employees to focus on the short term at the cost of long-term performance. Second, they encourage employees to focus on the individual rather than the collective organization. A culture that drives out fear begins at the top, just as paranoia does! Businesses that have successfully driven out fear from their corporate culture punish employees for inaction, not mistakes. Table 9-3 compares traditional and knowledge-friendly corporate cultures.

Table 9-3 Traditional Versus Knowledge-Centric Corporate Cultures

Cultural Dimensions	Traditional	Knowledge
Security derived from knowledge hoarding	High	Low
Trust among teams, departments, and business units	Low	High
Penalties for inaction	Low	High
Penalties for making honest mistakes	High	Low
Diversity of perspectives and cross-functional thinking	Low	High
Employee-level cross-functional and cross-institutional collaboration	Low	High
Rewards based on knowledge sharing and collaborative problem solving	Low	High
Compensation based on knowledge sharing/seeking customer relations	None	High

Empowered or Inspired?

When these employees are trusted, they do not need to be "empowered." Effective leaders need to inspire, not merely "empower" workers. Empowerment is an oxymoron that treats employees as detachable and disposable "human resources"— perhaps one of the most offensive terms coined in modern management. Table 9-4 describes several causes for employees not sharing what they know and compares which of these causes can be addressed by cultural change and which by revised

reward systems. Cultural alignment indeed solves more problems than purely financial incentives.

Table 9-3 Why People Do Not Share What They Know

Cause	Solutions	
	Cultural	Rewards
Knowledge hoarding is considered a source of job security		✔
Fear of not getting credit and suspicion	✔	✔
Loss of ownership of expertise		✔
Fear of making mistakes	✔	✔
Lack of comprehension of value of possessed knowledge	✔	
Lack of knowledge-sharing mechanisms	✔	
Lack of time to share insights, knowledge, "war stories," and experiences	✔	
Unwillingness to use existing technology to share knowledge	✔	✔

Culture *can* be enhanced by strong and visionary leadership that inspires
employees. Good leaders make employees feel like members of a cohesive social system that your business represents. Such empowerment comes from trusting them once
they are given the right set of motivations and tools to be trusted. In this respect, culture does not have to be created from scratch; instead, it has to be enhanced to sustain
knowledge sharing.

Getting From Here to There

Moving from the old knowledge-hoarding culture to one in which knowledge sharing
and relationship building thrive necessitates five fundamental touchstones: (1) setting
reasonable expectations, (2) using these expectations to arrive at requirements, (3) stabilizing procedures and then moving on to processes, (4) accuracy in assessing
resource inputs and time frames, and (5) alignment of reward systems and economic
incentives.

1. *Set reasonable expectations.* Set expectations from your employees that
   are not ridiculously unachievable. Lead your employees into suggesting
   what you can expect from them by way of improvements in customer
   retention and satisfaction when you introduce the new KCRM system.

2. *Begin by managing expectations, and then move on to requirements.* Arrive at your expectations in a collaborative manner, not a definitive or imposed manner. Use these expectations to demonstrate linkages with both technical and nontechincal requirements that have been incorporated into the CRM strategy and knowledge management system.

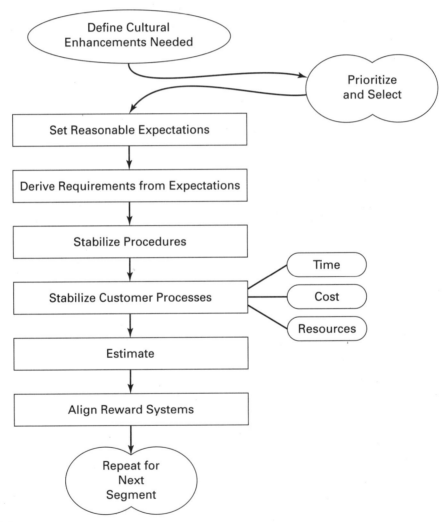

Figure 9-3
Adjusting your business to focus on knowledge and relationships.

3. *Stabilize procedures, and then move on to processes.* If your business does not have a clear-cut procedure for, say, handling customer complaints, creating entire process streams in a single shot will be a challenge. The approach then must be to look at practices (and best practices) and examine how work is actually done. Then use these procedures and work your way up to define processes that KCRM tools must support.

4. *Estimate the magnitude of effort, duration, and scale accurately.* Many organizations, especially those driven by projects, work on the basis of releases, products, editions, or programs. Estimates of work involved in managing and implementing cultural change through the use of CRM technology and processes must accurately take into account multifaceted dimensions including the magnitude of effort, duration to implement them, and the scale of the effort.

5. *Align reward systems.* Reward crisis managers and you will encourage more effective crisis management. Reward cost savings, and you will have more cost savings, maybe at the cost of losing customers. You must make a concerted effort to reward knowledge sharing, customer satisfaction generated by employees, and their efforts in customer retention. Rewards systems must encourage collaboration among front-line employees and customers that creates real-time agility and translates into more satisfied, loyal, and buying customers. A revised reward system must not only reward outcomes but also consider and reward efforts.

Figure 9-3 describes how this process is carried out for each change management phase before, during, and after the implementation of each KCRM business release.

Knowledge sharing and customer centricity must be imbibed as cultural values for KCRM to thrive. Four specifics for helping build each are discussed next.

Key Steps to Building a Knowledge-Centric Corporate Culture

Building a knowledge-sharing culture in your business begins with linking knowledge sharing to personal rewards for employees and partners, encouraging risk taking, educating, and addressing people before technology problems. These are discussed in further detail below:

1. *Link knowledge sharing and personal rewards*: Show employees how knowledge sharing will benefit them personally. Demonstrate this

using revised reward systems that reward them for both helping others solve problems, especially customer-related ones, and for sharing their expertise with co-workers. Second, show them how this can benefit them personally and professionally in their own work. Revamp reward structures for both creators and users of new knowledge, and recognize efforts to reuse existing knowledge rather than those that unnecessarily reinvent the wheel.

2. *Move beyond perfectionism and selectively reward mistakes.* Sharing best practices is not enough. In many companies, the best ideas for improvement come from analyzing their worst practices rather than their best. Cultivate a corporate culture where doors to knowledge sharing are not closed by unacceptability of honest mistakes, and not knowing.

3. *Educate.* Another reason people do not share knowledge is that they do not realize that they have something worth sharing. In PC technical support centers, almost 70 percent of calls are repeat problems. Knowing what is new in a given call can help document that in a way that an employee can pull up details of previous cases of the same problem when she receives the next call. With the Web, businesses like Dell and Apple have created knowledge-sharing forums where user communities can collaborate with employees on discussion forums— an approach that makes knowledge sharing efficient (maybe even more effective) and also increases the stickiness of customer communities and enhances the business' relationships with them. It comes as little surprise that Dell and Apple customers tend to be repeat buyers who often do not even consider alternative purchases.

4. *People, then technology.* Make sure that KCRM technology works for the people who use it, not the other way around. Technology can connect those who have expertise and those that need it, but it can also inhibit that transfer if it is too complex, difficult to use, needs a steep learning curve, or takes too much time and effort to be worth using. Make sure that these problems are unearthed well in advance during the pilot test stages of deployment (see Chapter 8).

Customer-Centric Cultures

Customer centricity is imbibed corporate culture by encouraging employees to truly think like their customers, by encouraging identification and differentiation among customers, managing expectations through internal and external metrics, and viewing complaints and problems as learning opportunities.

KNOWLEDGE MANAGEMENT AT RITZ CARLTON

A decade or two back, customer knowledge management infrastructure in the hospitality business included a dog-eared set of Rolodex cards, a few cash registers, and a guest book. Times have changed with knowledge management applications being used in hotel management systems. Ritz Carlton has an official *manager of guest recognition* on its payroll. The hotel chain calls its knowledge management system Class-Customer Loyalty Anticipation and Satisfaction System. The customer knowledge management system is interfaced with software modules and middleware that allow it to interact with all other systems such as food and beverage management, credit card authorization, energy management, remote check-in and check-out, group sales and catering, and transaction database systems. Although KM suffuses Ritz Carlton's customer information systems, the business still relies heavily on employee observations and input of customer-specific knowledge. The hotel chain has put in reward systems that actually motivate and reward employees for sharing and applying guest-specific knowledge.

The hotel gained the distinction of being the first ever chain in its line of business to have won the Malcolm Baldrige National Quality Award for its service quality.

1. *Think like a customer.* Encourage employees to think of your business processes as a continual service stream beginning with presales activities and continuing through postsales interaction.

2. *Encourage identification and differentiation.* No business can expect to succeed in satisfying all customers at all times. Identify customers by their lifetime value and encourage employees to differentiate and customize your business' offerings to them.

3. *Maintain internal and external metrics.* Manage customer relationships by evaluating your business' performance both against internal benchmarks and against competitors' performance. Manage not just outcomes but also customer expectations and perceptions.

4. *Encourage employees to view complaints as opportunities.* Complaints are simply another way of doing things, not necessarily wrong or right. Encouraging employees to listen more than talk drives home a customer-focused attitude at the corporate level.

Reconfiguring Reward Structures

Employees must have their expectations clearly laid out, must recognize why their opinions and contributions matter, and must know what is in it for them, before a well-developed customer knowledge management system will even begin to get used. Trust, cooperation, and a knowledge-focused culture in which fear is driven out and experimentation encouraged, are needed. Moreover, time to contribute, share, and learn must be given as a part of their paid work time. Clear-cut reward structures are needed that do at least the following:

1. Knowledge sharing is rewarded and recognized in performance evaluation, promotion, bonuses, and raises. Employees who add critical, new—short-term or long-term—value to the firm by building and enhancing relationships and customer-specific knowledge are recognized and rewarded.

2. Knowledge usage/reuse is rewarded and recognized.

3. Collaborative problem solving is encouraged and rewarded.

4. Accumulation of skills at a *group level* is linked to compensation packages.

5. Inaction, especially that involving customers, is penalized.

6. Time is officially allocated for sharing customer experiences, war stories, best practices, and indeed, worst practices.

CHANGE MANAGEMENT . . . .

Old culture dies hard. In *Leading Change*, John Kotter describes five tips for managers to help inculcate the new culture in employees and their business:

- Repeatedly highlight evidence that links performance improvements to new practices.

- Explain where the old culture came from, and why it served your business well then but how it is no longer helpful.

- Make sure that new hires are not screened using old criteria.

- Try hard not to promote and encourage those who blindly oppose new focal customer-centric ideas that have been accepted by others in the company.

- Make sure that senior management and top-level management do not carry on the old culture in their hearts and mind sat the cost of harboring the new one.

- Examine the enablers and impediments of KCRM in Table 9-5 and use this to identify additional enablers and impediments in your own organization.

Table 9-4 Enablers and Impediments of KCRM

Enablers	Impediments
Aligned mission, vision and values, and strategy	Individual accountability and reward
Collaborative and cross-functional	Incompatible
Eye on competition	Internal competition
Focus on customer satisfaction	Not-invented-here syndrome
Group accountability and rewards	Employee-owner interest conflict.
High levels of trust	Fear and suspicion
Interorganizational collaboration and trust	Organizational politics
Joint teamwide accountability and reward	Functional focus
Localized decision making	Centralized top-down decision making
Need to share	Compartmentalization of functional groups
Open to outside ideas	Too busy to share
Process focus	Lack of alignment
Rewarded for sharing	Unintentionally rewarded for hoarding
Team-based collaborative work	Individual effort without recognition and reward

SUMMARY . . . .

Success of your business' customer knowledge management initiative partly depends on strong leadership, cultural adjustment, and rewards that recognize and reward relationships enhancement with customers and partners, and knowledge sharing. The following six points summarize the crux of leadership and change management issues that are critical for KCRM.

- *Technology tools are artifacts, not your business' culture.* Successful KCRM initiatives need fundamental readjustment of corporate culture, strong leadership, and financial and nonfinancial reward structures that together gain the hearts and minds of employees and motivate them to share knowledge.

- *Fear inhibits knowledge sharing.* Fear for their job security is a single dominant inhibitor that can keep employees from sharing valuable knowledge to them. Reward structures must be reset to recognize and reward employees for sharing their knowledge and expertise with colleagues, customers, and channel partners. Building a knowledge-sharing culture in your business begins with linking knowledge sharing to personal rewards for employees and partners, encouraging risk taking, and educating and addressing people before technology problems.

- *The CRV's responsibilities span technology and organizational culture issues.* Customer relationship visionaries must champion customer knowledge management and relationship building, help devise appropriate metrics, eliminate collaborative impediments and technical barriers, integrate business processes, and support change management to put KCRM-embodying culture in place.

- *Cultural change cannot be mandated.* Customer support representatives, marketing managers, corporate sponsors, senior management, KCRM proponents, early adopters and zealots, and cynics must all be included. Repeatedly highlight evidence that links performance improvements to new practices; explain where the old culture came from, and why it served your business well then but how it is no longer helpful.

- *Remember the five touchstones.* Five fundamental touchstones must be kept in mind: (1) setting reasonable expectations, (2) using these expectations to arrive at requirements, (3) stabilizing procedures and then moving on to processes, (4) accuracy in assessing resource inputs and time frames, and (5) alignment of reward systems and economic incentives.

- *Encourage customer centricity.* Encourage employees to truly think like their customers by encouraging identification and differentiation among customers, managing expectations through internal and external metrics, and viewing complaints and problems as learning opportunities.

Successfully imbibing these norms in your organization's culture, practices, and work will provide the complementary assets that can help you build networks of accessible knowledge and lasting relationships with customers and channels partners—assets that provide inimitable advantage to traditional and e-businesses alike.

TEST YOUR UNDERSTANDING . . . .

1. What are the key drivers of KCRM success?

2. How do knowledge-focused managers typically differ from traditional managers? What does this imply in the context of their KCRM project leadership abilities?

3. What is the role of a customer relationship visionary in a customer knowledge management initiative?

4. What are the key technological imperatives that fall on the shoulders of the customer relationship visionary?

5. What are the key nontechnological organizational imperatives that fall on the shoulders of the customer relationship visionary?

6. How does fear prevent knowledge sharing and management? How can it be driven out of corporate culture?

7. How can personal and knowledge goals be linked? Why do they need to be linked?

8. How would an e-business know that it had a customer-centric culture?

9. How can change be effectively managed before, during, and after a KCRM plan is implemented?

10. How can top management slow down the growth of an e-business' digital capital?

PUTTING IT ALL TOGETHER: THE ROADMAP

Aligning strategy and technology is a crucial but often ignored link that determines the eventual business benefits of knowledge-enabled customer relationship management. Business environment, strategic context, strategy, and technology must be considered simultaneously while devising the KCRM game plan. The strategic framework (Chapter 4) integrates these four perspectives to help penetrate the four barriers that surround it: (1) interpretation barrier (environment), (2) expression barrier (strategy), (3) specification (strategy), and (4) implementation (technology). Three steps are then needed to build a strategy: (1) articulating a company vision and strategic intent, (2) translating this strategic intent into actionable business strategy, and (3) laying out discrete and measurable goals that lead your business in the direction of realizing its vision. Self-service, collaborative communities, intelligent personalization, and knowledge-based adaptation provide individualization at mass-market cost-efficiency.

You cannot know where you want your KCRM investments to take your business unless you know where your business stands. The knowledge audit provides a snapshot of the present state and a reference point for evaluating future investments in building networked knowledge and relationship capital. This consists of seven steps: defining audit goals, assembling an audit team, identifying all relevant constraints, defining customer clusters or segments, determining the ideal state, selecting audit dimensions and method, and documenting customer knowledge assets. Audit results form the basis for classifying customers into different categories based on their lifetime value to your business, and for differentiating among them. This provides the basis for planning, aligning, and implementing KCRM by taking both explicit and tacit knowledge about customers and business partners, and business processes into account.

KCRM teams themselves are boundary spanning and involve a variety of managerial and technical participants during different phases (in addition to a core team). This team applies the *Risk Assessment Framework* to determine and rank threats and risks that are within the team's control and those that are not.

Technology plays an important role in customer knowledge management. Not to be confused with intranets, extranets, data stores, or GroupWare, these systems serve several purposes: broadening reach, enhancing the speed of knowledge transfer and real-time knowledge application, enabling informed decision making, mapping various sources of tacit knowledge, communicating and integrating diverse channels and touchpoints, and facilitating collaborative success. The goal of technology in this context is that of maximizing relationships, not merely increasing efficiency. In e-business, customer knowledge management technology can be transparently integrated with the e-business system itself. The "customer" in KCRM is more representative of the channel, and must encompass suppliers, partners, and even competitors. Informal communications *(through* multimedia, pointers, e-communities, Voiceover IP, and intelligent routing) and business intelligence applications are facilitated by KCRM systems. Open standards, mission-focused design, results-driven design, modular integration, and a pragmatic approach can help build a future-proof system.

Deployment of these systems must consider *technology and nontechnology issues,* while explicitly considering training, reward systems, and integration of business processes and systems. Rather than using a "big-bang" approach, use a results-driven approach that helps build incremental but cumulative results through rapidly paced business releases, reduces risks of failure, and simultaneously addresses organizational and technical deployment issues. Execution excellence with short times-to-market—not perfection—is key.

Building the system might be the easier part, getting people to use it is the harder part. Success of your business' customer knowledge management initiative partly depends on strong leadership, cultural adjustment, and rewards that recognize and reward relationship enhancement with customers and partners, and knowledge sharing. Strong leadership qualities in a custom relationship visionary with infectious zeal help. Successfully imbibing these norms in your organization's culture, practices, and work will provide the complementary assets that can help you build networks of inimitable knowledge and strong relationships with customers and channel partners.

Part 3

Planning for Success

In this part…

Chapter 10: Evaluation, Measurement, and Refinement

- Understand the need for effective metrics.

- Understand the limitations of traditional metrics.

- Understand how benchmarking and Stages of Growth framework provide comparative measures.

- Understand the use of quality function deployment for evaluating KCRM success.

- Build a custom Balanced Scorecard for comprehensive evaluation and refinement.

- Understand and avoid the 10 most common pitfalls in devising KCRM metrics.

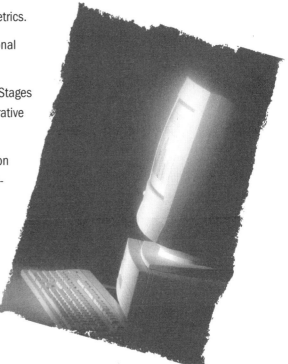

10 Evaluation, Measurement, and Refinement

In this chapter...

- Understand the need for effective metrics.

- Understand the limitations of traditional metrics.

- Understand how benchmarking and Stages of Growth framework provide comparative measures.

- Understand the use of quality function deployment for evaluating KCRM success.

- Build a custom Balanced Scorecard for comprehensive evaluation and refinement.

- Understand and avoid the 10 most common pitfalls in devising KCRM metrics.

FUNDAMENTAL METRICS . . . .

That what can be measured is not always important, and what is important cannot always be measured. Metrics essentially define KCRM success and serve as indicators of the business impact of customer knowledge management. Future investments and relationship building depend so heavily on these indicators of success that the poor choice of metrics can spell disaster. Unfortunately, many popular measurement systems do not handle intangible assets such as customer loyalty, relationship value, and knowledge sufficiently well. Many popular metrics tend to be overly focused on past events rather than the future, and many do not balance internal and external knowledge integration. Metrics that can be measured today with impact on future outcomes are the ones that are needed most.

This chapter explains the final step on the KCRM roadmap—that of determining how success is measured, how metrics (measures of success) are devised, and how this information is used to refine both KCRM strategy and technology. We begin by examining popular business metrics such as return on investment, Tobin's q, and total cost of ownership to understand why they are too limited to measure any aspect of digital capital—relationships and knowledge—in an accurate manner. We then analyze benchmarking, Roger Bohn's *Stages of Growth Framework*, and quality function deployment as a starter set of KCRM metrics. Finally, we examine how any combination of metrics must eventually build toward a comprehensive set of metrics such as the Balanced Scorecard to provide meaningful analysis and direction for future improvement. Ten common pitfalls that must be avoided on the way are finally discussed along with strategies for avoiding them.

TRADITIONAL METRICS . . . .

Four metrics, though useful for measuring IT returns, are rarely comprehensive enough to analyze KCRM investments. However, their undying popularity necessitates a short description to highlight their limitations for measuring KCRM performance.

Financial Return on Investment

Financial return on investment (ROI) reflects the "So, what do I get in return" mentality of capital investments whose performance could solely be measured in terms of financial returns. When ROI calculation methods are used to evaluate KCRM investments, one of two approaches prevail: (1) putting a dollar figure on intellectual assets and customer relationships and (2) additional dollars saved (cost reduction) or earned (revenue increases) as attributable to the system's use. Table 10-1 describes three key measures that constitute financial ROI calculations.

Table 10-1 Three Financial ROI Measures

ROI Figures	Description
Time to payback	Time required to recover the capital invested in the solution (i.e., the discounted cash flow benefits exceed the initial capital investment)
Raw ROI	Ratio of expected cash benefits (decreased costs and increased revenue) to the costs associated with the investment
Time to value	Lag between the system's acquisition and value delivery (this is often increased by integration and training hurdles)

Tobin's q

Tobin's q is the ratio between the firm's market valuation and the cost of replacing its physical assets. While Tobin's q provides a snapshot of the firm's state of intellectual health at a given point in time, it provides no direction for strategy development, does not lend focus, or highlight mistakes that might have been made. This measure does not tell a firm how it can create further value, prevent imitation or substitution, and leverage its customer knowledge assets to maximize its digital capital and to sustain its competitive advantage.

Total Cost of Ownership

Total cost of ownership (TCO) is the total lifecycle cost associated with the purchase, implementation, maintenance, and support of a system. This methodology identifies and measures components of IT expense beyond the initial cost of implementation. This includes software licensing fees, hardware expenditure, training costs, integration and design costs, and ongoing maintenance costs.

Unfortunately, this method leaves out significant cost categories (e.g., complexity costs, the implicit cost of supporting multiple vendors, the cost of dealing with compatibility issues), ignores benefits beyond pure costing, neglects strategic factors, and does not facilitate benchmarking across divisions, business units, and companies.

Limitations

Companies do not always demand solid business cases for IT investments but have trouble handling decisions based on *soft* gains and benefits. Maturity of judgment becomes a distinctive inhibiting factor that prevents them from making decisions where limited quantitative data exists. ROI, Tobin's q, and TCO-based approaches to measurement account for several hard measures; however, soft dimensions—which also are more difficult to observe and evaluate—are not measured *at all*. Table 10-2 illustrates these two broad categories with some examples.

Table 10-2 Examples of Hard and Soft Measures

Hard	Soft
Cost savings	Customer satisfaction
Customer retention	Customer loyalty
Repeat purchases	Customer and employee productivity
Market share	Employee loyalty
Customer acquisition rate	Employee empowerment
Cost of sales/expense reduction	Defection likelihood
Stock valuation	Market leadership
Bottom-line effects	Organizational stability
Profit margins	Cultural change

Metrics that incorporate soft measures provide managers the basis for decision-making and resource allocation after being informed by soft data that the aforementioned methods simply ignore. Benchmarking, discussed next, overcomes some of these problems but introduces others.

AGENCY PROBLEMS AND METRICS

Employees will maximize what is measured. If a customer service representative is evaluated on the basis of the number of calls answered per day, he will attempt to maximize precisely that—the number of calls answered—even if it means putting quality of interaction on the back seat. A service center that I observed used the following five measures to evaluate customer satisfaction with their support representatives: (1) the number of rings until the phone was answered, (2) average waiting time per customer, (3) number of calls answered per hour per representative, (4) number of times a customer was put on hold, and (5) minutes per hour spent talking to a customer. Customers were highly dissatisfied even though the company was doing well on all of these measures. Because customer satisfaction and accurate answers—two that mattered most—were not measured, employees were maximizing the rewarded metrics and giving their customers the most convenient answers rather than accurate ones. Poor metrics were therefore exacerbating the problem instead of fixing it.

The chosen metrics gain tremendous inertia, and employees who have painfully learned to maximize the chosen metrics fear to change course.

Benchmarking

Benchmarking is the search for industry-wide best practices—anywhere within or outside their firm, industry, or sector—which lead to superior performance. Businesses repeatedly expend time, resources, and money to solve problems that have already been solved in other offices or locations of the same company. Benchmarking often begins by identifying best practices, skills, and capabilities within your own company before looking outside. Benchmarking consists of four key steps:

1. *Select benchmark parameters.* Select the customer interaction processes, knowledge, service processes, and their scope for benchmarking.
2. *Select a benchmarking team.* Ensure that it is sufficiently diverse from a functional mix viewpoint.
3. *Select target partners.* Internal, from rival firms, from nonrival firms, or from averages representing your industry or sector. Table 10-3

Table 10-3 Benchmark Targets are internal or external to your business

Benchmark target	Advantages	Disadvantages
Internal business units	Breaks down internal communication barriers Easily accessible	Internal politics might impede use Compared internally, not against superior industry performers
Competing firms	Measured against direct competition Partners easily identified	Legal complexity "Escrows" impose additional costs
Industry	Measured against the overall market	Expensive Privacy threats might surface
Cross-industry	Insights from noncompeting firms	Comparative population not truly representative of industry/sector Harder sell More expensive

describes these benchmark targets and the tradeoffs involved in their selection. These target firms represent the ideal firm within each industry and have performance levels that others aspire to.

4. *Collect and analyze data.* Record this benchmark data for future comparisons and use it to iteratively improve the benchmarked processes.

Benchmarking can often provide insights into service quality, relative time-to-market, customer satisfaction and the operational level of customer service, customer relationships and relationship management, customer loyalty, and the likelihood of their defection. Benchmarking can be used for internal and external comparisons to provide measures that have no meaning in themselves, but will describe how your own business is performing *relative to* your benchmark targets. When used externally, role model firms are often used as the basis for comparison. Any changes in the value of selected benchmarks can be observed over time by comparing them with their preceding values. Examples of a few e-businesses are listed in Table 10-4.

A problem with benchmarks is that they do tell you what to do next, but not how to do it. A word of caution: If you select the wrong benchmark, you will end up focusing on the wrong set of processes. Benchmarking is most useful when you know what your expectations and objectives are and the process itself is closely tied to your firm's knowledge drivers for strategy.

Table 10-4 Prevalent Role Models for E-businesses

Performance Areas	E-business Role Models
Brand recognition	Ebay.com
Profitability	Cisco.com
Software development and marketing	Microsoft Corporation
Innovation and new product development	3M.com
Customer loyalty	Apple Computer
Brand management	Disney
Customer stickiness	Amazon.com
Logistics and enterprise-wide IT leverage	Outpost.com
Customer trust	NewYorkTimes.com
Apparel—satisfied customers	LandsEnd.com, Gap.com, Gear.com

BASIC KCRM METRICS . . . .

Before we delve into metrics that actually do measure KCRM processes well, let us take a quick look at some basic questions that effective performance metrics must be able to address:

1. Is the measure uniquely and directly linked to the area that you want to improve?

2. Can your employees understand this measure with minimal explanation?

3. Will it produce results that would be looked upon as being favorable by your customers?

4. Can it be implemented?

5. Can the results be communicated without undue delay?

6. Are there mechanisms for incorporating resultant feedback and learning?

Within each metric area, it is important to decide on the level of granularity at which you will analyze performance. For example, "Web usage" in the context of a business-to-consumer electronic commerce channel can mean one or many of the following:

- Overall e-commerce store (technical or sales) performance
- Advertising effectiveness of Web banners
- External referrals that generate (1) the most visits and (2) the most sales
- Shopper segmentation (e.g., shoppers from specific domains, shoppers who most frequently abandon shopping carts, etc.)
- Cross-up selling effectiveness and their contribution to overall revenue
- Design features that generate most activity or sales
- Search-to-sale conversion rates and the reasons underlying their differences

Again, simple frequency measures such as "click happiness" of a specific site design feature might mean either: (1) look-to-click rate, (2) click-to-basket insertion rate, or (3) basket-to-buy rate—all of which have very different implications. Although microlevel measurements are technologically feasible, you must balance the cost versus benefit of such excesses. Keep in mind that barely 2 percent of grocery store data is ever analyzed! Do not measure more than you can interpret *and apply* to decision-making processes. With these questions in mind, let us take a closer look at two basic KCRM measurement systems: the Stages of Knowledge Growth framework and quality function deployment.

Stages of Knowledge Growth Framework

Bohn's *Stages of Knowledge Growth* framework provides a readily usable methodology for measurement of process capability and technological knowledge. This relatively simple method is good at providing a 30,000-foot view and a clear *bigger picture*, though not at a low-level view. Because this framework was developed for knowledge that is used for delivering goods and services, it readily translates over to the e-business KCRM domain. Table 10-5 provides a basic description of the "stages" along which a business progresses (from stage 1, ignorance to stage 8, perfect knowledge) as it gains more knowledge about its customers, markets, and industry.

Table 10-6 provides the frame of reference against which you can precisely map, evaluate, and measure your own business relative to your competitors and your industry, and causal associations and prescriptive decisions.

As your customer relationship management process moves up this scale, you begin to build a robust and repeatable methodology that is very capable of handling unexpected and undocumented variations.

Table 10-5 The Stages of Knowledge Growth Framework

Stage	Name	Typical Form of Knowledge
1	Complete ignorance	Does not exist anywhere.
2	Awareness	Knowledge is primarily tacit (pure art).
3	Measure	Knowledge is primarily written (pretechnological).
4	Control of the mean	Written and embodied in methodological routines.
5	Process capability	Local recipes and operating manuals.
6	Process characterization	Empirical equations (cost-reducing tradeoffs are known).
7	Know why	Scientification: procedures, methodologies, and algorithms.
8	Complete knowledge	Knowledge nirvana; never happens.

Table 10-6 Stages of Knowledge Characteristics, and Learning Methods

Stage	Knowledge Stage	Knowledge Characteristic	Location of Knowledge	Work Processes	Learning Method
0	Total ignorance	Cannot tell the good state from the bad.	Undefined.	Undefined.	Undefined.
1	Pure art	Pure art.	Tacit, unarticulabel, and in the expert's head.	Trial-and-error based	Look for emergent patterns.
2	Awareness	List of *possibly* relevant variables exists.	Largely tacit; can be partially expressed in words, gestures and diagrams.	Experts dictated process execution that is still subject to randomness.	Experts keep repeating processes while looking for emergent patterns.
3	Measure	Pretechnological.	You are able to decide which variables are more important by noting their correlation with desirable outputs.	Casually ambiguous patterns begin to emerge.	Repetition and experimentation
4	Control of the mean	Scientific method feasible.	Written and embodied in hardware/software processes to some extent.	Some knowledge can be explicated and codified. You cannot measure the qualitative factors because a "recipe" is yet to emerge.	Records of processes and their outcomes are maintained.

Table 10-6 Stages of Knowledge Characteristics, and Learning Methods (cont.)

Stage	Knowledge Stage	Knowledge Characteristic	Location of Knowledge	Work Processes	Learning Method
5	Process capability	Local repeatable recipe.	A local procedural semireliable recipe based on experience is developed. It may be codified.	Methodology-based; *typically* produces "good" results.	Search for satisfaction patterns that produce satisfactory results.
6	Process characterization	Cost-effective, well-developed recipe capable of handling some contingencies.	Knowledge is documented in a methodology that usually works.	Mechanized, automated, time-proven, repeatable methodolgy that exhibits localized adaptablility.	Continuous application of the proven methodology will surface its weaknesses.
7	Know why	Formal or informal scientific quantitative model is developed.	Relevant knowledge is well explicated and codified; contingencies can be handled well.	Codifed in computer software and process manuals.	Iterative refinement.
8	Complete knowledge	Nirvana.	Rarely possible; any contingency can be handled perfectly.	KM becomes a natural part of work processes.	Occasional variations resulting in the inability to apply processes push it back to Stage 7.

Source: Based on Amrit Tiwana, *The Knowledge Management Toolkit,* Prentice Hall, Upper Saddle River, NJ, (1999) 246-248, and Roger Bohn, Measuring Technological Knowledge, *Sloan Management Review.* Fall 1994 61-73.

Quality Function Deployment

The second basic measurement method for KCRM effectiveness is quality function deployment (QFD). This method facilitates translation of high-level goals to discrete actions and integrates inputs such as individual goals, perceptions of significance, and desired outcomes from various stakeholders into decomposable, measurable, and more manageable actions. In other words, it can help turn vision into action during the strategy execution process.

Quality function deployment uses a QFD matrix (see Figure 10-1) to link customer needs to business processes and internal decisions.

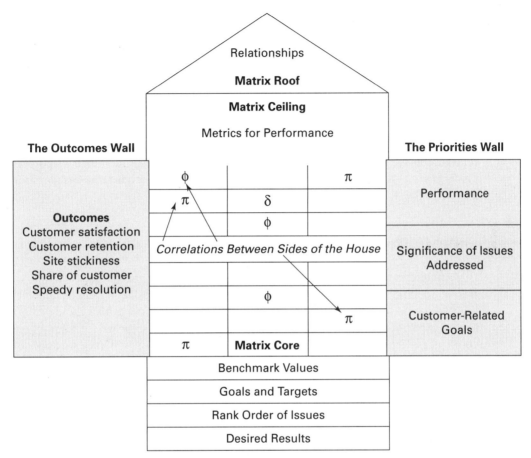

Figure 10-1
Quality function deployment uses a skeleton matrix as its measurement template.

The Outcomes Wall

Desirable outcomes are listed on the left wall of the matrix. As more outcomes are added over time, the *outcomes* wall of the *house* begins to build up. Whether high- or low-level, these outcomes must be clearly observable, and without much delay. Examples of such outcomes include the following:

- Increase customer retention by 6 percent by the end of this fiscal year.

- Reduce problem resolution times by 35 percent in 18 weeks.
- Increase customer satisfaction levels with our service by 18 percent by June 2003.

The Priorities Wall

Relative priority is assigned to each outcome by attaching weights that are listed on the right wall of the matrix. These weights are usually assigned on a scale of 1 to 5 or on a percentage scale. A 5-point scale is cognitively easier to track than a 100-point percentage scale, which makes some decisions and weight assignments both arbitrary and confusing.

Other Walls

Performance metrics are listed and clustered on the top of the matrix —that is, the matrix's ceiling. The matrix core indicates the levels of correlation between the metrics and the performance outcomes. The interrelationships between all these parameters are represented on the roof of the house. Decisions that improve the relevant outcome parameters are said to have a high level of correlation. High, medium, and low correlations are indicated by three different symbols in the QFD matrix shown in Figure 10-1. Once the goals of the KCRM project are set, customer-focused decisions can be made by focusing on the parameters that exhibit high likelihood of impact or have the highest priority level in the matrix core.

Limitations

While QFD can help relate high-level goals to the discrete steps that must be taken to produce them, the method can get overly complex over time. Several commercial software tools facilitate easier implementation and requirements management. However, the method itself does not distinguish between financial and nonfinancial outcomes—a problem that the Balanced Scorecard method discussed in the next section addresses well.

COMPREHENSIVE METRICS . . . .

Although various metrics described in the preceding sections are straightforward to deploy, they are not comprehensive. The Balanced Scorecard method is truly comprehensive, but it cannot be taken out of the box and deployed. It requires extensive customization and polishing before you can begin to use it in your own business' context. The following sections describe this method and its usability for KCRM evaluation at an introductory level.

The Balanced Scorecard Technique

Tech Talk

Balanced Scorecard: Measurement method that simultaneously tracks internal and external focus, financial and nonfinancial measures, and past, present, and future goals. Each "card" of the scorecard represents one dimension being tracked.

The Balanced Scorecard is a well-suited method for measuring KCRM impact because it comprehensively links strategy, technology, competitiveness, customer centricity, and knowledge management. It provides a technique to maintain a balance between long-term and short-term objectives, financial and nonfinancial measures, lagging and leading indicators, and internal and external perspectives. Like QFD, the Balanced Scorecard begins with a template scorecard as illustrated in Figure 10-2. The

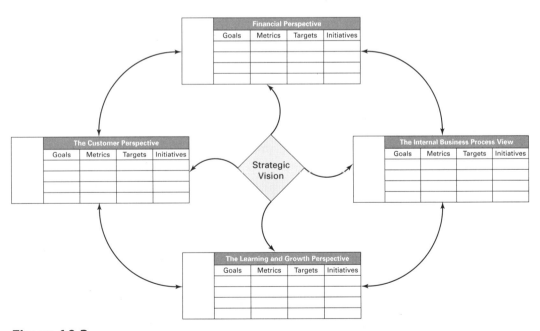

Figure 10-2
The basic Balanced Scorecard template simultaneously tracks four dimensions.

Balanced Scorecard can also be used to evaluate the impact of customer knowledge management on four complementary criteria.

The Balanced Scorecard approach lets you accomplish several measurement-related actions that other metrics do not track:

- Direct linkages between financial (e.g., profits, margins, and revenue) and non-financial (e.g., customer satisfaction and employee competencies) value drivers of your business
- Translation of a lofty business vision into more doable, realistic, manageable, and specific performance-driven goals
- The ability to provide a snapshot of the health of your firm at any point in time
- Built-in cause-and-effect relationships that help guide your e-business strategy
- A *sufficient* number of performance drivers and metrics
- Capability to communicate the KCRM strategy throughout the firm and to link individual goals with the overall e-business strategy

The choice and the number of dimensions in your Balanced Scorecard are flexible. Though the original Balanced Scorecard model uses four dimensions, more can be added. However, this number must be kept below seven to avoid informational overload and inclusion of non-critical dimensions. Note that customized Balanced Scorecards are more difficult to develop and can rarely be directly adopted from other businesses that use them. Although the Balanced Scorecard was developed long before e-business evolved, a large number of e-businesses have had a positive experience in using it to build a comprehensive picture.

The KCRM Balanced Scorecard is an adaptation of the original Balanced Scorecard. As illustrated in Figure 10-3, it helps translate the KCRM vision into action, facilitates bottom-up communication of this vision, continually validates your choice of metrics, and robustly links your company's clients, markets, people, results, and profitability.

Implementing the KCRM Balanced Scorecard requires four key steps: (1) vision translation, (2) communication, (3) reality checks, and (4) feedback incorporation as described in Table 10-7.

To implement the Balanced Scorecard, you must take various metrics for each scorecard and individually determine what you will analyze, intensify all associated ROI drivers, and then decide which of those can be quantified and which must be qualitatively assessed.

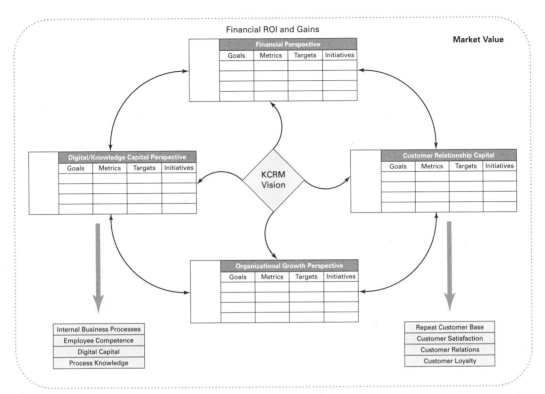

Figure 10-3
The KCRM Balanced Scorecard and its basic dimensions.

YOU DON'T BRING ME FLOWERS ANYMORE...

Garden.com does not grow its own products. It has a test garden in Des Moines, Iowa; it does not sell anything from there. Garden.com's servers in Austin, Texas, take all orders, but a complex virtual supply chain actually delivers them. The system connects 70 suppliers from around the United States, automatically routing orders as appropriate. The company retains expertise of the fancy Latin botanical names of its flowers in house, and every supplier deals with a simple barcode that is attached to each item that the site sells. To the customer, the company presents one face; every order's progress can be tracked in real time through its Website without having to know whether it is being shipped from the opposite end of the country or a city that is next door.

Table 10-7 Implementation of the Balanced Scorecard requires four key steps.

Step	What Must Be Done
Translate the vision	Reach managerial consensus on the key objectives behind the plan
	Decompose the vision into concrete goals and objectives
	Create short-term, specific goals for individual employees and relate them to organizational vision
Communicate and link	Communicate vision-derivative goals and employee performance targets to the relevant departments and individual employees
	Clarify metric rewards linkages to demonstrate what is in it for them
Do a reality check	Evaluate how well your chosen metrics, individual-level goals, business unit targets, and allocated resources align with the initial vision
Incorporate feedback	Evaluate your goals, metrics, and targets based feedback from customers and employees
	Incorporate this feedback to incrementally refine and refocus performance targets

Two assessment examples are described in Tables 10-8 and 10-9. Table 10-8 describes several generic dimensions of B2C electronic commerce transactions that can be analyzed, their ROI drivers, and quantifiable metrics.

Similarly, Table 10-9 describes several benefits that can be analyzed in the context of a new customer interaction support tool, their ROI drivers, and quantifiable metrics.

Several other employee and customer-related measures are worth considering as you develop your own version of the Balanced Scorecard. Examples include:

- Average expense per dollar earned
- Competence development expenses per employee in dollars
- Customer satisfaction
- Delivery time deviation rate
- Dollar figure value of employee attrition

Table 10-8 B2C E-commerce Transaction Analysis for the Balanced Scorecard

Analysis	ROI Drivers	Quantified Metrics
Shopping patterns	Higher customer acquisition	Increased revenue/sales
Visitor behavior	Higher customer retention	Lower churn
Buyer: Browser ratio	Churn reduction	Higher acquisition rates
Cross-selling/up-selling	Effective personalization	Higher sales/customer
Fulfillment	Improved targeting	Reduced operations costs
Product returns	Finer market segmentation	Improved profit margins
Advertising effectiveness	Reduced fulfillment time	
Business rule performance	Increased value to customer	
Customer profiling	Higher stickiness	
Segment-level targeting	Advertising effectiveness	
Product affinity		
Demographics and geographics		

Note: Rows in this table are not corresponding to values populating adjacent columns.

Table 10-9 Customer Service Benefits Analysis for Balanced Scorecard Deployment

Analysis	ROI Drivers	Quantified Metrics
Root cause	CSR throughput	Lower support costs
High and low performers	Schedule optimization	Higher support volume
Process bottlenecks	Resource allocation	High MVC retention rates
Scheduling	MVC retention and loyalty	Price premiums
Up-sell/cross-sell	Higher service levels	
Customer profiling/satisfaction	Faster problem identification	
Escalations/hot cases		
Call scheduling		
Customer satisfaction		

- Employee attrition rate
- Employee satisfaction
- Expense of business development per dollar spent on overheads
- Expense of reinventing problem solutions per year
- Information-gathering expenses per existing customer
- Level of customer attrition
- Marketing expense per customer
- Number of ideas implemented from customer suggestions
- Pay-back on development activities
- Problem-solving time/customer
- Renewal expense per existing customer
- Time spent on systematic packaging of know-how for future use
- Time spent per unsuccessful sales lead
- Training expenses per customer per year in dollars
- Training expenses per employee

Actual implementation and use of the Balanced Scorecard approach are beyond the intended scope of this chapter. For implementation level details, I highly recommend reading, *Translating Strategy Into Action: The Balanced Scorecard* (Harvard Business School Press, 1996) by Robert Kaplan and David Norton. Several software tools such as Gentia's (www.gentia.com) scorecard software and application services (such as www.balancedscorecard.com) simplify the maintenance of these scorecards once the initial set of dimensions have been internally established.

PITFALLS . . . .

Having *no* metric is better than relying on one that is *absolutely wrong*. The choice of a wrong metric can have more ill effects than positive ones. Metrics, when applied to knowledge work, or in general, are vulnerable to 10 common pitfalls, as described in Table 10-10.

To avoid these pitfalls, concentrate on what your *customers* value, not what you want to sell. Insightful data analysis can feed your company's bottom line; however, to deliver insights, you must begin with a clear appreciation for the questions that your company needs answered. Start with the big picture, gain senior management support, make sure that the KCRM initiative is well aligned with your business strategy, and incrementalize the project. These qualities can be brought into your KCRM initiative only if they are reflected in the metrics deployed to measure their degree.

Table 10-10 Common Pitfalls in Developing Knowledge-Based Metrics

Pitfall	Description and Avoidance Tactics
Using too many metrics	Use a few robust metrics rather than several marginally significant ones.
	Use metrics that focus on past performance, present processes, and future results simultaneously.
	Choose metrics that can be tracked effectively, accurately, and efficiently.
	Link measures to strategic capabilities, competitive positioning, customer expectations, and financial indicators.
Risky reward ties	Tie metrics to long-term performance but accommodate short-term rewards for employees who sustain them.
	Keep the long view—select metrics that can be measured today but impact future outcomes.
Hard to control	Do not choose metrics that are beyond the control of employees.
	Do not fall for metrics that look good only on paper!
Hard to focus on	Select metrics that encourage decisions that move your company in the same direction as the long-term goals.
Neglect the "soft stuff"	Do not place overly strong emphasis on hard, financial results.
	Track financial, process capability, employee performance, and customer-relationship measures.
	Set soft goals for managing people, suppliers, customers, and innovation.
	Ensure that your hard and soft measures are well balanced.
Focus on past performance	Select metrics that can serve as early warning signals for future problems.
	Select metrics that can signal future opportunities.
Measure the wrong things	Have employees maximize what is measured, not what is important.
	Wrong metrics can be more damaging than helpful.
	Ensure that your metrics actually measure what you intended to measure.

Table 10-10 Common Pitfalls in Developing Knowledge-Based Metrics (cont.)

Pitfall	Description and Avoidance Tactics
Perfect metric syndrome	Do not delay choosing metrics hoping to come across the perfect set later. A few good metrics today are better than a perfect one tomorrow.
Obsess over narrow e-business metrics	Whether the focus is on marketing, customer service, support, or sales, make your e-business metrics also applicable to *all* customer touchpoints other than the Web.
Measure quantity but not quality	Purely quantitative metrics tend to ignore the "soft stuff." Measure both quality and quantity using the selected set of metrics.

SUMMARY . . . .

Effective metrics help organizations build KCRM strategies and solutions that help understand customer needs, differentiate between customers via customer segmentation, predict customer loyalty, identify problems, predict future events, understand the true customer value, and monitor marketing effectiveness.

- *Measures reflect success.* Metrics define success and failure. Effective metrics must reflect what is important to customers, and in turn, to your business. Employees will maximize things that are measures, which may not necessarily be those that are important.

- *Traditional financial metrics are insufficient.* ROI, NPV, Tobin's *q*, and total cost of ownership measure only the hard and quantitative factors at the cost of soft, qualitative ones.

- *Benchmarking is a starting metric but not an end in itself.* Benchmarking allows you to compare the performance of different business units but is subject to problems related to selecting the right targets and the lack of detailed analysis. Although you can begin with benchmarking, you must eventually adopt a more comprehensive set of measures. The Stages of Knowledge Growth framework provides a high-level assessment of your customer relationship management capability and customer knowledge to determine areas that need most attention.

- *Devise a Balanced Scorecard customized to your business.* The Balanced Scorecard method provides the most comprehensive set of measures that take long-term and short-term objectives, financial and nonfinancial measures, lagging and leading indicators, and internal and external perspectives into account. Your business' initial set of metrics must eventually lead toward the formulation of the cards within a custom-built Balanced Scorecard.

Effective metrics can facilitate the right customer-focused initiatives if they are analyzed using an integrative relational cause-effect approach such as the Balanced Scorecard.

TEST YOUR UNDERSTANDING . . . .

1. What are metrics? Can you think of any examples in your own job?

2. What is the need for the need for effective metrics? What must they measure?

3. Why do traditional metrics not work well for knowledge-driven e-businesses?

4. What is the fundamental idea behind benchmarking? Where does it begin to fall apart?

5. How does the Stages of Growth framework serve as a comparative measure? What are its limitations?

6. How is quality function deployment (QFD) used for evaluating KCRM success?

7. What is the fundamental idea behind the Balanced Scorecard approach? Why is it well suited for measuring digital capital assets in e-businesses?

8. Why can Balanced Scorecards not be copied from your competitors? What problems can one expect if you copied them?

9. What are the most common pitfalls in devising KCRM metrics?

10. Why are soft measures necessary? Why can we not manage with hard measures like return on investment alone?

PUTTING IT ALL TOGETHER: EVALUATION AND REFINEMENT . . . .

You cannot control what you cannot measure. Metrics help businesses measure performance, understand customer needs, differentiate between customers via customer segmentation, predict customer loyalty, identify problems, predict future events, understand true customer value, monitor marketing effectiveness, and incrementally refine their strategies. Unfortunately, businesses that attempt to apply metrics from the brick-and-mortar world (e.g., . ROI, NPV, Tobin's q, and total cost of ownership) to e-business might be in for an unpleasant surprise.

Poorly chosen metrics will encourage employees to maximize the metrics themselves, not necessarily things that you want maximized. Remember the example of the telephone support office in which management measured the number of calls answered per hour. Employees began hanging up on callers and gave convenient (and often incorrect) answers to maximize the number of calls answered per hour. Satisfaction plummeted.

Metrics for knowledge management and CRM necessarily take both hard (quantitative) and soft (qualitative) factors into account. Benchmarking is a good starter metric. It can be followed by the *Stages of Knowledge Growth* measure and eventually by a comprehensive Balanced Scorecard that combines long-term and short-term objectives, financial and nonfinancial measures, lagging and leading indicators, and internal and external perspectives.

Remember that acquiring customers is often an expensive proposition on the Web. These customers must be judged on the basis of their lifetime value, not the value of a single transaction. CDNow.com, a popular music retailer, suffered precisely because its metrics could not warn the company early enough that its customer acquisition costs were not justified by their lifetime values. Similarly, knowledge management investments have both financial and competitive utility; make sure that you take both of them into account. When measured well, metrics serve as a compass for improving the performance of your investments in knowledge-enabled relationship management.

Glossary

Agricultural economy
Traditionally, a land and labor-intensive economy primarily aimed at the production of food.

Analytical applications
Help analyze information. These include fishbone diagrams, cash cow analysis using Boston Consulting Group (BCG) grids, mind maps, critical path analysis tools, decision trees, force-field analysis, strengths, weaknesses, opportunities, system thinking tools, etc.

Artificial Intelligence
Use of human models for cognition and perception to create computer systems to solve humanlike problems.

B2B
See business-to-business

B2C
See business-to-consumer.

Basket-to-buy rate
Percentages of shopping cart placements that are converted to purchases.

Benchmarking
Search for industry-wide best practices—anywhere within or outside their firm, industry, or sector—that lead to superior performance.

Broadcast marketing
Marketing practices and norms developed for selling mass-produced products to broad, homogeneous markets and market segments.

Browser
Program that allows users to access documents on the World Wide Web, typically using the HTTP protocol. Browsers can be either text or graphic. They read HTML and interpret the code into what we see as Web pages. The two popular browsers in use are Microsoft's Internet Explorer and America Online's Netscape Navigator. Browsers are often used as the primary front-end interface for knowledge management systems that rely on intranet technology.

Business intelligence systems
Systems that collectively hold explicated formal and informal knowledge and the rules

associated with them for accumulation, refining, managing, validating, maintaining, annotating (adding context), and distributing the contents.

Business process reengineering

Focuses on detecting the core processes that make up the business and then reassemble them more efficiently in a way that is free of functional divides and reduces complexity by reengineering operational and customer-directed activities into processes.

Business value orientation

Determines where a company principally derives value from.

Business-to-business (B2B)

E-businesses that primarily conduct business transactions with other businesses.

Business-to-consumer (B2C)

E-Businesses that primarily conduct transactions with consumers (e.g., Amazon.com, Buy.com, Drugstore.com).

C2C

See consumer-to-consumer.

Case-based reasoning (CBR)

System that searches a collection of previous cases known as its case base for past cases with attributes that match the current case. The user defines the problem to be solved based on some attributes (each with varying degrees of importance as indicated by their user-assigned weights). A search engine then searches through all the cases in the case base and retrieves those that match closely.

Channel integration

Integrating touchpoints such as Web browsers (HTML, ASP, etc.), voice (telephones, call centers, interactive voice response systems, and VoIP interfaces),

wireless hand-held devices (such as WAP-protocol-enabled cellular phones), hand-held computing platforms such as PalmPilots, direct contact (brick-and-mortar stores and mail), and WebTV interfaces.

Chief knowledge officer (CKO)

Along with other senior management members, responsible for creating the vision of what is possible and designing the framework for realizing the results.

Chunks

Set of technology modules that fit together and can be implemented together as a single whole.

Click-through rate

Percentage of users who click on a link, banner, or picture.

Click-to-basket rate

Percentage of click-throughs that are converted to placement in the shopping cart.

Clustering

Automatically finding groups of related documents and knowledge elements such as technical reports, news feeds, patents, manuals, and press releases by analyzing key concepts in textual and nontextual information (using tags).

Communication processes

Information technology and cultural processes that enable people to share information in an efficient and effective manner. Remember that the term *process* does not describe just the technical process underlying message delivery, but the whole act of communicating. If I were to describe it as a purely technical process, I would be straying too far away from knowledge management, where the human and cultural side is as important, if not more important, than the technological side.

Components of knowledge

Intuition, ground truth, judgment, experience, values, assumptions, beliefs, and intelligence.

Consumer-to-consumer (C2C)

E-businesses that facilitate transactions between consumers (e.g., eBay, Half.com, napster.com, and iwant.com).

Content directors

Executive management levels that design, set, and execute strategies on issues for which they provide focus regarding the process of knowledge sharing.

Content organizers

Organizational unit (usually the corporate office of a company) that coordinates, controls, and communicates knowledge by combining and connecting strategy to operations.

Control processes

Enable a company to create and maintain stability within business performance and legal and financial systems.

Coordination processes

Activities that link strategic and operational processes in an efficient, effective, financially acceptable, timely, and value-adding manner.

Core Competencies

Company's unique combination of available knowledge capabilities that represent its key strength. They reflect key strengths of companies to such an extent that they allow the company to sustain its competitive advantage in order to add value to customers. Often considered semipermanent in nature —that is, sustainable over a period of time.

Corporate processes

Corporate processes are coordination, control and communication processes that allow companies to link strategic processes to operational processes and vice versa.

CRM

See customer relationship management.

Cross-selling

Offering related products at the time of sale. For example, offering a camera carrying case to a customer who is purchasing a camera.

CRV

See customer relationship visionary.

Customer capital

Value of an organization's relationships with its customers.

Customer knowledge cycle

Process of knowledge management involving three broad phases that often run in parallel: (1) acquisition, (2) sharing, and (3) utilization.

Customer profitability analysis

Measurement and ranking of customers based on their long-term profitability calculated by measuring accumulated customer revenue less operational costs and acquisition costs.

Customer relationship management (CRM)

Combination of business processes and technology that seeks to understand a company's customers from multiple perspectives to competitively differentiate a company's products and services. The focus of CRM is to improve levels of customer satisfaction, boost their loyalty, and increase revenues from *existing* customers.

Customer relationship visionary (CRV)

Managerial leader who plays the role of the *organizational glue* that brings together many overlapping groups across your business: customer support representatives, and marketing managers; corporate sponsors and senior management; knowledge and customer-centricity proponents and cynics (who do not agree on the value of customer knowledge management); KCRM technology early adopters and zealots (that often include IT staff, intranet zealots, human resources managers) versus laggards, each of which might pull your customer relationship management efforts in different directions.

Data mining

Technique to analyze data in very large databases with the goal of revealing trends and patterns.

Data slam

Onslaught of meaningless pieces of data that attack and clog corporate intranet sites and databases. Mucks up internal databases and can also dangerously slow down management decision making by making systems slow, unwieldy, and difficult to navigate.

Data warehouse

Acts as a unifier of a multitude of isolated, distributed databases and aggregates, cleans, scrubs, and consolidate disparate data. Although data warehouses do not possess the ability to deliver real-time data, Web-enabled Web houses overcome this limitation to some extent.

Data

Raw transactional representations and outputs without inherent meaning.

Digital capital

Networked knowledge and relationship capital in e-business.

Document management

System that makes vast amounts of documents such as product literature, electronic forms, specifications, and correspondence easily accessible and adaptable through electronic media (often a Web front end). These systems often include workflow functionality that allows documents to be intelligently routed to select, relevant employees.

E-business

Internet-facilitated execution, coordination, and management of business processes and activities. Electronic commerce is a subset of e-business.

Expertise

Ability to take information and apply it to a particular situation.

Exploitation of knowledge

Extent to which a business uses its existing knowledge and relationship assets to create short-term gains.

Exploration of knowledge

Degree to which a business engages in creating new knowledge and building relationships with a long-term focus.

Expression barrier

Inability to express the influence of the business environment in explicitly worded strategic needs.

Firewall

Device that protects a private network from the public domain. A computer that monitors traffic between an Internet site and the Internet. It's designed to prevent unauthorized people from tampering with a computer system thereby increasing security.

4 Ps of marketing
Product, price, place, and promotion that were considered essentials of marketing in the old economy.

Functional alignment
Remember that companies are not in the business of building knowledge but in the business of creating value; functional disciplines are increasingly redesigned to become more business- and process-oriented. By ensuring functional alignment, functional expertise has a clearer and more direct impact on strategic and operational performance.

Gap analysis
Process of analyzing what is and what should be in terms of strategy, markets, knowledge assets, and relationship assets.

Gaps
Differences between what is and what is needed. KCRM strategy formulation depends on three types of gaps: (1) strategic gaps, (2) knowledge gaps, and (3) relationship gaps.

Genetic computing
Use of DNA strings to perform computations. Its four basic materials, adenine, guanine, thymine and cytosine are combined to form strings of information. A closely related concept is that of genetic algorithms. The strength of this emerging technique for arriving at the best-fitting solutions comes from the notion of Darwin's theory of natural selection: A test tube of one billion DNA strings has a capacity of one billion parallel computations per second.

Hard networks
Distribute data and information by connecting computers through a variety of systems.

Human Capital
Knowledge, skills, and competencies of people in an organization.

Implementation barrier
Inability to implement technology solutions that may be caused by a combination of incompatible infrastructure, time pressures, or unfeasible technology solution, or technical skills, analysis skills, and expertise.

Impression count
Measure of click-through rate obtained from an external source (such as a partner site).

Individualization
Using customer knowledge to identify, track, learn from, and interact with each customer on an individual basis *and then* customizing and configuring your product or service package to meet each customer's specific needs.

Integrated knowledge environment
Information technology that supports the flow of knowledge throughout the enterprise.

Intellectual capital (IC)
Intangibles such as information, knowledge, and skills that can be leveraged by an organization to produce an asset of equal or greater importance than land, labor, and capital. Skilled people, their competencies, market positions, goodwill, recognition, achievements, patents, contacts, support, collaborators, market innovation leadership, a repeat customer base, and reputation represent various facets of IC.

Intelligent personalization

Artificial intelligence techniques applied for learning about consumer behavior through passive observation and adapting to the customer's preferences.

Just-in-case delivery

Just-in-case systems devalue knowledge as users become used to receiving information that is not relevant to their immediate work or task in hand. They may ignore the messages or spend time following threads that are interesting but not applicable or useful to them in their work. The underlying idea is to make information available just in case users might need it.

Just-in-time delivery

Knowledge delivered at the moment it is needed rather than being available at all times, just in case it might be needed.

KCRM roadmap

Conceptually simplified way of explaining the seven key topics relating to KCRM, and a logical way of explaining how it relates to knowledge management and customer relationship management in general. See Chapter 3 or the opening page for an illustrated description.

KCRM

See Knowledge-enabled customer relationship management.

Knowledge repository

Collection of information or knowledge, usually centered on specific issues of interest to the company and accessible through technologies such as intranets and browsers.

Knowledge segment

Everything a company's professionals and systems know about a specific domain.

Knowledge

Fluid mix of framed experience, values, contextual information, expert insight, and grounded intuition that provides an environment and framework for evaluating and incorporating new experiences and information. It originates and is applied in the minds of knowers. In organizations, it often becomes embedded not only in documents or repositories but also in organizational routines, processes, practices, and norms.

Knowledge-enabled customer relationship management (KCRM)

Lies at the intersection of knowledge management, collaborative relationship management (with customers *and* partners), and e-business.

K-spots

These represent the knowledge niches on which a company must focus its knowledge management efforts. Based on how the audit process populates the Strategic Capability framework (see Chapter 8), you can identify promising processes that stand to gain the most through knowledge management.

Laterality

Ability to cut across functional boundaries and relate to people from different areas. Lateral team members have often worked in many roles, in many divisions of your company, so they know what it is like to be in other participants' shoes because they have "been there."

Lessons learned and best practices

Databases in which examples of previous experiences are stored, the reasons why they worked best or failed miserably and the lessons that were learned from them.

Look-to-click rate
Percentage of product impressions that are converted to click-throughs.

Migratory knowledge
Knowledge that is independent of its owner or creator. As knowledge becomes more and more extensively codified, its capacity to move increases. Codification implies some kind of capture — in documents, databases, pictures, illustrations, or spreadsheets on a disk, in e-mails, on videotapes, or on a Web page on the corporate intranet. When knowledge is migratory, we have the ability to transfer knowledge from one person or organization to another without losing its context and meaning.

Neural network
Networked computing architecture in which a number of processors are interconnected in a manner suggestive of the connections between neurons in a human brain and that can learn by a process of trial and error.

Operational processes
Logically grouped support activities that, together, form a core operational process.

Path dependence
Unique historical chain of events that led to a certain capability or outcome. If competitors want to develop the same capability, they must go "through the same path" or sequence of events.Knowledge delivered at the moment it is needed rather than being available at all times, just in case it might be needed.

Performance appraisal
Provides an overall evaluation of how well a team or an individual is doing in the eyes of its members and as well as its customers.

PRM
Partner relationship management.

Process organization
Characterized by its horizontal flow of information and communication and its decentralized authority over decisions.

Process team
Group of professionals responsible for a company's operational, corporate, and/or strategic processes.

Push delivery
Systems that distribute and deliver knowledge to their audience, after filtering it through highly customized filters.

RDI methodology
Results-driven incremental methodology suited for complex projects such as knowledge management system deployment. The key idea is that each phase incrementally builds upon a learning experience gained from the preceding phase.

Reflecting
Act of playing back and thinking about the lessons learned each day. Also called action replay or rationale reconstruction in some software engineering circles.

Response analysis
Measurement of the effectiveness of a customized campaign or promotion within a specific customer segment.

Retention likelihood
Measuring how likely the customer is not to churn, and engage in repeat transactions with your business.

Segmentation
Subdivision of customer populations into finer groups defined by their characteristics.

Sensing
Ability to observe and perceive without passing judgment.

Smart networks

Combine hard and soft networks. Results in effective linking of smart business strategies to every employee throughout the company. Smart organizations are entirely process and team based and use knowledge as their primary asset and are characterized by such smart networks.

Soft networks

Process of establishing a community of practice and collating a number of people who can be called upon when expertise is required.

Strategic holding

Corporate office acts as a strategic holding when its core purpose is not to direct operational processes but to prepare, design, and implement a long-term business strategy.

Strategic knowledge management

Links the building of a company's knowledge to a business strategy.

Structural capital

Processes, structures, and systems that a firm owns less its people. Skandia reported its structural capital in its 1996 annual report intellectual asset supplement.

Synergy

Ability to produce a result that is greater than the sum of individual components. In the context of knowledge management, synergy refers to the ability of the knowledge management system to allow different groups of users, representing different functional departments, to produce results exceeding those that they would produce working without the support of such a system.

TCO

See total cost of ownership.

Team synergy

Process of working together as a team that creates synergy by combining each member's unique knowledge. The combination is capable of producing results exceeding those possible if each member's capabilities and productivity measures were summed up.

360° performance appraisal

Concept that smart knowledge workers regularly request mentors, team leaders, peers and customers to appraise their performance by providing them formal and informal feedback.

Tobin's *q*

Ratio between the firm's market valuation and the cost of replacing its physical assets.

Total cost of ownership (TCO)

Total lifecycle cost associated with the purchase, implementation, maintenance, and support of a system. This methodology identifies and measures components of IT expense beyond the initial cost of implementation. This includes software licensing fees, hardware expenditure, training costs, integration and design costs, and ongoing maintenance costs.

Transformation of knowledge

Knowledge is complex and initially tacit; however, it can be externalized and embedded in a company's products and processes. One of the aspects of tacit knowledge is the cognitive dimension that comprises beliefs, ideals, values, schemata, and mental models that are deeply ingrained in participants; often taken for granted by the possessors. While this cognitive component, like any other aspect of tacit knowledge, is difficult to articulate, it shapes the perception of the participants. This cognitive component should be extracted to retain context and fullness of the captured explicit knowledge.

Up-selling
Offering higher-end products at the time of sale. For example, offering the professional version of a program to a customer who is buying a basic version of the same.

Virtual competence center
Virtual team of people organized around a specific knowledge domain.

Web house
Web-enabled data warehouse.

Wrappers
Scripts and connection modules that allow personal computers and modern networks to access legacy data.

References

Chapter 1

Alajoursijarvi, K., "Customer Relationships and the Small Software Firm: A Framework for Understanding Challenges Faced in Marketing," *Information & Management*, 37 (2000), 153–159.

Arndt, J., "Role of Product Related Conversations in the Diffusion of a New Product," *Journal of Marketing Research*, 4, August (1967), 291–295.

Bitner, M., "Evaluating Service Encounters: The Effect of Physical Surroundings and Employee Responses," *Journal of Marketing*, 54, April (1990), 69–82.

Brown, S., *Customer Relationship Management: A Strategic Imperative in the World of E-Business,* John Wiley & Sons, Toronto, (2000).

Drucker, P., *Management Challenges for the 21st Century*, Harper Business, New York, 1999.

Hansen, M., "The Search-Transfer Problem: The Role of Weak Ties in Sharing Knowledge Across Organizational Subunits," *Administrative Science Quarterly*, 44 (1999), 83–111.

Kimmel, P., J. Weygandtand, and D. Kieso, *Financial Accounting: Tools for Business Decision Making*, Wiley, New York, 1998.

Lynn Gary, S., Abeland, Kate D., and Wright, Robert C., "Key Factors in Increasing Speed to Market and Improving New Product Success Rates," *Industrial Marketing Management*, 28, 4 (1999), 319.

McKenna, R., "Real-Time Marketing," *Harvard Business Review*, July–August, (1995), 87–95.

Peppers, D. and Rogers, M,, "As Products Get Smarter Companies Have to Focus on Relationships," *Forbes ASAP*, Feburary 26 (1996) 69.

Peppers, D. and. Rogers, M., "Enterprise One to One: Tools for Competing in the Interactive Age," Currency Doubleday, New York (1997).

Peppers, D. and. Rogers, M,, *Information Rules*, Harvard Business School Press, Boston (1999).

Reichheld, F. and Schefter, P., "E-Loyalty: Your Secret Weapon on the Web," *Harvard Business Review*, July–August (2000), 105–113.

Riesenberger, J., "Knowledge—The Source of Sustainable Competitive Advantage," *Journal of International Marketing*, 6, 3 (1998), 94–107.

Shapiro, C. and H. Varian, *Information Rules: A Strategic Guide to the Network Economy*, Harvard Business School Press, Boston, 1999.

Shapiro, Carl, and Varian, H., "Versioning: The Smart way to Sell Information," *Harvard Business Review*, November–December, (1998), 16–114.

Tapscott, D., Ticolland, D., and Lowy, A., *Digital Capital: Harnessing the Power of Business Webs*, Harvard Business School Press, Boston, 2000.

Tiwana, A., *The Knowledge Management Toolkit: Practical Techniques for Building a Knowledge Management System*, Prentice Hall, Upper Saddle River, NJ, 2000.

Tiwana, A., "Managing Micro- and Macro-level Design Process Knowledge Across Emergent Internet Information System Families," In *Industrial Knowlwdge Management—A Micro Level Approach*, R. Rajkumar (Ed.), Springer U.K., London, 2000,

Todd, Ann, "Managing Radical Change," *Long Range Planning*, 32, 2 (1999), 237.

Tomas, Jose, and Gomez, Arias, "Do Networks Really Foster Innovation?" *Management Decision*, 33, 9 (1995), 52–56.

Vijayasarathy, Leo R. and Robey, Daniel, "The Effect of EDI on Market Channel Relationships in Retailing," *Information & Management*, 33, December 5 (1997) 73–86.

Chapter 2

Garvin, D., "Building a Learning Organization," *Harvard Business Review*, July–August, (1993) 78–91.

Kalakota, R., and Robinson, M., *E-Business: Roadmap for Success*, Addison Wesley, Reading, MA, 1999.

Kogut, B. "The Network as Knowledge: Generative Rules and the Emergence of Structure," *Strategic Management Journal* (21), (2000), 405–425.

McDermott, R., "Why Information Technology Inspired but Cannot Deliver Knowledge Management," *California Management Review* 41:4, (1999) 103–117.

McEvily, S., Das, S. and McNabe, K., "Avoiding Competence Substitution Through Knowledge Sharing," *Academy of Management Review*, 25,2, (2000) 294–311.

Peppers, D., and Rogers, M., "Is Your Company Ready for One-to-One Marketing, *Harvard Business Review*, January–February (1999), 3–12.

Pine, J., *Mass Customization: The New Frontier in Business Competition*, Harvard Business School Press, Boston, (1993).

Pine, J., Peppers, D. and Rogers, M., "Do You Want to Keep Your Customers Forever?" *Harvard Business Review*, March–April, (1995), 103–114.

Pine, J., *The Experience Economy*, Harvard Business School Press, Boston (1999).

Schilling, M. "Toward a General Modular Systems Theory and Its Application to Interfirm Product Modularity," *Academy of Management Review*, 25:2, (2000), 312–334.

Storck, J. and Hill, P., "Knowledge Diffusion Through "Strategic Communities," *Sloan Management Review*, Winter (2000) 63–74.

Tapscott, D., Ticoll, D., and Lowy, A. *Digital Capital: Harnessing the Power of Business Webs*, Harvard Business School Press, Boston, 2000.

Tiwana, A., "Custom KM: Implementing the Right Knowledge Management Strategy for Your Organization," *Cutter IT Journal* (formerly *American Programmer*), 12,11, (1999), 6–14.

Tiwana, A., "Knowledge-enabled Customer Relationship Management: Beyond "Word of Mouse," *Cutter IT Journal* (formerly *American Programmer*) 13,10, (2000), 17–25.

Tiwana, A., *The Knowledge Management Toolkit: Practical Techniques for Building a Knowledge Management System*, Prentice Hall, Upper Saddle River, NJ, 2000.

Tiwana, A., "Managing Micro- and Macro-Level Design Process Knowledge Across Emergent Internet Information System Families," In *Industrial Knowledge Management—A Micro Level Approach*, R. Rajkumar (Ed.), Springer U.K., London, 2000,

Tiwana, A., and Bush, A. "Peer-to-Peer Valuation as a Mechanism for Reinforcing Active Learning in Virtual Communities: An Application of Social Exchange Theory," *Proceedings of the HICSS–33*, Maui, Hawaii, 2000,

Tiwana, A., and Ramesh, B., "Supporting Distributed Information Product Development With Design Decision Knowledge," *Proceedings of the International Conference on Intelligent Decision Support Systems*, Melbourne, Australia, 1999,

Tiwana, A., and Ramesh, B., "Toward a Composite Metric for Electronic Commerce ROI: An Extension of the Balanced Scorecard," *Proceedings of the International Conference of Electronic Commerce Measurement*, Singapore, 1999.

Tiwana, A., and Ramesh, B., "A Design Knowledge Management System to Support Collaborative Information Product Evolution," *Decision Support Systems* (forthcoming).

Tiwana, A., and Ramesh, B., "From Intuition to Institution: Supporting Collaborative Diagnoses in Telemedicine Teams," *Proceedings of the HICSS–33*, Maui, Hawaii, 2000.

Tiwana, A. and Ramesh, B. "Supporting Distibuted Information Product Development with Design Decision Knowledge," *Proceedings of the International Conference on Intelligent Decision Support Systems*, Melbourne, Australia (1999).

Chapter 3

Brown, S., "Customer Relationship Management: A Strategic Imperative in the World of E-Business," John Wiley & Sons, Toronto, (2000),

Kalakota, R. and M. Robinson, E-*Business: Roadmap for Success*, Addison Wesley, Reading, MA, 1999.

Rust, R., and Zahorik, A., "Customer Satisfaction, Customer Retention, and Market Share," *Journal of Retailing*, 69, 2 (1993), 193–215.

Tiwana, A., "Custom KM: Implementing the Right Knowledge Management Strategy for Your Organization," *Cutter IT Journal (formerly American Programmer)*, 12, 11 (1999), 6–14.

Tiwana, A., *The Knowledge Management Toolkit: Practical Techniques for Building a Knowledge Management System*, Prentice Hall, Upper Saddle River, NJ, 2000.

Tiwana, A., "Managing Micro- and Macro-Level Design Process Knowledge across Emergent Internet Information System Families," In *Industrial Knowledge Management—A Micro-Level Approach*, R. Rajkumar (Ed.), Springer U.K., London, 2000.

Zack, M., "Developing a Knowledge Strategy," California Management Review, 41(3), 125–145.

Chapter 4

Alajoursijarvi, K., "Customer Relationships and the Small Software Firm: A Framework for Understanding Challenges Faced in Marketing," *Information & Management* 37 (2000), 153–159.

Christensen, C., *The Innovator's Dilemma*, Harvard Business School Press, Boston (1997).

Christensen, C., Suarez, F., Utterback, J., "Strategies for Survival in Fast-Changing Industries," *Management Science*, 45 (12), 375–387.

Davenport, T., Jarvenpaa, S., and Beers, M., "Improving Knowledge Work Processes," *Sloan Management Review* Summer (1996) 53–65.

Davenport, T., and Klahr, P., "Managing Customer Support Knowledge," *California Management Review*, 40,3 (1998) 195–208.

Davenport, T., and Prusak, L., *Working Knowledge*, Harvard Business School Press, Boston, 1998.

Drew, S., "Strategy at the Leading Edge—Building Knowledge Management Into Strategy: Making Sense of a New Perspective," *Long Range Planning* 32:1 (1999) 130.

Eisenhardt, K., "Strategy as Strategic Decision Making," *Sloan Management Review*, Spring, (1999) 65–72.

Fahey, L., and Prusak, L., "The Eleven Deadliest Sins of Knowledge Management," *California Management Review*, 40:3, (1998) 265–279.

Garvin, D. "Building a Learning Organization," *Harvard Business Review*, July–August, (1993) 78–91.

Gupta, Y., Karimi, J., and Somers, T., "Alignment of a Firm's Competitive Strategy and Information Technology Management Sophistication: The Missing Link," *IEEE Transactions on Engineering Management*, 44:4 (1997) 399–413.

Hansen, M., Nohria, N. and Tierney, T., "What's Your Strategy for Managing Knowledge?" *Harvard Business Review* March–April (1999) 106–116.

Hoffman, D., and Novak, T., "How to Acquire Customers on the Web," *Harvard Business Review*, May–June (2000) 3–8.

Ives, B., Jarvenpaa, S. L. and Mason, R. O. "Global Business Drivers: Aligning Information Technology to Global Business Strategy," *IBM Systems Journal*, 32,1 (1993).

Kim, W. C. and Mauborgne, R., "Strategy, Value Innovation, and the Knowledge Economy," *Sloan Management Review* 40,3 (1999) 41.

Lowendahl, B., and Revang, O., "Challenges to Existing Strategy Theory in a Postindustrial Society," *Strategic Management Journal* 19 (1998) 755–773.

McEvily, S., Das, S. and McNabe, K. "Avoiding Competence Substitution Through Knowledge Sharing," *Academy of Management Review*, 25,2 (2000) 294–311.

McKenna, R. "Real-Time Marketing," *Harvard Business Review* July–August (1995) 87–95.

Smith, T., and Reece, J., "The Relationship of Strategy, Fit, Productivity, and Business Performance in a Services Setting," *Journal of Operations Management*, 17 (1999) 145–161.

Tiwana, A., "Custom KM: Implementing the Right Knowledge Management Strategy for Your Organization," *Cutter IT Journal (formerly American Programmer)* 12,11 (1999) 6–14.

Tiwana, A., *The Knowledge Management Toolkit: Practical Techniques for Building a Knowledge Management System*, Prentice Hall, Upper Saddle River, NJ, 2000.

Tiwana, A., "Managing Micro- and Macro-Level Design Process Knowledge across Emergent Internet Information System Families," In *Industrial Knowledge Management—A Micro-Level Approach*, R. Rajkumar (Ed.), Springer U.K., London, 2000,

Venkatraman, N., "The Concept of Fit in Strategy Research: Toward Verbal and Statistical Correspondence," *The Academy of Management Review*, 14,3 (1989) 423–444.

Zack, M. H., "Developing a Knowledge Strategy," *California Management Review* 41:3 (1999) 125–145.

Chapter 5

Bohn, Roger E., "Measuring and Managing Technological Knowledge," *Sloan Management Review*, 36, Fall (1994), 61–73.

Brown, John Seely, and Dugid, Paul, "Balancing Act: How to Capture Knowledge Without Killing It," *Harvard Business Review*, May–June (2000), 3–7.

Glazer, Rashi, "Measuring the Knower: Towards a Theory of Knowledge Equity," *California Management Review*, 40, 3 (1998), 175–194.

Hoopes, D., and Postrel, S., "Shared Knowledge, 'Glitches,' and Product Development Performance," *Strategic Management Journal*, 20, (1999), 837–865.

Lahti, R., and Beyerlein, M., "Knowledge Transfer and Management Consulting: A Look at the Firm," *Business Horizons*, January–February, (2000), 65–74.

McEvily, S., Dasand, S., and McNabe, K., "Avoiding Competence Substitution through Knowledge Sharing," *Academy of Management Review*, 25, 2 (2000), 294–311.

Peppers, D. and Rogers, M., "Enterprise One-to-One," Currency Doubleday, New York (1997).

Simonin, B., "Ambiguity and the Process of Knowledge Transfer in Strategic Alliances," *Strategic Management Journal*, 20 (1999), 595–623.

Storck, J., and Hill P.,, "Knowledge Diffusion through 'Strategic Communities,'" *Sloan Management Review*, Winter (2000), 63–74.

Straub, Detmar W., Karahanna, Elena "Knowledge Worker Communications," *Organization Science*, 4,2, (1998), 160–175.

Terwiesch, Christian, and Loch, Christoph H., "Measuring the Effectiveness of Overlapping Development Activities," *Management Science*, 45, 4 (1999), 455.

Tiwana, A., *The Knowledge Management Toolkit: Practical Techniques for Building a Knowledge Management System*, Prentice Hall, Upper Saddle River, NJ, 2000.

Tiwana, A., "Managing Micro- and Macro-Level Design Process Knowledge Across Emergent Internet Information System Families," In *Industrial Knowledge-Management—A Micro-Level Approach*, R. Rajkumar (Ed.), Springer U.K., London, 2000,

Wah, Louisa, "Making Knowledge Stick," *Management Review*, 88, 5 (1999), 24.

Wallham, Steven, "The Importance of Measuring Intangible Assets: Public Policy Implications," In *Capital for Out Time*, N. Imparato (Ed.), Hoover Institution Press, Stanford, CA, 1999, 181–191.

Chapter 6

Anacona, D., and D. Caldwell, "IT and Work Groups: The Case of New Product Teams," In *Intellectual Teamwork*, Galegher, J., Kraut, R., and Egido, C. (Ed.), Erlbaum, Hillsdale, 1990, 173–190.

Brown, S., *Customer Relationship Management: A Strategic Imperative in the World of E-Business,* John Wiley & Sons, Toronto, (2000),

Ciborra, Claudio, *Teams, Markets, and Systems: Business Innovation and Information Technology*, Cambridge University Press, Cambridge, England, 1993.

Ciborra, Claudio and Suetens, Nicole, "Groupware for the Emerging Virtual Organization," In *Groupware and Teamwork*, C. Ciborra (Ed.), Wiley, New York, 1996, 61–86.

Jassawalla, A. and Sashittal, H., "Building Collaborative Cross-Functional New Product Teams," *Academy of Management Executive*, 13, 3 (1999), 50–63.

Keil, M., Cule, P., Lyytinen, K., Schmidt, R., "A Framework for Identifying Software Project Risks," *Communications of the ACM,* 41 (11), 76–83.

Lee, Jintae, and Malone, Thomas W., "Partially Shared Views: A Scheme for Communicating among Groups That Use Different Type Hierarchies," *ACM Transactions on Information Systems*, 8, 1 (1990), 1–26.

Mandivalla, M., and Olfman, L. "What Do Groups Need? A Proposed Set of Generic Groupware

Requirements," *ACM Transactions on Human-Computer Interaction*, 1, 3 (1994), 245–268.

Meyer, Christopher, "How the Right Measures Help Teams Excel," *Harvard Business Review*, May–June, (1994), 95–103.

Orlikowski, Wanda J., "Learning From Notes: Organizational Issues in Groupware Implementation," *The Information Society*, 9, 2 (1993), 237–250.

Pare, Guy, and Dube, Line, "Ad Hoc Virtual Teams: A Multi-Disciplinary Framework and a Research Agenda," *Ecole des Hautes Etudes Commercialies, Montreal, Canada: Working Paper*, June (1998), 1–25.

Robey, Daniel, Farrowand, Dana and Franz, Charles, "Group Processes and Conflict in System Development," *Management Science*, 35, 10 (1989), 1172–1191.

Satzinger, John W., Garfieldand, Monica J., and Nagasundaram, Murli, "The Creative Process: The Effects of Group Memory on Individual Idea Generation," *Journal of Management Information Systems*, 15, 4 (1999), 143.

Townsend, Anthony, DeMarieand, Samuel, and Hendrickson, Anthony, "Virtual Teams: Technology and the Workplace of the Future," *Academy of Management Executive*, 12, 3 (1998), 17–29.

Chapter 7

Antonelli, C., "New Information Technology and the Knowledge-based Economy," *Journal of Evolutionary Economics*, 8, 2 (1998), 177–198.

Brown, S., "Customer Relationship Management: A Strategic Imperative in the World of E-Business," John Wiley & Sons, Toronto, , (2000), Chaps. 10, 12, 18.

Davenport, T., and Klahr, P., "Managing Customer Support Knowledge," *California Management Review*, 40, 3 (1998), 195–208.

Davenport, T., and Prusak, L., *Working Knowledge*, Harvard Business School Press, Boston, 1998.

Davenport, Thomas H., "Saving ITs Soul: Human-Centered Information Management," *Harvard Business Review*, March–April, (1994), 119–131.

Deeds, David L., "Firm-Specific Resources and Wealth Creation in High-technology Ventures: Evidence from Newly Public Biotechnology Firms," *Entrepreneurship Theory and Practice* (1998).

Dhar, Vasant, and Stein, Roger, *Intelligent Decision Support Methods: The Science of Knowledge Work*, Prentice Hall, Upper Saddle River, NJ, 1997.

Grant, R., "Prospering in Dynamically-Competitive Environments: Organizational Capability as Knowledge Integration," *Organization Science*, 7, 4 (1996), 375–387.

Huber, George P., "A Theory of the Effects of Advanced Information Technologies on Organizational Design, Intelligence, and Decision-Making," *Academy of Management Review*, 15, 1 (1990), 47–71.

Iansiti, M., *Technology Integration: Making Critical Choices in a Dynamic World*, Harvard Business School Press, Boston, 1998.

Kogut, B., and Zander, U., "Knowledge of the Firm, Combinative Capabilities, and the Replication of Technology," *Organization Studies*, 3 (1992), 383–397.

Linthicum, D., *Enterprise Application Integration*, Addison-Wesley Longman, Reading, MA 2000.

Lynch, Patrick, and Horton, Sarah, *Web Style Guide: Basic Design Principles for Creating Web Sites*, Yale University Press, New Haven, CT, 1999.

Orlikowski, Wanda J., "The Duality of Technology: Rethinking the Concept of Technology in Organizations," *Organization Science*, 3, (3) August (1992) 398–427.

Peppers, D. and Rogers, M., "As Products Get Smarter Companies Have to Focus on Relationships," *Forbes ASAP*, February 26 (1996) 69.

Ramesh, B., and Tiwana, A., "Supporting Collaborative Process Knowledge Management in New Product Development Teams," *Decision Support Systems*, 27, 1–2 (1999), 213–235.

Robey, D., Boudreau, M. and Rose, G., "Information Technology and Organizational Learning: A Review and Assessment of Research," *Accounting, Management, and Information Technology*, 10 (2000), 125–155.

Saviotti, R., "Technology Mapping and Evaluation of Technical Change," *International Journal of Technology Management*, 10, 4/5/6 (1995), 423.

Simon, H., "Applying Information Technology to Organizational Design," *Public Administration Review*, 33, 3 (1973), 268–278.

Tiwana, A., *The Knowledge Management Toolkit: Practical Techniques for Building a Knowledge Management System*, Prentice Hall, Upper Saddle River, NJ, 2000.

Tiwana, A., *Web Security*, Butterworth
Hiennmann/Digital Press, Boston, MA, 1999.

Chapter 8

Ciborra, Claudio, *Teams, Markets, and Systems:
Business Innovation and Information Technology*,
Cambridge University Press, Cambridge, England,
1993.

Ewusi-Mensah, Kweku, "Critical Issues in
Abandoned Information Systems Development
Projects," *Communications of the ACM*, 40, 9
(1997), 74–80.

Fichman, R. and Moses, S., "An Incremental Process
for Software Implementation," *Sloan Management
Review*, Winter (1999), 39–52.

Field, Tom, "When Bad Things Happen to Good
Projects," *CIO*, October 15 (1997),

Gruca, T., Nathand, D., and Mehra, A., "Exploiting
Synergy for Competitive Advantage," *Long Range
Planning*, 30, 4 (1997) 605–611.

Keil, Mark, Cule, Paul E., and Lyytinen, Kallie, and
Schmidt, Roy C., "A Framework for Identifying
Software Project Risks," *Communications of the
ACM*, 41, 11, (1998), 76–83.

Khurana, Anil, "Managing Complex Production
Processes," *Sloan Management Review*, Winter
(1999), 85–97.

Mankin, Don, Cohenand, Susan, and Bikson,, Tora
Teams and Technology, Harvard Business School
Press, Boston, 1996.

Tiwana, A., *The Knowledge Management Toolkit:
Practical Techniques for Building a Knowledge
Management System*, Prentice Hall, Upper Saddle
River, NJ, 2000.

Verganti, Roberto, "Planned Flexibility: Linking
Anticipation and Reaction in Product
Development Projects," *The Journal of Product
Innovation Management*, 16, 4 (1999), 363.

Watson, H. and Haley, B., "Data Warehousing: A
Framework and Survey of Practices," *Journal of
Data Warehousing*, 2, 1, 1997, 10–17.

Yourdon, E., "Best Practices for E-Business Projects:
Introduction to Special Issue," *Cutter IT Journal
(formerly American Programmer)*, 13, 4 (2000), 2–4.

Chapter 9

Earl, M., and Scott, I., "What is a Chief Knowledge
Officer?" *Sloan Management Review*, Winter
(1999), 29–38.

Kettinger, William, Tengand, James, and Guha,
Subashish, "Business Process Change: A Study of
Methodologies, Techniques, and Tools," *MIS
Quarterly*, 14, 2 (1997), 55–80.

Kotter, J., *Leading Change*, Harvard Business School
Press, Boston, 1996.

Kuwanda, Kotaro, "Strategic Learning: The Continuous
Side of Discontinuous Strategic Change,"
Organization Science, 9, 6 (1998), 719–736.

Orlikowski, W. J., "CASE Tools as Organizational
Change: Investigating Incremental and Radical
Changes in Systems Development," *MIS
Quarterly*, 17 (1993), 309–340.

Sridharan, Uma V. and St John,, Caron H., "The
Effects of Organizational Stability and Leadership
Structure on Firm Performance," *Journal of
Managerial Issues*, 10, 4 (1998), 469–484.

Tiwana, A. and Bush, A., "Peer-to-Peer Valuation as a
Mechanism for Reinforcing Active Learning in
Virtual Communities: An Application of Social
Exchange Theory," *Proceedings of the HICSS–33*,
Maui, Hawaii, 2000,

Todd, Ann, "Managing Radical Change," *Long Range
Planning*, 32, 2 (1999), 237.

Von Krogh, G., "Develop Knowledge Activists!"
European Management Journal, 15, 5, (1997),
475–483.

Von-Glinow, M. A., and Mohrman, S.A., *Managing
Complexity in High Technology Organizations*,
Oxford University Press, New York. 1990.

Zack, Michael H., "Developing a Knowledge
Strategy," *California Management Review*, 41, 3
(1999), 125–145.

Chapter 10

Baru, A., Whinston, A. and Yin, F. "Value and
Productivity in the Internet Economy," *Computer*
May, (2000) 102–105.

Blose, Laurence, and Shieh, Joseph, "Tobin's Q-ratio
and Market Reaction to Capital Investment
Announcements," *The Financial Review*, 32, 3,
(1997), 449–476.

Bohn, Roger E., "Measuring and Managing
Technological Knowledge," *Sloan Management
Review*, 36, Fall (1994), 61–73.

Brownlie, Douglas, "Benchmarking Your Marketing
Process," *Long Range Planning*, 32, 1 (1999), 88.

Chamberlain, Trevor W, "Business Investment and
the Measurement of Profit Expectations," *The*

Mid-Atlantic Journal of Business, 33, March (1997), 5–18.

Garrity, Edward J. and Lawrence Sanders, G., *Information Systems Success Measurement*, Idea Group Publishing, Hershey, PA., 1998.

Hauser, J., and Gerald, K., "Metrics: You Are What You Measure!" *European Management Journal*, 16, 5 (1998), 517–528.

Kaplan, R., Norton, D., *Translating Strategy into Action: The Balanced Scorecard,* Harvard Business School Press, Boston (1996).

Lewellen, Wilbur G., and Badrinath, S. G., "On the Measurement of Tobin's Q," *Journal of Financial Economics*, 44, 1 (1997), 77–122.

McEvily, S., Das, S. and McNabe, K. "Avoiding Competence Substitution through Knowledge Sharing," *Academy of Management Review* 25:2 (2000) 294–311.

McKenna, R., "Real-time Marketing," *Harvard Business Review*, July–August (1995), 87–95.

Mishra, Chandra, and Gobeli, David, "Managerial Incentives, Internalization, and Market Valuation of Multinational Firms," *Journal of International Business Studies*, 29, 3 (1998), 583–597.

Morell, Jonathan, "Metrics and Models for the Evaluation of Supply Chain Integration," *EDI Forum*, 10, 1 (1997), Electronic version.

Mullins, J. and Sutherland, D., "New Product Development in Rapidly Changing Markets: An Exploratory Study," *Journal of Product Innovation Management*, 15, 3 (1998), 224–236.

Pfeffer, Jeffrey, and Sutton, Robert, "Knowing "What" To Do Is Not Enough: Turning Knowledge into Action," *California Management Review*, 42, 1 (1999), 83–108.

Reich, B. and Benbasat, I., "Factors that Influence the Social Dimension of Alignment Between Business and Information Technology Objective, *MIS Quarterly* 24:1,(2000) 81–111.

Rosen, K. and Howard, A., "E-Retail: Gold Rush or Fool's Gold?" California Management Review 42:3 (2000) 72–100.

Tapscott, D., Ticoll, D. and Lowy, A., *Digital Capital: Harnessing the Power of Business Webs,* Harvard Business School Press, Boston (2000).

Teece, D., "Capturing Value from Knowledge Assets: The New Economy, Markets for Know-how, and Intangible Assets," *California Management Review*, 40, 3 (1998), 55–79.

Thompson, M., "The Economic Impact of E-Commerce," *The Industry Standard*, April 26, 1999.

Tiwana, A., *The Knowledge Management Toolkit: Practical Techniques for Building a Knowledge Management System*, Prentice Hall, Upper Saddle River, NJ, 2000.

Tiwana, A., and Ramesh, B., "A Design Knowledge Management System to Support Collaborative Information Product Evolution," *Decision Support Systems:* forthcoming (2000).

Tiwana, A., and Ramesh, B., "Supporting Distributed Information Product Development with Design Decision Knowledge," *Proceedings of the international Conference on Intelligent Decision Support Systems,* Melbourne, Australia (1999).

Tiwana, A., and Ramesh, B., "Toward a Composite Metric for Electronic Commerce ROI: An Extension of the Balanced Scorecard," *Proceedings of the International Conference of Electronic Commerce Measurement, Singapore* (1999).

Venkatraman, N., "Strategic Orientation of Business Enterprises: The Construct, Dimensionality, and Measurement," *Management Science*, 35, 8 (1989), 942–962.

Venkatraman, N., and Ramanujam, Vasudevan, "Measurement of Business Economic Performance: An Examination of Method Convergence," *Journal of Management*, 13, 1, Spring (1987), 109–122.

Index

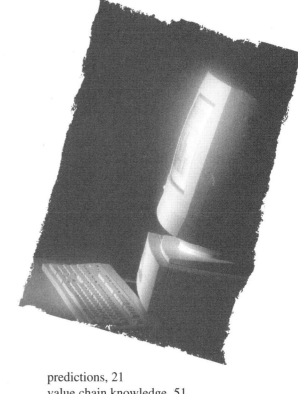

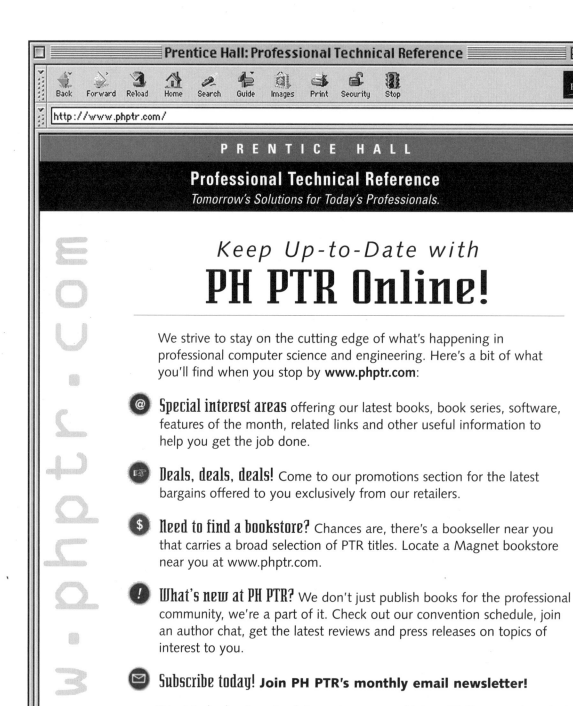